Printed at the Mathematical Centre, 49, 2e Boerhaavestraat, Amsterdam.

The Mathematical Centre, founded the 11-th of February 1946, is a non-profit institution aiming at the promotion of pure mathematics and its applications. It is sponsored by the Netherlands Government through the Netherlands Organization for the Advancement of Pure Research (Z.W.O).

MATHEMATICAL CENTRE TRACTS 68

P.P.N. DE GROEN

SINGULARLY PERTURBED DIFFERENTIAL OPERATORS OF SECOND ORDER

MATHEMATISCH CENTRUM AMSTERDAM 1976

AMS(MOS) subject classification scheme (1970): 34E20, 35B25, 34B25, 35P20, 47A55

ISBN 90 6196 120 3

CONTENTS

ACKNOWLEDGEMENTS

The research, leading to this publication, was carried out at the "Vrije Universiteit van Amsterdam". The author is indebted to professor G.Y. Nieuwland for reading and criticizing the text, to professor W. Eckhaus and E.M. de Jager and to dr. A. van Harten for valuable discussions on the subject.

I thank the Mathematical Centre for the opportunity to publish this monograph in their series Mathematical Centre Tracts and all those at the Mathematical Centre who have centributed to its technical realization.

ABSTRACT

This tract is devoted to spectral properties and asymptotics of the singularly perturbed two-point boundary value problems on the interval (-1,1)

$$(1\pm) \qquad \varepsilon(au''+bu'+cu) \pm xu' - \lambda u = f, \quad u(\pm 1) = A \pm B, \quad a > 0,$$

with $0 < \varepsilon \ll 1$, with $\lambda \in \mathbb{C}$ and with C^∞-coefficients. This problem is often referred to as a turning point problem. Moreover, we consider its two-dimensional analogue on the unit disk Ω,

$$(2) \qquad \varepsilon Lu + \ell u - \lambda u = f, \quad u_{|\partial\Omega} = g,$$

where L is a uniformly elliptic operator with C^∞-coefficients and where ℓ is a first order operator with one non-degenerate critical point at (x,y) = = (0,0). We take for ℓ the following operators:

$$\ell = \pm(x\partial_x + \mu y\partial_y) \quad \text{and} \quad \ell = \pm\big((x-\mu y)\partial_x + (y+\mu x)\partial_y\big),$$

which have a critical point of nodal ($\mu>0$), saddle-point ($\mu<0$) and vortex ($\kappa \neq 0$) type respectively. We prove that problems (1±) have discrete spectra for every $\varepsilon > 0$ and that the n-th eigenvalues ($n \in \mathbb{N}$) of (1±) converge for $\varepsilon \to +0$ to $- n + \frac{1}{2} \mp \frac{1}{2}$, if they are arranged in order of magnitude, thus showing that the phenomenon of "resonance", observed by many authors in problems of this type, is a spectral effect. The proof is based on the perturbation theory for linear operators in a Hilbert space. Similarly the spectrum of (2) converges to a discrete set in $\mathbb{C}$. Moreover, we construct asymptotic approximations to the solutions of (1±) and (2) and we prove their validity for all $\lambda \in \mathbb{C}$ outside the spectrum by variational inequalities.

INTRODUCTION

In the wide variety of singular perturbation problems considerable attention has been devoted to the asymptotic behaviour for $\varepsilon \to +0$ of the solution of the real two-point boundary value problem on the interval $(-1,1)$

(1) $$\varepsilon u'' + pu' + qu = f, \quad u(\pm 1) \text{ prescribed}, \quad 0 < \varepsilon \ll 1,$$

with p and q in C^∞. The analogous boundary value problem on a bounded domain Ω in several dimensions has long been of interest also; this problem is as follows:

(2) $$\varepsilon Lu + \sum_{j=1}^{n} p_j \partial_j u + qu = f, \quad u_{|\partial\Omega} \text{ prescribed}, \quad 0 < \varepsilon \ll 1,$$

with p_j and q in $C^\infty(\Omega)$ and L a uniformly elliptic operator.

If the coefficient p of u' in (1) is (real and) bounded away from zero, the behaviour of the solution of (1) for $\varepsilon \to +0$ is well understood. The solution of (1) converges for $\varepsilon \to +0$ to the solution of the reduced problem

(3) $$pu' + qu = f$$

which satisfies the boundary condition at $+1$ if $p > 0$ and at -1 if $p < 0$. Convergence is non-uniform at the other boundary point and a boundary layer of width $\mathcal{O}(\varepsilon)$ is located there. We can construct uniformly valid asymptotic approximations to the solution of (1) of order $\mathcal{O}(\varepsilon^n)$ for every $n \in \mathbb{N}$, cf. WASOW [30], O'MALLEY [23] and other works quoted by them.

Similarly, the asymptotic behaviour of the solution of problem (2) is well known if the coefficients p_j of the first order operator $\sum p_j \partial_j$ do not have a simultaneous zero, i.e. if the associated system of ordinary differential equations

(4) $$\frac{dx_j}{ds} = p_j, \quad j = 1,\dots,n,$$

which determines the characteristics, does not have a critical point. In that case, the problem (2) has a solution for every $\varepsilon > 0$ and this solution converges to the solution of the reduced equation

(5) $$\sum_{j=1}^{n} p_j \partial_j u + qu = f$$

which takes the boundary condition of (2) at a part of the boundary; if the quadratic form, associated with the principal part of L, is positive, this part of the boundary consists of those points of $\partial\Omega$ where the inner product of the vector $\vec{p} := (p_1,\ldots,p_n)$ with the outward drawn normal $\vec{n}$ at $\partial\Omega$ is positive. At the remainder of the boundary, a boundary layer is located. Asymptotic approximations of order $\mathcal{O}(\varepsilon^n)$ can be constructed for any $n \in \mathbb{N}$ and they are uniformly valid, at least outside neighbourhoods of characteristics which are somewhere tangent to $\partial\Omega$, cf. ECKHAUS & DE JAGER [8], LIONS [21], GRASMAN [11], VAN HARTEN [17] and [18] and BESJES [5].

We can formulate the problems (1) and (2) differently and consider the differential operators associated with them in a Hilbert (or Banach) space. In connection with (1) we define the differential operator T_ε by

(6) $$T_\varepsilon u := \varepsilon u'' + pu' + qu \qquad \text{for all } u \in \mathcal{D}(T_\varepsilon),$$

where the domain of definition is defined by

$$\mathcal{D}(T_\varepsilon) := \{v \in L^2(-1,1) \mid v'' \in L^2(-1,1) \text{ and } v(\pm 1) = 0\}.$$

The obvious question now is whether $T_\varepsilon - \lambda$ (with $\lambda \in \mathbb{C}$) is invertible and whether this inverse converges to the inverse of an operator associated with the reduced equation (3). It is easy to show that the spectrum of T_ε ($\varepsilon>0$) is contained in the left half-plane and that it moves away to the left for $\varepsilon \to +0$ if p is bounded away from zero. If p is positive we define in connection with (3) the operator T_o,

(7) $$T_o u := pu' + qu \qquad \text{for all } u \in \mathcal{D}(T_o),$$

$$\mathcal{D}(T_o) := \{v \in L^2(-1,1) \mid v' \in L^2(-1,1) \text{ and } v(1) = 0\}.$$

The spectrum of this operator is empty and we can show that the resolvent operator $(T_\varepsilon-\lambda)^{-1}$ converges strongly to $(T_o-\lambda)^{-1}$ for all $\lambda \in \mathbb{C}$, cf. KATO [19]. We can consider problem (2) from a similar point of view, cf. LIONS [21].

In the second chapter of this tract we describe this approach to problem (1). We show that the spectrum of T_ε disappears at infinity for $\varepsilon \to +0$ and that the resolvent operator $(T_\varepsilon-\lambda)^{-1}$ converges to $(T_o-\lambda)^{-1}$ in the uniform operator topology for every λ. This analysis applies to the case where ε, p and q are complex valued, provided the real part of p is bounded away from zero and ε/p tends to zero within a (fixed) closed sector in $\mathbb{C}$ not containing the imaginary axis.

If the assumption that the coefficient p does not have a zero (and p_j, $j = 1...n$, do not have a simultaneous zero), is abandoned, problem (1) (and (2)) is much more complicated, since the usual method of proving convergence by a maximum principle or by Gårdings inequality does not apply for non-negative q.

Recently a large number of papers have been published on problem (1), in which p is assumed to have (at least) one zero in the interior of the interval (-1,1). In most of the contributions, only formal approximations are computed, i.e. functions are computed which satisfy the differential equation and the boundary conditions up to some order of ε, and no effort is made to prove validity of the approximations. In [3], ACKERBERG & O'MALLEY indicate that a formal approximation of the solution of (1) with $p(0) = 0$, $p'(x) < 0$ and $f \equiv 0$ shows a peculiar behaviour if $q(0)/p'(0)$ is equal to a non-negative integer. In that case the formal approximation is of order unity in the interior of the interval, while otherwise it is exponentially small (with respect to ε). They call this phenomenon (internal) resonance. Others, e.g. COOK & ECKHAUS [7], show by more refined (formal) asymptotic techniques that "resonance" can be expected if $q(0)/p'(0)$ is somewhere in an $\mathcal{O}(\sqrt{\varepsilon})$-neighbourhood of a non-negative integer. MATKOVSKY [22] suggests that the conditions for resonance may be connected with the eigenvalues of a related boundary value problem. In [14] we state that resonance is caused by a neighbouring eigenvalue of the problem and in [15] we prove this; we reformulate problem (1) with $p(0) = 0$, and $p'(x) \neq 0$, as an eigenvalue problem, and we show convergence of its eigenvalues. Moreover, we prove convergence of its solutions, if the system is not at an eigenvalue. RUBENFELD & WILLNER [25] state a recursive procedure by which for each $n \in \mathbb{N}$ can be decided whether system (1) (with $p' < 0$) has an eigenvalue inside an $\mathcal{O}(\varepsilon^n)$-neighbourhood of zero. They show that no resonance occurs, if this eigenvalue is outside an $\mathcal{O}(\varepsilon^{n+1})$-neighbourhood of zero; i.e. they prove that the solution of (1) with $f \equiv 0$, $p(0) = 0$ and $p' < 0$ is exponentially small, if a positive constant α exists such that the disk of radius $\alpha\varepsilon^n$ in $\mathbb{C}$ around zero does not contain an eigenvalue of (1) for some $n \in \mathbb{N}$ and for all sufficiently small positive ε. They use LANGER's method for approximating turning point problems. However they formulate their criterion in a different way and they do not seem to realize that by doing so they are in fact approximating the eigenvalues of problem (1). ABRAHAMSSON [1] proves convergence of the solution of (1) with $p(0) = 0$ and $p'(x) \neq 0$, provided $q(0)/p'(0)$ is not equal to a non-negative integer.

In this tract we give a detailed analysis of the problems (1) and (2) in which $\underline{p}$ and $\sum|p_j|$ respectively have exactly one zero in the interior of the domain under consideration. Such problems are often referred to as turning point problems. We reformulate the boundary value problems in terms of linear operators in a Hilbert space and we study the behaviour of the spectrum of these operators in the limit for $\varepsilon \to +0$. We then consider strong convergence of the resolvent operators outside the spectrum and we give asymptotic expansions of the solutions of the boundary value problems. We stipulate that it is necessary first to determine the spectrum and its limiting behaviour for $\varepsilon \to +0$. Otherwise we are completely in the dark as regards the existence (and the unicity) of a solution and we are faced with such apparently curious phenomena as "resonance" (in the sense of [3]) was thought to be.

In the first chapter we deal with abstract perturbation theorems for linear operators in a Hilbert space, with spaces of functions (Sobolev spaces) and elliptic operators on them and with critical points of first order partial differential operators on $\mathbb{R}^2$. We restrict ourselves to such results as are needed in the subsequent chapters.

In the second chapter we consider problem (1) with $p > 0$. With this additional condition, the problem is comperatively easy and the asymptotics of its solution are well understood, as stated above. We present the problem more or less along the lines of KATO [19] and LIONS [21]. This chapter aims to illustrate, in a fairly straightforward case, methods to be used later on. Moreover, some of the results derived here can be used in the subsequent chapters.

In chapter 3 we study the singularly perturbed turning point problem, i.e. problem (1) with the assumptions $p(0) = 0$ and $p'(x) \neq 0$. For convenience, we transform it into the following equivalent form:

$$(8\pm) \qquad \varepsilon\{(au')' + bu' + cu\} \pm xu' - \lambda u = f, \qquad u(1) = 0,\ u(-1) = 0,$$

where a, b and c are C^∞-functions with $a > 0$, where λ is a complex "spectral" parameter and ε is a small positive parameter. In connection with the boundary value problems (8±) we define differential operators T_ε and U_ε for any u in the domains

$$\text{(9a)} \qquad \mathcal{D}(T_\varepsilon) := \mathcal{D}(U_\varepsilon) := \{v \in L^2(-1,1) \mid v'' \in L^2(-1,1) \text{ and } v(\pm 1) = 0\}$$

by

$$\text{(9b)} \qquad T_\varepsilon u = \varepsilon\{(au')' + bu' + cu\} + xu', \quad U_\varepsilon u := \varepsilon\{(au')' + bu' + cu\} - xu'.$$

The spectra of T_ε and U_ε are discrete for any $\varepsilon > 0$. We show that if the eigenvalues are arranged in order of magnitude, the n-th eigenvalues of T_ε and of $U_\varepsilon - 1$ converge to $-n$ for $\varepsilon \to +0$ and for each $n \in \mathbb{N}$. The proof assumes full knowledge of the eigenvalues and eigenfunctions of the Hermite operator (harmonic oscillator in Quantum Mechanics) and we show, using perturbation theory for linear operators, cf. KATO [19], that the limits of the eigenvalues cannot change when we change the operator continuously into T_ε (or into $U_\varepsilon-1$).

If λ is not an eigenvalue, the problems (8±) have unique solutions and we can consider their convergence for $\varepsilon \to +0$. We show that the reduced problem of (8+), $xu' - \lambda u = f$ and $u(\pm 1) = 0$, has one continuous solution if f is continuous and if $Re\lambda > 0$ and that the analytic continuation (in the λ-plane) of this solution approximates $(T_\varepsilon-\lambda)^{-1}f$ up to the order $\mathcal{O}(\varepsilon)$ in the weighted uniform norm

$$\text{(10)} \qquad u \mapsto \max_{-1\le x\le 1} \left| |x|^{k+\frac{1}{2}} u(x) \right| ,$$

provided $-\lambda \notin \mathbb{N}$ and $Re\lambda > -k + 3/2$ with $k \in \mathbb{N}$. Similarly, the reduced problem of (8−), $-xu' - \lambda u = f$ (without boundary conditions), has one continuous solution, if f is continuous and $Re\lambda > 0$; if f is k times continuously differentiable, this solution can be continued analytically to all $\lambda \in \mathbb{C}$ with $Re\lambda > -k$ and this analytic continuation approximates the solution of (8−) uniformly up to $\mathcal{O}(\varepsilon)$ on each subinterval $(-\delta,\delta)$ with $0 < \delta < 1$. By constructing ordinary boundary layers at $x = \pm 1$ we obtain uniform approximations of the solution of (8−) on the entire interval. If $Re\lambda$ is larger than the first eigenvalue, the convergence of the approximations can be proved by standard techniques, such as the maximum principle, Gårding's inequality or the variational inequality. If $Re\lambda$ is smaller, we have to consider related boundary value problems with other boundary conditions in the larger Sobolev space $H^{-n}(-1,1)$ of n-th order distributions for problem (8+) and in the smaller space $H^{+n}(-1,1)$ of functions, whose n-th derivative is square integrable, for problem (8-). If n is large enough, we can construct approximations to the solutions of the auxiliary boundary value problem and prove their validity by a variational inequality. Hereafter we can compare the solutions of the original and the auxiliary problems and prove convergence of the approximation of the original problems.

The remaining chapters 4, 5 and 6 are devoted to problems of type (2) in which the first order operator $\sum p_j \partial_j$ has one critical point inside Ω. For simplicity, we limit the analysis to two-dimensional problems; the results obtained can easily be extended to problems in $\mathbb{R}^n$ with $n > 2$. We assume that the quadratic form associated with the elliptic operator L is positive. We formulate problem (2) in a manner similar to (8) and we study it with the following three first order operators

$$(11a\pm) \qquad \pm(x\partial_x + \mu y \partial_y), \qquad \mu \in \mathbb{R}^+,$$

$$(11b\pm) \qquad \pm\big((x-\kappa y)\partial_x + (y+\kappa x)\partial_y\big), \qquad \kappa \in \mathbb{R},$$

$$(11c) \qquad x\partial_x - \mu y \partial_y, \qquad \mu \in \mathbb{R}^+,$$

whose critical points are a node, a vortex and a saddle-point respectively; the fields of characteristics associated with these three operators represent the three structurally stable (under topological transformations) classes in $\mathbb{R}^2$. The results obtained are analogous to the results in the one-dimensional case, but the proofs are more complicated.

In chapter 4 we study problem (2) with the first order operators (11a+) and (11a-). The eigenvalues converge to the numbers $-n-\mu m$ with $n,m \in \mathbb{N}$ in the first and $n,m \in \mathbb{N}_o$ in the latter case. Qualitatively, the asymptotic behaviour of the solutions can be read from figure 1, in which a domain is sketched with (directed) characteristics and with shadings indicating the position of the boundary layers. We prove that the solution of (2) & (11a+) converges to the solution of the reduced equation, which satisfies the boundary condition at the entire boundary, uniformly on subdomains not containing the critical point (0,0) for all λ outside the spectrum. We make no effort to clarify the structure of the boundary layer at (0,0), which can be very complicated, cf. [13] and [14]. For $Re\lambda > 0$ we construct an asymptotic approximation to the solution of (2) & (11a-); it consists of the solution of the reduced equation which is continuous at (0,0) plus boundary layer terms at $\partial\Omega$. This approximation is an analytic function of λ, which can be continued into the negative half-plane, if the right-hand side f is smooth enough; we prove that this analytic continuation converges uniformly in Ω to the solution of (2) & (11a-) for all λ outside the spectrum by considering related boundary value problems in spaces of sufficiently smooth functions.

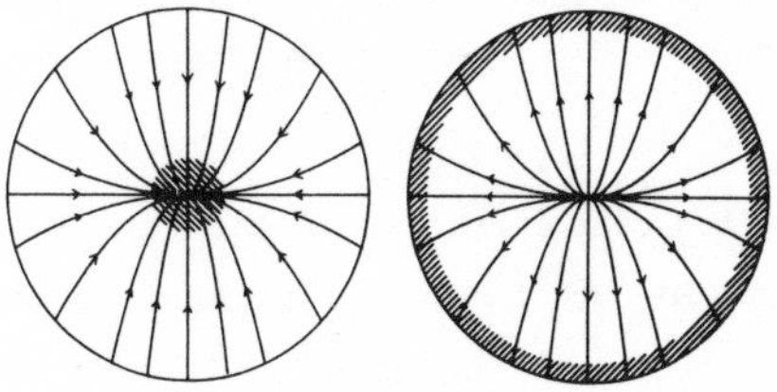

fig. 1: characteristics and boundary layers in the case of a first order operator with an attracting (11a+) and a repelling (11a-) node.

In chapter 5 we study problem (2) with the first order operators (11b+) and (11b-). The eigenvalues converge to the numbers $- 2n - |m| + i\kappa m$ with $m \in \mathbb{Z}$ and $n \in \mathbb{N}$ and $n \in \mathbb{N}_0$ respectively; the proof is more complicated than in the nodal case, since the limits are non-real. Qualitatively, the asymptotic behaviour of the solution can be read from fig. 2.

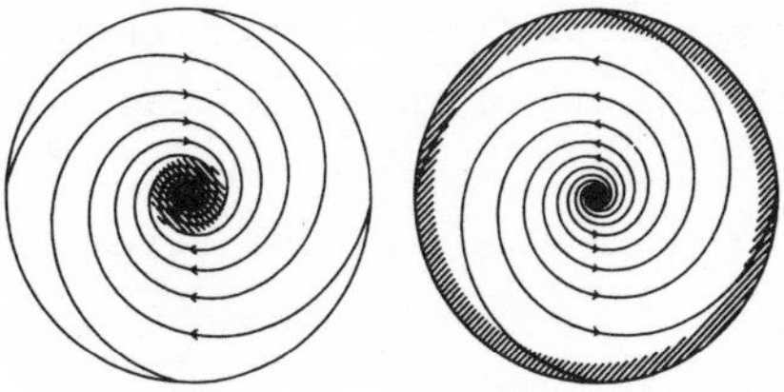

fig. 2: characteristics and boundary layers in the case of a first order operator with an attracting (11b-) and a repelling (11b-) vortex.

The asymptotic behaviour of the solutions is similar to that of the nodal case.

In chapter 6 we study problem (2), with the first order operator (11c). The eigenvalues converge to the number $- n - \mu m + \mu$ with $n,m \in \mathbb{N}$. Qualitatively, the asymptotic behaviour can be read from fig. 3. We construct

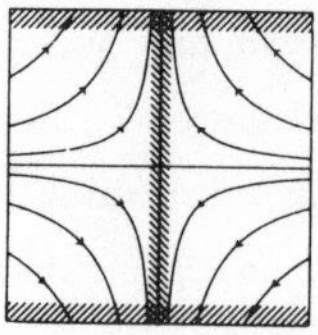

fig. 3: characteristics and boundary layers for a first order operator with a critical point of saddle-point type.

an approximation comprising 1°: the solution of the reduced equation satisfying the boundary conditions at the left- and right-hand sides of the domain, and 2°: boundary layer terms at the upper and lower sides. We prove that it converges uniformly on (closed) subdomains not containing the line $x = 0$, at which an interior boundary layer occurs, for all λ outside the spectrum. In the special case $L = \Delta$ we can study related boundary value problems in non-isotropic function spaces and we use them to prove convergence of the approximation in the weighted uniform norm

$$u \mapsto \max_{(x,y)\in\Omega} \left| |x|^{k+\frac{1}{2}} u(x,y) \right| ,$$

provided $Re\lambda > - k + 3/2$ and f has sufficiently many continuous derivatives with respect to y.

We have limited our analysis of "turning point problems" to linear problems in which the coefficient(s) of the first order operator has (have) one simple (simultaneous) zero and in which all coefficients are real. What happens, when one or more of these conditions are relaxed?

In [16] we study problem (1) in which p does not have a simple zero, i.e. we study the spectrum of the problems

$$(12) \qquad \varepsilon(au')' \pm x|x|^{\nu-1}u' - \lambda u = f, \qquad u(\pm 1) = 0, \qquad \nu \in \mathbb{R}^+ .$$

We show that the spectrum shifts away to $-\infty$ for $\varepsilon \to +0$ if ν is smaller than one and that it tends to a dense set in $(-\infty,0)$ for $\varepsilon \to +0$ if $\nu > 1$. It does not seem difficult to show that the asymptotic behaviour of the solutions of (12) is similar to that of the solutions of (8), provided either $\nu < 1$ or $Re\lambda > 0$; if $\nu > 1$ and $Re\lambda \leq 0$, the density of the limit of the spectrum may cause additional problems.

If the coefficients of (8±) are non-real, our analysis remains valid -at least so we expect-, provided ε and a satisfy the same condition as in chapter 2, namely that $\mathcal{Re}\,a$ is bounded away from zero and that εa tends to zero within a fixed closed sector in $\mathbb{C}$ not containing the imaginary axis.

Where the interval (-1,1) or the domain Ω contains several "turning points", we expect (1°) that the limiting spectrum is the union of the limiting spectra of the restrictions of the problem to disjoint neighbourhoods of the turning points and (2°) that an approximation of the solution can be constructed by pasting together approximations on subdomains containing only one turning point, cf. [14] §8.

DEFINITIONS AND NOTATIONS

Numbers

$\mathbb{Z}$: integers.

$\mathbb{N}$: positive integers, ($-\mathbb{N}$: negative integers).

$\mathbb{N}_o$: non-negative integers.

$\mathbb{R}$: real numbers.

$\mathbb{R}^+$: positive real numbers.

$\mathbb{C}$: complex numbers (with absolute value $|\cdot|$).

$Re\lambda$: real part of $\lambda \in \mathbb{C}$.

$Im\lambda$: imaginary part of $\lambda \in \mathbb{C}$.

$arg\lambda$: the argument of $\lambda \in \mathbb{C}$, $\lambda \neq 0$.

$D(z,r)$: is the open disk in $\mathbb{C}$ with center $z \in \mathbb{C}$ and radius $r \in \mathbb{R}^+$.

$\mathrm{dist}(V,W) := \inf\{|x-y| \mid x \in V \text{ and } y \in W\}$ with V and W subsets of $\mathbb{C}$.

${}^t(\alpha)$: transposed of the vector $\alpha \in \mathbb{C}^2$.

$|S|$: number of elements of the set S, provided S is a finite set.

Norms and inner products

We assume that Ω is a bounded open set in $\mathbb{R}$ or $\mathbb{R}^2$ with boundary $\partial\Omega$ and that u,v are (sufficiently smooth) functions on Ω. The subscript Ω in norms and inner products is skipped, if it is clear from the context to what domain is referred to.

$$\langle u,v\rangle_\Omega := \langle u,v\rangle_{o,\Omega} := \int_\Omega u(\vec{x})\bar{v}(\vec{x})d\vec{x}.$$

$$\langle u,v\rangle_{k,\Omega} := \begin{cases} \langle u^{(k)},v^{(k)}\rangle_{o,\Omega}, & \text{if } \Omega \subset \mathbb{R}, \\ \sum_{j=0}^{k} \langle \partial_x^j\partial_y^{k-j}u, \partial_x^j\partial_y^{k-j}v\rangle_{o,\Omega}, & \text{if } \Omega \subset \mathbb{R}^2. \end{cases} \qquad k \in \mathbb{N}.$$

$$[u]_\Omega := \max_{\vec{x}\in\Omega} |u(\vec{x})|.$$

$$\|u\|_\Omega := \|u\|_{o,\Omega} := |u|_{o,\Omega} := |u|_{o,2,\Omega} := \langle u,u\rangle_\Omega^{\frac{1}{2}}.$$

$$\|u\|_{k,\Omega} := \left\{\langle u,u\rangle_{k,\Omega} + \langle u,u\rangle_{o,\Omega}\right\}^{\frac{1}{2}}.$$

$$|u|_{k,\Omega} := \langle u,u\rangle_{k,\Omega}^{\frac{1}{2}}.$$

$$|u|_{o,p,\Omega} := \left\{ \int_\Omega |u(\vec{x})|^p d\vec{x} \right\}^{1/p}, \quad 1 \le p < \infty.$$

$$|u|_{k,p,\Omega} := \begin{cases} |u^{(k)}|_{o,p,\Omega}, & \text{if } \Omega \subset \mathbb{R}, \quad 1 \le p < \infty, \quad k \in \mathbb{N}, \\ \left\{ \sum_{j=0}^{k} |\partial_x^j \partial_y^{k-j} u|^p_{o,p,\Omega} \right\}^{1/p}, & \text{if } \Omega \subset \mathbb{R}^2. \end{cases}$$

$|u|_{o,\infty,\Omega} := \operatorname{ess.sup}_{\vec{x}\in\Omega} |u(\vec{x})| = \lim_{p\to\infty} |u|_{o,p,\Omega}$; $|u|_{k,\infty,\Omega} := \lim_{p\to\infty} |u|_{k,p,\Omega}$, $k \in \mathbb{N}$.

$$\|u\|_{k,p,\Omega} = \left\{ |u|^p_{o,p,\Omega} + |u|^p_{k,p,\Omega} \right\}^{1/p}.$$

$|u|_{-k,\Omega} := \sup\left\{ |\langle u,v\rangle| \;\middle|\; v \in C^\infty(\Omega),\ \|v\|_{k,\Omega} = 1 \right\}$, $k \in \mathbb{N}$, cf. (1.3b).

$\langle u,v\rangle_{-k,\Omega} := \frac{1}{4}\left\{ |u+v|^2_{-k,\Omega} - |u-v|^2_{-k,\Omega} + i|u+iv|^2_{-k,\Omega} - i|u-iv|^2_{-k,\Omega} \right\}$, cf. (1.6b).

$\langle u,v\rangle^{(1)}_k$ and $|u|^{(1)}_k$, cf. (1.17).

$\langle u,v\rangle^{(\nu)}_k$ and $|u|^{(\nu)}_k$, cf. (1.28).

$|||u|||_k$ and $\nmid u \nmid_k$, cf. (6.51).

$\left[[u]\right]$, cf. (4.51b).

$\|\nabla u\|_\Omega := |u|_{1,\Omega}$, provided $\Omega \subset \mathbb{R}^2$.

Spaces of functions

$C(\Omega)$: space of continuous functions on $\overline{\Omega}$, equipped with the maximum norm.

$C^k(\Omega)$: space of continuous functions on $\overline{\Omega}$, whose k-th derivatives are continuous, $k \in \mathbb{N}_o$, equipped with the norm $u \mapsto |u|_{o,\infty,\Omega} + |u|_{k,\infty,\Omega}$.

$C^\infty(\Omega) := \bigcap_{j=o}^{\infty} C^k(\Omega)$.

$C^\infty_o(\Omega)$: the subset of functions in $C^\infty(\Omega)$ with compact support in Ω.

$C^k_o(\Omega)$: closure of $C^\infty_o(\Omega)$ in $C^k(\Omega)$, $k \in \mathbb{N}_o$.

$L^p(\Omega)$: closure of $C(\Omega)$ in the norm $u \mapsto |u|_{o,p,\Omega}$, $1 \le p \le \infty$.

$H^k(\Omega)$: closure of $C^k(\Omega)$ in the norm $u \mapsto \|u\|_{k,\Omega}$, $k \in \mathbb{N}_o$.

$H^k_o(\Omega)$: closure of $C^k_o(\Omega)$ in the norm $u \mapsto \|u\|_{k,\Omega}$, $k \in \mathbb{N}_o$.

$H^{-k}(\Omega)$: dual of $H^k_o(\Omega)$ or closure of $L^2(\Omega)$ in the norm $u \mapsto |u|_{-k,\Omega}$, $k \in \mathbb{N}$, cf. ch.1§2a.

$H_1^k(\Omega)$: subspace of $H^k(\Omega)$, $k \in \mathbb{N}$, cf. ch.1 §2b.

$H^{(o,k)}(\Omega)$: cf. (1.43a).

$H_1^{(o,k)}(\Omega)$: cf. (1.45).

supp(f) := closure in Ω of the set $\{\vec{x} \in \Omega \mid f(\vec{x}) \neq 0\}$

Formal differential operators

We assume that the domain of definition of a formal differential operator $\mathcal{t}$ in a space $\mathcal{B}$ is maximal, i.e. that it is equal to the set $\{u \in \mathcal{B} \mid \mathcal{t}u \in \mathcal{B}\}$.

$\tau u := (au')' + bu' + cu;$ (' = d/dx)

with a,b and $c \in C^\infty(\mathbb{R})$ and a strictly positive.

$\partial_x u := \frac{\partial u}{\partial x}$, $\partial_y u = \frac{\partial u}{\partial y}$.

$\nabla u := \begin{pmatrix} \partial_x u \\ \partial_y u \end{pmatrix}$.

$\Delta u := \partial_x^2 u + \partial_y^2 u$.

$Lu := a\partial_x^2 u + 2b\partial_x\partial_y u + c\partial_y^2 u + d_1\partial_x u + d_2\partial_y u + d_3 u$

with a,b,c,d_1,d_2 and $d_3 \in C^\infty(\Omega)$, such that a and $ac-b^2$ are strictly positive.

$L_p u := \partial_x a\partial_x u + \partial_x b\partial_y u + \partial_y b\partial_x u + \partial_y c\partial_y u$ is the formally symmetric principal part of L.

$A(\cdot,\cdot)$: sesquilinear form in $\mathbb{C}^2$ connected with L, cf. (1.33b).

$\mathcal{A}(\cdot,\cdot)$: sesquilinear form in $H^1(\Omega)$ connected with L, cf. (1.33a).

$\mathcal{B}(\cdot,\cdot)$: sesquilinear form in $H^1(\Omega)$, cf. (4.86).

τ^*, L^* : formal adjoints of τ and L.

Linear operators

We assume that T and A are linear operators in a Banach space $\mathcal{B}$, equipped with the norm $\|\cdot\|$.

$\mathcal{D}(T)$: domain of definition of T.

$\mathcal{R}(T)$: range of T $(= T\mathcal{D}(T))$.

$\mathcal{N}(T)$: null-space of T.

$T_{|W}$: restriction of T to W, provided $W \subset \mathcal{D}(T)$.

$TW := \mathcal{R}(T_{|W})$, provided $W \subset \mathcal{D}(T)$.

$\rho(T) := \{\lambda \in \mathbb{C} \mid T - \lambda$ has a bounded inverse$\}$, resolvent set of T.

$\sigma(T) := \mathbb{C}\backslash\rho(T)$, spectrum of T.

$\|T\| := \sup\{\|Tu\| \mid u \in \mathcal{D}(T) \text{ and } \|u\| = 1\}$, norm of T.

T^* dual of T in the dual space of $\mathcal{B}$ (adjoint if $\mathcal{B}$ is a Hilbert space), provided $\mathcal{D}(T)$ is dense in $\mathcal{B}$.

T-*bounded* : an operator A is called T-bounded with "T-bound"β, if $\mathcal{D}(A) \supset \mathcal{D}(T)$ and if numbers α and $\beta \in \mathbb{R}^+$ exist such that

$$\|Au\| \leq \alpha\|u\| + \beta\|Tu\| \qquad \text{for all } u \in \mathcal{D}(T).$$

Semibounded : an operator T in a Hilbert space H with inner product $\langle \cdot,\cdot \rangle$ is called semibounded from above with upper bound $d \in \mathbb{R}$ if

$$\langle Tu-du,u \rangle \leq 0 \qquad \text{for all } u \in \mathcal{D}(T)$$

Special functions

P_k : Legendre polynomials
H_k : Hermite polynomials
} cf. [2] ch. 22.

$F(\cdot;\cdot;\cdot)$: Confluent hypergeometric function, cf. [27].

Y : Heaviside's unit step function: $Y(x) = \begin{cases} 1, & \text{of } x > 0, \\ 0, & \text{if } x < 0. \end{cases}$

δ : Dirac distribution, $\delta := Y'$.

Pf.: pseudo-function, cf. (3.26) and [26] ch. 5.6.

O-symbols

If S_α is the sector $\{\lambda \in \mathbb{C} \; |Im\lambda| \leq \alpha Re\lambda\}$ with $\alpha \geq 0$ and if f and g are continuous functions on S_α, then the expression

$$f(x) = O(g(x)) \qquad \text{for} \begin{cases} x \to 0,\; x \in S_\alpha, & \text{if } \alpha > 0, \\ x \to +0 & \text{if } \alpha = 0, \text{ i.e. if } S_\alpha = \mathbb{R}^+, \end{cases}$$

means that numbers $r \in \mathbb{R}^+$ and $C \in \mathbb{R}^+$ exist, such that $|f(x)| \leq C|g(x)|$ for all $x \in S_\alpha$ with $|x| \leq r$. Let f and g depend on several parameters; the order estimate is called *uniform* with respect to some of these, if C does not depend on these parameters. Moreover, the expression

$$f(x) = o(g(x)) \qquad (x \to +0)$$

means: $\lim_{x \to +0} f(x)/g(x) = 0$.

REMARK. All derivatives are taken in the generalized (distributional) sense. If the classical derivative exists, the generalized derivative is identified with it.

CHAPTER I

PRELIMINARIES

This chapter contains a number of results on abstract perturbation theorems and on Sobolev spaces, which we will subsequently require.

1.1. ABSTRACT PERTURBATION THEOREMS

Let $(H,\langle\cdot,\cdot\rangle)$ be a Hilbert space and let T be a densely defined closed linear operator on H, then T satisfies the following well-known results:

THEOREM 1.1. *If* $\|Tu\| \geq d\|u\|$ *for all* $u \in \mathcal{D}(T)$ *and some* $d \in \mathbb{R}^+$, *then* $R(T)$ *is closed; if, in addition,* $N(T^*) = \{0\}$ *then* T *has a bounded inverse and* $\|T^{-1}\| \leq 1/d$.

PROOF. cf. [29] ch. 7.5. □

THEOREM 1.2. *If* T *is normal, then* $\|(T-\lambda)^{-1}\| \leq 1/\mathrm{dist}(\lambda,\sigma(T))$ *for all* $\lambda \in \rho(T)$.

PROOF. cf. [19] ch. 5.3.8. □

THEOREM 1.3. *Let* Γ *be a closed curve of finite length* $|\Gamma|$ *in* $\rho(T)$ *which separates* $\sigma(T)$ *in the parts* Σ^1 *and* Σ^2 *and which encloses* Σ^1, *then the operator* $P := \frac{1}{2\pi i}\int_\Gamma (T-\lambda)^{-1}\, d\lambda$ *is a bounded projection which commutes with* T *and is such that* $H = PH \oplus (1-P)H$ *and* $\sigma(T_{|PH}) = \Sigma^1$ *and* $\sigma(T_{|(1-P)H}) = \Sigma^2$, *where* $T_{|PH}$ *means the restriction of* T *to the space* PH. *If, in addition,* $T - \lambda$ *has a compact inverse for some* $\lambda \in \mathbb{C}$ *then* P *is of finite rank and if* T *is normal then* P *is orthogonal and* $\|P\| = 1$.

PROOF. cf. [19] ch. 3, th. 6.17. □

Let A be a T-bounded operator satisfying

$$\|Au\| \leq \alpha\|u\| + \beta\|Tu\| \quad \text{for all } u \in \mathcal{D}(T) \text{ and for some } \alpha,\beta \in \mathbb{R}^+,$$

let $0 \in \rho(T)$ and $\gamma := \|T^{-1}\|$, then the family of operators $T_t := T + tA$ satisfies the following results:

THEOREM 1.4. *If* $|t| < (\alpha\gamma+\beta)^{-1}$, *the operator* T_t *is closed and has a bounded inverse; this inverse satisfies*

(1) $$\| T_t^{-1} \| \le \gamma(1-|t|(\alpha\gamma+\beta))^{-1}$$

(2) $$\| T_t^{-1}-T_s^{-1} \| = \|(s-t)T_s^{-1}AT_t^{-1}\| \le \frac{\gamma|s-t|(\alpha\gamma+\beta)}{(1-|s|(\alpha\gamma+\beta))(1-|t|(\alpha\gamma+\beta))} .$$

If in addition T^{-1} *is compact, then* T_t^{-1} *is compact.*

PROOF. cf. [19] ch. 4, th. 1.6. □

COROLLARY 1.5. *If* $\beta < \frac{1}{2}$, *if* T *is semibounded from above with semibound* $d \in \mathbb{R}$ *and if* $T - \lambda$ *has a bounded (compact) inverse for some* $\lambda \in \mathbb{C}$ *(with* $Re\lambda > d$ *if* $(T-\lambda)^{-1}$ *is not compact), then there is a* $\mu \in \mathbb{C}$ *such that* $T + A - \mu$ *has a bounded (compact) inverse.*

PROOF. Since T satisfies for all $u \in \mathcal{D}(T)$

$$\|Tu-\lambda u\| \ge |Re\langle Tu-\lambda u,u\rangle|/\|u\| \ge (Re\lambda-d)\|u\| \quad \text{if } Re\lambda > d,$$

$\rho(T)$ contains the set $\{\lambda \in \mathbb{C} \mid Re\lambda > d\}$ by the previous theorem. Since

$$\|Au\| \le (\alpha+\beta|\lambda|)\|u\| + \beta\|Tu-\lambda u\| \qquad \text{with } \beta < \tfrac{1}{2}$$

we can find by the previous theorem a positive real number ξ such that $T + A - \xi$ has a bounded (compact) inverse. □

THEOREM 1.6. *Let* Γ, Σ^1 *and* Σ^2 *be as in theorem 1.3 and define* $d := \max_{\lambda\in\Gamma} \|(T-\lambda)^{-1}\|$. *If* $t \in \mathbb{R}$ *and* $|t| < (\alpha d+\beta)^{-1}$, *then*

$$P_t := \frac{1}{2\pi i}\int_\Gamma (T_t-\lambda)^{-1}\, d\lambda$$

is a family of bounded projections which is continuous in t. P_t *commutes with* T_t, $H = P_tH \oplus (1-P_t)H$ *and* $\Sigma_t^1 := \sigma(T_t|_{P_tH})$ *and* $\Sigma_t^2 := \sigma(T_t|_{(1-P_t)H})$ *are separated by* Γ. *If, in addition,* $T - \lambda_o$ *has a compact inverse for some* $\lambda_o \in \mathbb{C}$, *then* P_t *is of finite constant rank and* Σ_t^1 *depends continuously on* t.

PROOF. From (1) it is clear that $\Gamma \subset \rho(T_t)$ for all $|t| < (\alpha d+\beta)^{-1}$, hence according to theorem 1.3 the operator P_t is a well-defined bounded projection which commutes with T_t (and is of finite rank if $(T-\lambda_o)^{-1}$ is compact). The continuity of P_t with respect to T is a direct consequence of formula (2),

$$\|P_t - P_s\| \leq \frac{d|s-t| \ |\Gamma|(\alpha d+\beta)}{(1-|t|(\alpha d+\beta))(1-|s|(\alpha d+\beta))} .$$

If $(T-\lambda_o)^{-1}$ is compact, the rank of P_t is finite and hence it is constant and equal to the total multiplicity of Σ^1; furthermore $P_t T_t$ is an operator of finite rank which depends continuously on t, hence the eigenvalues of T_t contained in Γ depend continuously on t, cf. [19] ch. 2, th. 5.1. □

1.2. SOBOLEV SPACES

a. The space $H_o^k(-1,1)$ with $k \in \mathbb{N}$ is the closure of $C_o^\infty(-1,1)$ with respect to the norm $u \longmapsto \|u\|_k$. It consists of those functions $f \in H^k(-1,1)$, for which $f^{(j)}(\pm 1) = 0$ for $0 \leq j \leq k-1$. In it we introduce the inner product $\langle \cdot,\cdot \rangle_k$ and norm $|\cdot|_k$ by

$$\langle u,v \rangle_k := \langle u^{(k)}, v^{(k)} \rangle \quad \text{and} \quad |u|_k := \| u^{(k)} \| = \langle u,u \rangle_k^{\frac{1}{2}} .$$

Since positive numbers γ_k exist such that

(3a) $$\|u\|_o \leq \gamma_k |u|_k \quad \text{for all } u \in H_o^k(-1,1) \text{ and } k \in \mathbb{N}_o ,$$

the norm $|\cdot|_k$ is on $H_o^k(-1,1)$ equivalent to the norm $\|\cdot\|_k$ and H_o^k is a Hilbert space with respect to the inner product $\langle \cdot,\cdot \rangle_k$. Since

$$\langle u,h \rangle \leq \|u\| \ \|h\| \leq \gamma_k |u|_k \ \|h\|$$

for all $u \in H_o^k(-1,1)$ and $h \in L^2(-1,1)$, each $h \in L^2(-1,1)$ defines the continuous anti-linear functional $u \longmapsto \langle h,u \rangle$ on $H_o^k(-1,1)$, which we will identify with h. Its norm

(3b) $$|h|_{-k} := \sup\{ |\langle h,u \rangle| \mid u \in H_o^k(-1,1) \ \& \ |u|_k = 1\}$$

satisfies

$$|h|_{-k} \leq \gamma_k \|h\| \quad \text{for all } h \in L^2(-1,1) \text{ and } k \in \mathbb{N}.$$

$H^{-k}(-1,1)$ is defined as the completion of $L^2(-1,1)$ with respect to the norm $|\cdot|_{-k}$; it is the $\langle \cdot,\cdot \rangle$-dual of $H_o^k(-1,1)$, cf. YOSIDA [29] ch. 3.10.

The differentiation operator $(\frac{d}{dx})^j$ is extended to an operator on $H^{-k}(-1,1)$ by duality; for $h \in H^{-k}$ we define $h^{(j)} := d^jh/dx^j$ by

(4) $$\left\langle h^{(j)},u\right\rangle := (-1)^j \left\langle h,u^{(j)}\right\rangle \qquad \text{for all } u \in H_o^{k+j}(-1,1).$$

By this definition $(d/dx)^j$ is an operator of $H^{-k}(-1,1)$ onto $H^{-k-j}(-1,1)$, whose kernel is the span of $\{1,x,\ldots,x^{j-1}\}$. Hence its adjoint $(-d/dx)^j$ is a one-to-one mapping of $H_o^{k+j}(-1,1)$ into $H_o^k(-1,1)$ whose range is the $\langle\cdot,\cdot\rangle$-orthogonal complement of $\{1,x,\ldots,x^{j-1}\}$ and which is isometric by definition of the norms $|\cdot|_{k+j}$ and $|\cdot|_k$.

Since $(H_o^k(-1,1), \langle\cdot,\cdot\rangle_k)$ is a Hilbert space, we can find for every $h \in H^{-k}(-1,1)$ exactly one $v \in H_o^k(-1,1)$ such that $\langle u,h\rangle = \langle u,v\rangle_k$ for all $u \in H^k(-1,1)$, and we have

$$\left\langle u,h\right\rangle = \left\langle u,v\right\rangle_k = \left\langle u^{(k)},v^{(k)}\right\rangle = \left\langle u,(-1)^k\, v^{(2k)}\right\rangle .$$

We conclude that the mapping $D_k := (-1)^k(d/dx)^{2k}$ is an isometric isomorphism of $H_o^k(-1,1)$ onto $H^{-k}(-1,1)$. We define the operator $J_k : H^{-k}(-1,1) \longrightarrow H^o(-1,1)$ by

(5) $$J_kh := (d/dx)^k\, D_k^{-1}h;$$

this operator satisfies

(6a) $$\|J_kh\| = \|(D_k^{-1}h)^{(k)}\| = |D_k^{-1}h|_k = |h|_{-k}$$

and it enables us to define in $H^{-k}(-1,1)$ the inner product

(6b) $$\left\langle g,h\right\rangle_{-k} := \left\langle J_kg,J_kh\right\rangle \quad (\text{with } \left\langle h,h\right\rangle_{-k}^{1/2} = |h|_{-k}).$$

The mapping J_k is an isometric isomorphism of $H^{-k}(-1,1)$ onto the orthogonal complement of the set $\{1,x,\ldots,x^{k-1}\}$ in $L^2(-1,1)$; we can also say that J_k stands for a k-fold repeated integration, corrected so that J_kh is orthogonal to the set $\{1,x,\ldots,x^{k-1}\}$. Define the operator P_k as the orthogonal projection onto the span of $\{1,x,\ldots,x^{k-1}\}$, i.e.

$$P_ku := \sum_{j=0}^{k-1} (j+\tfrac{1}{2})\left\langle u,P_j\right\rangle P_j, \qquad \text{for all } u \in L^2(0,1),$$

where P_j is the j-th Legendre polynomial, then $\mathcal{P}_k J_k = 0$ and $(1-\mathcal{P}_k)J_k = J_k$. This results in the commutation relation

$$(7) \qquad J_k (d/dx)^j u = (1-\mathcal{P}_k)(d/dx)^j J_k u, \qquad \text{for all } u \in H^{-k+j}(-1,1) \text{ and } j \le k.$$

Hence for any pair $u \in H^{j-k}(-1,1)$ and $v \in H^{-k}(-1,1)$ with $0 \le j \le k$ we find the identity

$$(8a) \qquad \left\langle u^{(j)}, v \right\rangle_{-k} = \left\langle J_k u^{(j)}, J_k v \right\rangle = \left\langle (d/dx)^j J_k u, J_k v \right\rangle$$

and any $u \in L^2(-1,1)$ satisfies the inequality

$$(8b) \qquad |u^{(k)}|_{-k} = \|(1-\mathcal{P}_k)(d/dx)^k J_k u\| = \|(1-\mathcal{P}_k)u\| \le \|u\|.$$

By formula (8a) we are able to compute the $\left\langle \cdot,\cdot \right\rangle_{-k}$-adjoint of a differential operator on H^{-k} and to decide whether it is invertible or not, cf. (15).

<u>THEOREM 1.7</u>. *The operator* S *on* $H^{-k}(-1,1)$, *defined by*

$$(9) \qquad Su := \tau u \quad \textit{for all } u \in \mathcal{D}(S) := \{u \in H^{-k+2}(-1,1) \mid (J_k u)(\pm 1) = 0\},$$

is semibounded from above and $S - \lambda$ *has a compact inverse for some* $\lambda \in \mathbb{C}$.

<u>PROOF</u>. Since by definition $J_k u \in H^2(-1,1)$ for all $u \in \mathcal{D}(S)$, the boundary conditions $u \mapsto (J_k u)(\pm 1)$ are well-defined continuous functionals (with respect to the graph norm of S) on $\mathcal{D}(S)$ by the lemma of Sobolev (lemma 2.6).

From Leibniz' rule we easily derive

$$(10) \qquad p\left(\frac{d}{dx}\right)^k q = \sum_{j=0}^{k} (-1)^j \binom{k}{j} \left(\frac{d}{dx}\right)^{k-j} (p^{(j)} q),$$

hence any $u \in \mathcal{D}(S)$ satisfies by (6b) and (8a)

$$(11a) \qquad \left\langle (au')', u \right\rangle_{-k} = -\left\langle J_k au', J_k u' \right\rangle = -\left\langle J_k a\left(-\frac{d}{dx}\right)^k J_k u', J_k u' \right\rangle =$$

$$= -\sum_{j=0}^{k} (-1)^{k-j} \binom{k}{j} \left\langle J_k \left(\frac{d}{dx}\right)^{k-j} (a^{(j)} J_k u'), J_k u' \right\rangle \le$$

$$\le -[1/a]^{-1} \|J_k u'\|^2 + \sum_{j=1}^{k} \binom{k}{j} [a^{(j)}] \|J_k u'\| \left\|\left(\frac{d}{dx}\right)^{k-j+1} D_k^{-1} u\right\|,$$

(11b) $$\left\langle bu',u\right\rangle_{-k} \le \sum_{j=0}^{k} \binom{k}{j} [b^{(j)}] \| J_k u' \| \, \| (\tfrac{d}{dx})^{k-j} D_k^{-1} u \| ,$$

(11c) $$\left\langle cu,u\right\rangle_{-k} \le \sum_{j=0}^{k} \binom{k}{j} [c^{(j)}] \| J_k u \| \, \| (\tfrac{d}{dx})^{k-j} D_k^{-1} u \| .$$

From (3) we infer

(12) $$\| (\tfrac{d}{dx})^{k-j} D_k^{-1} u \| \le \gamma_j | (\tfrac{d}{dx})^{k-j} D_k^{-1} u |_j = \gamma_j \| J_k u \| .$$

Using the inequality

(13) $$pq \le \tfrac{1}{2} p^2/r + \tfrac{1}{2} q^2 r \qquad \text{for all } p,q,r \in \mathbb{R}^+ ,$$

we find from (11) and (12) a positive constant C_k such that

(14) $$\left\langle \tau u,u\right\rangle_{-k} \le C_k \left\langle u,u\right\rangle_{-k} \qquad \text{for all } u \in \mathcal{D}(S),$$

hence S is semibounded.

In order to prove that $S - \lambda$ is invertible for some $\lambda \in \mathbb{C}$ and has a compact inverse, we consider the special operator $S_o := d^2/dx^2$. By (8a) it satisfies

(15) $$\left\langle S_o u,v\right\rangle_{-k} = \left\langle J_k u'', J_k v\right\rangle = \left\langle J_k u, J_k v''\right\rangle = \left\langle u, S_o v\right\rangle_{-k}$$

for all u and $v \in \mathcal{D}(S)$, hence S_o is selfadjoint and, since

$$\left\langle S_o u,u\right\rangle_{-k} = - |u'|^2_{-k} < 0,$$

$S_o - \lambda$ is invertible by theorem 1.1 at least for all $\lambda \in \mathbb{C}$ with $Re\lambda > 0$. This inverse is compact, for $J_k S_o J_k^{-1}$ is the restriction of an operator on $L^2(-1,1)$ with a compact inverse. By defining the continuous chain $S_t := tS + (1-t)S_o$ with $t \in [0,1]$ we can deduce constants α_k and β_k from the inequalities (14) such that

$$|S_s u - S_t u|_{-k} \le |s-t| (\alpha_k |u|_{-k} + \beta_k |S_t u|_{-k}),$$

for all $u \in \mathcal{D}(S)$ and $s,t \in [0,1]$. Since S_t is semibounded for all $t \in [0,1]$ and $S_o - \lambda$ has a compact inverse if $Re\lambda > 0$, we find from corollary 1.5 numbers t_o and $\lambda_o \in \mathbb{R}^+$ such that $S_t - \lambda$ has a compact inverse for all

$t \in [0,t_o]$ and λ with $Re\lambda > \lambda_o$. Doing this repeatedly we find increasing sequences $\{t_j\}$ and $\{\lambda_j\}$ in $\mathbb{R}^+$ such that $S_t - \lambda$ has a compact inverse for all $t \in [0,t_j]$ and $\lambda \in \mathbb{C}$ with $Re\lambda > \lambda_j$. Since we can choose $t_j - t_{j-1} > 1/4\beta_k$, the value $t = 1$ is attained in a finite number of steps. $\square$

<u>REMARK</u>. The way in which we defined the spaces $H_o^k(-1,1)$ with $k \in \mathbb{Z}$ implies not only that $H_o^k(-1,1)$ is the $\langle\cdot,\cdot\rangle$-dual of $H^{-k}(-1,1)$ and that $H_o^k(-1,1)$ is $\langle\cdot,\cdot\rangle_k$-self dual, but also that the form $\langle\cdot,\cdot\rangle_k$ can be extended to a sesquilinear form on $H_o^{k+n}(-1,1) \times H_o^{k-n}(-1,1)$, such that $H_o^{k+n}(-1,1)$ is the $\langle\cdot,\cdot\rangle_k$-dual of $H_o^{k-n}(-1,1)$. This implies the inequality

(16) $$|\langle u,v\rangle_k| \le |u|_{k+n}|v|_{k-n},$$

if $u \in H_o^{k+n}$ and $v \in H_o^{k-n}$. N.B. The subindex o in H_o^k has to be skipped if $k \le 0$.

b. The space $H_1^k(-1,1)$ is the set of functions $u \in H^k(-1,1)$ which satisfy $u^{(j)}(0) = 0$ for $j \in \mathbb{N}_o$ and $0 \le j < k$. With respect to the inner product $\langle\cdot,\cdot\rangle_k$ it is a Hilbert space; in order to prove this we have to show only that the norms $u \mapsto |u|_k$ and $u \mapsto \|u\|_k$ are equivalent on $H_1^k(-1,1)$. In case $k = 1$ we define the operators A and B by

$$Au := u' \quad \text{for all } u \in \mathcal{D}(A) := \{v \in H^1(0,1) \mid v(0) = 0\}$$

$$Bu := u' \quad \text{for all } u \in \mathcal{D}(B) := \{v \in H^1(-1,0) \mid v(0) = 0\}$$

and we observe that $H_1^1(-1,1) = \mathcal{D}(A) \oplus \mathcal{D}(B)$. By formula (2.4b) we find the inequality

$$|u|_1^2 = \|Au\|^2_{(0,1)} + \|Bu\|^2_{(-1,0)} \ge e^{-2}\|u\|^2_{(-1,1)},$$

which proves the equivalence of $|\cdot|_1$ and $\|\cdot\|_1$ on $H_1^1(-1,1)$. In case $k > 1$, we take the k-th powers of A and B and proceed in the same way.

In the space $H^k(-1,1)$ we can now define the inner product

(17) $$\langle u,v\rangle_k^{(1)} := \langle u,v\rangle_k + \sum_{j=0}^{k-1} u^{(j)}(0)\, \bar{v}^{(j)}(0);$$

with respect to this inner product $H^k(-1,1)$ is a Hilbert space. The norm $|\cdot|_k^{(1)}$ belonging to this inner product is equivalent to the original $\|\cdot\|_k$-norm, for any $u \in H^k(-1,1)$ satisfies

(18) $$\|u\|_k^2 = \|u\|_{k,(0,1)}^2 + \|u\|_{k,(-1,0)}^2 =$$

$$= \|A^{-k}u^{(k)} + \sum_{j=0}^{k-1} u^{(j)}(0)x^j/j!\|_k^2 + \|B^{-k}u^{(k)} + \sum_{j=0}^{k-1} u^{(j)}(0)x^j/j!\|_k^2$$

and the equivalence of $|\cdot|_k^{(1)}$ and $\|\cdot\|_k$ is a simple consequence of this identity and Sobolev's lemma. The space $H^k(-1,1)$ admits the decomposition

(19) $$H^k(-1,1) = H_1^k(-1,1) \oplus \bigoplus_{j=0}^{k-1} sp\{x^j\}$$

and it is easily seen that this decomposition is orthogonal with respect to the inner product $\langle \cdot,\cdot \rangle_k^{(1)}$.

In the space $H^k(-1,1)$ we define the differential operator $S^{(k)}$ by

(20) $$S_u^{(k)} := \tau u \quad \text{for all } u \in \mathcal{D}(S^{(k)}) := \{v \in H^{k+2}(-1,1) \mid v^{(k+1)}(\pm 1) = 0\}$$

and it satisfies:

THEOREM 1.8. *The operator* $S^{(k)}$ *is semibounded from above and has a compact inverse for some* $\lambda \in \mathbb{C}$.

PROOF. We proceed in a way analogous to thm. 1.7. In order to prove the semiboundedness we use the inner product $\langle u,v \rangle_k + \langle u,v \rangle_o$ in $H^k(-1,1)$; we have

$$\langle (au')',u \rangle_k = \langle (au')^{(k+1)}, u^{(k)} \rangle_o =$$

$$= -\langle au^{(k+1)}, u^{(k+1)} \rangle + \langle \sum_{j=0}^{k-1} \binom{k}{j} \left(a^{(k-j)}u^{(j+1)} + a^{(k-j+1)}u^{(j)}\right), u^{(k)} \rangle$$

and we obtain semiboundedness by straightforward computations with use of inequalities of type (16).

In order to prove the invertibility we consider the special operator $S_o^{(k)} := d^2/dx^2$. Let u_λ be a solution of the equation

(21) $$S_o^{(k)}u - \lambda u = f, \qquad u^{(k+1)}(\pm 1) = 0$$

with $f \in H^k(-1,1)$, then $v_\lambda := u_\lambda^{(k)}$ is a solution of the equation

$$S_o^{(0)}v - \lambda v = f^{(k)}, \qquad v'(\pm 1) = 0.$$

It is well-known that $S_o^{(0)} - \lambda$ has a compact inverse if $\lambda \notin \sigma(S_o^{(0)})$, hence u_λ can be written as

$$u_\lambda(x) = \int_0^x (x-t)^k v_\lambda(t)dt/k! + \sum_{j=0}^{k-1} u_\lambda^{(j)}(0)x^j/j!\,.$$

Inserting this expression in eq.(21), we obtain the set of equations

$$u_\lambda^{(j+2)}(0) - \lambda u_\lambda^{(j)}(0) = f^{(j)}(0), \qquad 0 \le j \le k-3,$$

$$v_\lambda(0) - \lambda u_\lambda^{(k-2)}(0) = f^{(k-2)}(0),$$

$$v_\lambda'(0) - \lambda u_\lambda^{(k-1)}(0) = f^{(k-1)}(0),$$

from which the numbers $u_\lambda^{(j)}(0)$ can be solved uniquely if $\lambda \neq 0$ and $\lambda \notin \sigma(S_o^{(0)})$. We conclude that eq.(21) has a unique solution for all $f \in H^k(-1,1)$ and hence that $S_o^{(k)} - \lambda$ has a compact inverse, if $\lambda \notin \sigma(S_o^{(0)}) \cup \{0\}$. As in the previous theorem we can continue this invertibility-property along the chain $tS^{(k)} + (1-t)S_o^{(k)}$. □

c. In the space $H^k(\Omega)$, $k \in \mathbb{N}$, where Ω is the unit disk in $\mathbb{R}^2$, we define the sesquilinear form

(22) $$\langle u,v\rangle_k := \sum_{j=0}^{k} \langle \partial_x^j\partial_y^{k-j}u, \partial_x^j\partial_y^{k-j}v\rangle$$

and the (semi)norm connected with it,

(22b) $$|u|_k := \langle u,u\rangle_k^{1/2}, \qquad \|u\|_k := \{\langle u,u\rangle_o + \langle u,u\rangle_k\}^{1/2}.$$

The form $\langle u,v\rangle_o + \langle u,v\rangle_k$ constitutes an inner product and $u \mapsto \|u\|_k$ a norm in $H^k(\Omega)$.

The restriction of a function defined on Ω to the boundary is a continuous operator form $H^k(\Omega)$ into $H^{k-1}(\partial\Omega)$ (onto $H^{k-1/2}(\partial\Omega)$, cf. [20]); by way of example we show

LEMMA 1.9. *Every function* $u \in H^1(\Omega)$ *satisfies the inequality*

(23) $$\|u\|_{\partial\Omega}^2 \le 2\|u\|_\Omega^2 + 2\|u\|_\Omega\,|u|_{1,\Omega}\,.$$

PROOF. Let (r,ϕ) be the polar coordinates; any $u \in C^1(\Omega)$ satisfies

$$\|u\|^2_{\partial\Omega} = \int_0^{2\pi} |u|^2 \, d\phi = \int_0^{2\pi}\int_0^1 \partial_r(r^2|u|^2)dr\, d\phi \le$$

$$\le 2\|u\|^2 + 2\|r^2u\|\,|u|_1$$

and since $C^1(\Omega)$ is dense in $H^1(\Omega)$, this inequality can be extended to all $u \in H^1(\Omega)$. □

REMARK. This lemma is a special example of a large class of "trace theorems", which deal with the continuity of the restriction operator to spaces of functions on subdomains of lower dimension, cf. [20] ch. 1 §8 and [4] §7.58.

LEMMA 1.10. *If* $u \in H^k(\Omega)$ with $k \in \mathbb{N}$ *is such that* $(\partial_x^i\partial_y^j u)(0,0) = 0$ *for all* $i,j \in \mathbb{N}_o$ *with* $i + j \le k - 2$ *then* $r^\nu u \in H^o(\Omega)$ *for all* $\nu > -k$. *Moreover, constants* C_k *not depending on* ν *and* u *exist such that*

$$\|r^\nu u\| \le C_k(\nu+k)^{-1}\|u\|_k . \tag{24}$$

PROOF. We begin with the case $k = 1$. If $u \in C^1(\Omega)$, integration by parts yields

$$\|r^\nu u\|^2 = \int_0^{2\pi}\int_0^1 r^{2\nu+1}\, u\bar{u}\, dr\, d\phi =$$

$$= \frac{1}{2\nu+2}\int_0^{2\pi} |u|^2 d\phi - \frac{1}{2\nu+2}\int_0^{2\pi}\int_0^1 r^{2\nu+2}\,\partial_r(u\bar{u})dr\, d\phi,$$

provided $\nu > -1$. By lemma 1.9 and by Schwarz' inequality we find

$$\|r^\nu u\|^2 \le (\nu+1)^{-1}\Big\{\|u\|\,(\|u\| + |u|_1) + \|r^\nu u\|\,\|r^{\nu+1}\nabla u\|\Big\} \le \tag{25}$$

$$\le \tfrac12\|r^\nu u\|^2 + (\tfrac12 + (\nu+1)^{-1})\|u\|^2 + (\nu+1)^{-2}|u|_1^2 .$$

Since $C^1(\Omega)$ is dense in $H^1(\Omega)$ this inequality extends to all $u \in H^1(\Omega)$.

If $u \in H^2(\Omega)$ and $u(0,0) = 0$, we have the identity

$$(26)\qquad u(x,y) = x(\partial_x u)(x,y) + y(\partial_y u)(x,y) + \\ - \int_0^1 ((x^2\partial_x^2+2xy\partial_x\partial_y+y^2\partial_y^2)u)(xt,yt)\,tdt.$$

We apply the result of the first part of the proof to the first and second term of the right-hand side and we apply to the integral a result for the inverse of the operator $-(x\partial_x+y\partial_y+2)$ proved in lemma 4.11. By (4.64) and (4.65) we find that any $v \in \overset{o}{H}(\Omega)$ satisfies the inequality

$$\left\| \int_0^1 v(xt,yt)\,tdt \right\| = \| (x\partial_x+y\partial_y+2)^{-1} v \| \le \|v\| ,$$

hence we find for all $\nu > -2$

$$\| r^\nu u \| \le \| r^{\nu+1}\partial_x u \| + \| r^{\nu+1}\partial_y u\| + \| \partial_x^2 u\| + 2\| \partial_x\partial_y u \| + \| \partial_y^2 u \| .$$

In conjunction with (25) this yields (24) for $k = 2$. In order to avoid suspicion of a circular reasoning, we stipulate that the proof of lemma 4.11 does not depend on the contents of this section.

If $k > 2$ we proceed the same way; instead of (26) we use the identity

$$(27a)\qquad u(x,y) = \sum_{j=0}^{k-2}\sum_{i=0}^{k-j-2} \frac{x^i y^j}{i!\,j!}\,\partial_x^i\partial_y^j u(0,0) + \frac{1}{(k-1)!}\left(\frac{d}{ds}\right)^{k-1} u(xs,ys)\Big|_{s=1} + \\ + \frac{1}{(k-1)!}\int_0^1 \sum_{j=1}^{k} \binom{k}{j}(-t)^j\left(\frac{d}{ds}\right)^k u(xs,ys)\Big|_{s=t}\,dt.$$

This formula is proved by iteration of the formula for a function of one variable

$$(27b)\qquad w(x) = w(0) + x\int_0^1 w'(xt)dt = w(0) + xw'(0) + x^2\int_0^1 (1-t)w''(xt)dt = \\ = w(0) + xw'(x) - x^2\int_0^1 tw''(xt)dt$$

and application of it to $u(r\cos\phi, r\sin\phi)$ considered as a function of r alone. □

In $H^k(\Omega)$ we introduce the second innerproduct $\langle\cdot,\cdot\rangle_k^{(\nu)}$:

(28a) $$\left\langle u,v\right\rangle_k^{(\nu)} := \sum_{j=0}^{k-2}\sum_{m=0}^{k-j-2} (j!\,m!)^{-2}(\partial_x^j\partial_y^m u)(0,0)(\partial_x^j\partial_y^m \bar{v})(0,0) + \left\langle r^{\nu-k}Z_k u, r^{\nu-k}Z_k v\right\rangle_o + \left\langle u,v\right\rangle_k ,$$

where $Z_k u$ is the remainder of the Taylor expansion of order k-1 in (0,0),

$$Z_k u := u - \sum_{j=0}^{k-2}\sum_{m=0}^{k-j-2} \frac{x^j y^m}{j!\,m!}(\partial_x^j\partial_y^m u)(0,0);$$

the norm connected with this inner product is denoted by $|\cdot|_k^{(\nu)}$

(28b) $$|u|_k^{(\nu)} := (\left\langle u,u\right\rangle_k^{(\nu)})^{\frac{1}{2}} .$$

This norm is equivalent to $\|\cdot\|_k$ in $H^k(\Omega)$:

<u>LEMMA 1.12</u>. *For each* $k \in \mathbb{N}$ *a constant* C_k *exist such that*

(29) $$\|u\|_k \le 2|u|_k^{(\nu)} \le C_k\nu^{-1}\|u\|_k$$

for all $u \in H^k(\Omega)$ *and* $\nu \in (0,k]$.

<u>PROOF</u>. The left-hand inequality of (29) is a consequence of the identity (27) and the right-hand inequality follows from lemma 4.11. □

With respect to this new inner product $H^k(\Omega)$ admits the orthogonal decomposition in the $\frac{1}{2}k(k-1)$-dimensional subspace of polynomials of degree $\le$ k-2 and the subspace of functions u which satisfy $u = Z_k u$:

(30) $$H^k(\Omega) = Z_k H^k(\Omega) \oplus (1-Z_k)H^k(\Omega).$$

Moreover, the monomials $x^i y^j$ and $x^m y^n$ are orthogonal with respect to this inner product for all i, j, m and n, provided $i+j \le k-2$, $m+n \le k-2$ and $m+n\pi \neq i+j\pi$.

If k is an even number, say $k = 2j$ with $j \in \mathbb{N}$, we can introduce in $H^k(\Omega)$ the third inner product

(31) $$u,v \longmapsto \left\langle \Delta^j u, \Delta^j v\right\rangle + \left\langle u,v\right\rangle.$$

As is well-known, the norm $u \mapsto (\|\Delta^j u\|^2 + \|u\|^2)^{\frac{1}{2}}$, defined by this inner product, is equivalent to the norm $u \mapsto \|u\|_k$. In $H^{2j}(\Omega)$ we define the operator $S^{(j)}$,

$$\text{(32)} \qquad S^{(j)}u := Lu$$

$$\text{for all } u \in \mathcal{D}(S^{(j)}) := \{v \in H^{2j+2}(\Omega) \mid (x\partial_x + \mu y\partial_y)\Delta^j v\big|_{\partial\Omega} = 0\};$$

it satisfies:

<u>THEOREM 1.13</u>. *The operator* $S^{(j)}$ *is semibounded from above and* $S^{(j)} - \lambda$ *has a compact inverse for some* $\lambda \in \mathbb{C}$.

<u>PROOF</u>. In connection with L_p we define the sesquilinear form A in $H^1(\Omega)$ by

$$\text{(33a)} \qquad A(u,v) := \iint_\Omega A(\nabla u, \nabla v)\,dxdy, \qquad u,v \in H^1(\Omega),$$

where A is the sesquilinear form in $\mathbb{C}^2$:

$$\text{(33b)} \qquad A(\alpha,\beta) := a\alpha_1\overline{\beta}_1 + b\alpha_1\overline{\beta}_2 + b\alpha_2\overline{\beta}_1 + c\alpha_2\overline{\beta}_2,$$

$$\alpha := (\alpha_1,\alpha_2) \quad \text{and} \quad \beta := (\beta_1,\beta_2) \in \mathbb{C}^2.$$

Since L_p is uniformly elliptic, a constant $\gamma > 0$ exists such that

$$\text{(33c)} \qquad A(u,u) \geq \gamma|u|_1^2 \quad (u \in H^1(\Omega)) \quad \text{and} \quad A(\alpha,\alpha) \geq \gamma|\alpha|^2, \quad (\alpha \in \mathbb{C}^2).$$

L_p satisfies for all pairs $(u,v) \in H^2(\Omega)$ Green's formula,

$$\text{(34)} \qquad \left\langle L_p u, v\right\rangle + A(u,v) =$$

$$= \int_0^{2\pi} \{(ax^2+2bxy+cy^2)\overline{v}\partial_r u + (bx^2-by^2+cxy-axy)\overline{v}\partial_\phi u\}\big|_{r=1}\, d\phi,$$

where (r,ϕ) denote the polar coordinates. If u and v satisfy the boundary condition

$$0 = (x\partial_x + \mu y\partial_y)w\big|_{\partial\Omega} = \left((x^2+\mu y^2)\partial_r + (\mu-1)xy\partial_\phi\right)w\big|_{\partial\Omega},$$

we can eliminate the normal derivative ∂_r from the boundary term of (34); integrating by parts again, we find

$$\left\langle L_p u,v\right\rangle + \left\langle u,L_p v\right\rangle + 2A(u,v) = -\int_0^{2\pi} h'(\phi)u\bar{v}d\phi, \tag{35a}$$

where h is defined by

$$h(\phi) := \{cxy - axy + bx^2 - by^2 + (1-\mu)xy(x^2a+2xyb+y^2c)/(x^2+\mu y^2)\}\Big|_{r=1}. \tag{35b}$$

Setting u = v, we find by lemma 1.9 the estimate for the boundary term

$$\left|\int_0^{2\pi} h'(\phi)u\bar{u}d\phi\right| \le 2[h']\|u\|(\|u\|+|u|_1). \tag{36}$$

Since constants C_{ij} exist such that

$$\left\langle L_p\Delta^j u - \Delta^j Lu,\Delta^j u\right\rangle \le C_{1j}A^{\frac{1}{2}}(\Delta^j u,\Delta^j u)|\Delta^j u|_o + C_{2j}|u|_o^2\ , \tag{37}$$

we deduce from the formulae (33c), (34), (35a) and (36) a constant K_j such that L satisfies for all $u \in \mathcal{D}(S^{(j)})$ the inequality

$$\left\langle \Delta^j Lu,\Delta^j u\right\rangle + \left\langle Lu,u\right\rangle \le K_j(\|\Delta^j u\|^2 + \|u\|^2). \tag{38}$$

This implies that the operator $S^{(j)}$ is semibounded from above.

In order to show that $S^{(j)} - \lambda$ is invertible for some $\lambda \in \mathbb{C}$, we consider the special operator $S_o^{(j)}$:

$$S_o^{(j)}u := \Delta u \qquad \text{for all } u \in \mathcal{D}(S_o^{(j)}) := \mathcal{D}(S^{(j)}).$$

It is well-known that $S_o^{(0)} - \lambda$ has a compact inverse if $Re\lambda > 0$, cf. [20] ch. 2 §5, so we define for some $f \in C^\infty(\Omega)$ and $j \in \mathbb{N}$ the function $v_\lambda := (S_o^{(0)}-\lambda)^{-1}\Delta^j f$. Let us now assume that a solution of the equation

$$\Delta u - \lambda u = f, \qquad (x\partial_x+\mu y\partial_y)\Delta^j u\Big|_{\partial\Omega} = 0, \qquad Re\lambda > 0,$$

exists and let us denote it by u_λ; it clearly satisfies $\Delta^j u_\lambda = v_\lambda$. Applying Δ j times to the equation $\Delta u_\lambda = \lambda u_\lambda + f$ we find at the boundary the set of relations

$$(39)\qquad \lambda\Delta^i u_\lambda\big|_{\partial\Omega} = \Delta^{i+1}u_\lambda\big|_{\partial\Omega} - \Delta^i f\big|_{\partial\Omega}, \qquad 0 \le i \le j-1,$$

which can be solved recursively for $\lambda \neq 0$, since $\Delta^j u_\lambda\big|_{\partial\Omega} = v_\lambda\big|_{\partial\Omega}$ is known. Because $f \in C^\infty(\Omega)$, the boundary values $\Delta^i u_\lambda\big|_{\partial\Omega}$ are elements of $C^\infty(\partial\Omega)$.

For each $s \in \mathbb{R}$, $s \ge 2$ the operator $\mathcal{D}$ which assigns to $u \in H^s(\Omega)$ the pair $(\Delta u, u|_{\partial\Omega})$ is a one-to-one continuous mapping with a continuous inverse from $H^s(\Omega)$ onto the cartesian product $H^{s-2}(\Omega) \times H^{s-\frac{1}{2}}(\partial\Omega)$, cf. [20] ch 2 §5 (for non-integral s the space H^s is defined by interpolation; it satisfies $H^s \subset H^t$ if $s > t$). By iteration we find that the operator $\mathcal{D}_j$, which assigns to $u \in H^{2j}(\Omega)$ the n+1-tuple

$$(40)\qquad (\Delta^j u, \Delta^{j-1}u\big|_{\partial\Omega}, \ldots, u\big|_{\partial\Omega}) \in H^0(\Omega) \times \prod_{i=1}^{j} H^{2i-\frac{1}{2}}(\partial\Omega)$$

is continuous and has a continuous inverse. Hence u_λ exists and is defined uniquely for each $f \in C^\infty(\Omega)$ by v_λ and by the set of relations (39), provided $Re\lambda > 0$. Since $C^\infty(\Omega)$ is dense in $H^{2j}(\Omega)$ and since we find from (38)

$$\| S_o^{(j)}u - \lambda u\|_n \ge (\text{constant})\ Re\lambda \|u\|_n ,$$

this implies that $S_o^{(j)} - \lambda$ is invertible, if $Re\lambda > 0$. Since $(S_o^{(0)}-\lambda)^{-1}$ is compact and since $\mathcal{D}_j^{-1}$ is bounded, $(S_o^{(j)}-\lambda)^{-1}$ is compact too.

By the continuity method, used in the proof of theorem 1.7, we extend the result to $S^{(j)}$. □

If M is a uniformly elliptic formal differential operator of second order on Ω, then

$$(41)\qquad u,v \mapsto \langle M^j u, M^j v\rangle + C^j\langle u,v\rangle$$

defines an inner product in $H^{2j}(\Omega)$ and a norm which is equivalent to the original one, provided the constant $C \in \mathbb{R}^+$ is large enough. If, moreover, M is formally selfadjoint (or has real coefficients) and does not contain a zero-th order derivative, then all eigenvalues of the restriction of M to $H^2(\Omega) \cap H_o^1(\Omega)$ have a negative real part and we can assume $C = 1$. By analogy to (32) we define the operator $S_M^{(j)}$ as the restriction of L to

$$(42)\qquad \mathcal{D}(S_M^{(j)}) := \left\{u \in H^{2j+2}(\Omega)\ \middle|\ (x\partial_x + \mu y\partial_y)M^j u\big|_{\partial\Omega} = 0\right\}.$$

Replacing Δ in the previous proof by M we find:

COROLLARY 1.14. *The operator* $S_M^{(j)}$ *is semibounded from above and* $S_M^{(j)} - \lambda$ *has a compact inverse for some* $\lambda \in \mathbb{C}$.

d. On the square $\Omega := (-1,1) \times (-1,1)$ we define the non-isotropic space $H^{(o,n)}(\Omega)$, with $n \in \mathbb{N}$, as the set of functions

$$H^{(o,n)}(\Omega) := \{u \in L^2(\Omega) \mid \|\partial_y^n u\| < \infty\}. \tag{43a}$$

It is a Hilbert space with respect to the inner product

$$u,v \mapsto \langle u,v\rangle + \langle \partial_y^n u, \partial_y^n v\rangle \tag{43b}$$

The restriction of an element of $H^{(o,n)}(\Omega)$ to a line y = constant is a continuous operation onto $L^2(-1,1)$; by way of example we show

LEMMA 1.15. *Every* $u \in H^{(o,1)}(\Omega)$ *satisfies the inequality*

$$\|u_{|y=0}\|^2_{(-1,1)} \le \|u\|^2_\Omega + 2\|u\|_\Omega \|\partial_y u\|_\Omega . \tag{44}$$

PROOF. If $u \in C^1(\Omega)$, then we find

$$\|u(\cdot,0)\|^2_{(-1,1)} = -\int_{-1}^{1}\int_0^1 \partial_y (1-y)|u(x,y)|^2 dydx \le$$

$$\le \|u\|^2_\Omega + 2\|u\|_\Omega \|\partial_y u\|_\Omega .$$

Since $C^1(\Omega)$ is dense in $H^{(o,1)}(\Omega)$, this inequality implies (44) for all $u \in H^{(o,1)}(\Omega)$. □

Analogously to subsection 1.2b we define $H_1^{(o,n)}(\Omega)$ as the subset

$$H_1^{(o,n)}(\Omega) := \{u \in H^{(o,n)}(\Omega) \mid \partial_y^j u_{|y=o},\ j \in \mathbb{N}_o,\ j < n\}. \tag{45}$$

According to lemma 1.15 it is a closed subspace of $H^{o,n}(\Omega)$. In $L^2((-1,1) \times (0,1))$ and $L^2((-1,1) \times (-1,0))$ we define the operators A and B as the restrictions of ∂_y to the domains

$$\mathcal{D}(A) := \{u \in L^2((-1,1)\times(0,1)) \mid \partial_y u \in L^2((-1,1)\times(0,1)) \ \&\ u_{|y=0} = 0\}$$

$$\mathcal{D}(B) := \{u \in L^2((-1,1)\times(-1,0)) \mid \partial_y u \in L^2((-1,1)\times(-1,0)) \ \&\ u_{|y=0} = 0\}$$

and we observe the identity

$$H_1^{(o,n)}(\Omega) = \mathcal{D}(A^n) \oplus \mathcal{D}(B^n).$$

By analogy to (2.4b) we find for any $u \in \mathcal{D}(A)$:

$$\| Au\|_{(-1,1)\times(0,1)} \| e^{2y}u\|_{(-1,1)\times(0,1)} \geq |\tfrac{1}{2}\int_{-1}^{1}\int_{0}^{1} e^{2y}\partial_y(u\bar{u})\,dydx| =$$

$$= \| e^{y}u\|^2_{(-1,1)\times(0,1)} \geq e^{-1}\| e^{2y}u\|_{(-1,1)\times(0,1)} \| u\|_{(-1,1)\times(0,1)} ;$$

B satisfies an analogous formula. For any $u \in H_1^{(o,n)}(\Omega)$ this implies the inequality

$$\| \partial_y^n u\|^2_\Omega = \| A^n u\|^2_{(-1,1)\times(0,1)} + \| B^n u\|^2_{(-1,1)\times(-1,0)} \geq e^{-2n}\| u\|^2$$

and we find that the norms

$$\text{(46)} \qquad u \mapsto \| \partial_y^n u\| \quad \text{and} \quad u \mapsto \{\| u\|^2 + \| \partial_y^n u\|^2\}^{\frac{1}{2}}$$

are equivalent on $H_1^{(o,n)}(\Omega)$. Moreover, in conjunction with (44) this implies that the inner products (43b) and

$$\text{(47)} \qquad u,v \mapsto \left\langle \partial_y^n u, \partial_y^n v\right\rangle + \sum_{j=0}^{n-1}(j!)^{-2}\left\langle \partial_y^j u\big|_{y=0}, \partial_y^j v\big|_{y=0}\right\rangle_{(-1,1)}$$

define equivalent norms in $H^{(o,n)}(\Omega)$, see also formula (17).

As a variant on Sobolev's lemma we find

<u>LEMMA 1.16</u>. *If* u *and* $\partial_x u$ *are elements of* $H^{(o,1)}(\Omega)$, *then*

$$\text{(48)} \qquad |u(x,y)|^2 \leq \| u\|^2 + 2\| \partial_x u\| \| \partial_y u\| + 2\| u\| \| \partial_y\partial_x u\|$$

for all $(x,y) \in \Omega$.

PROOF. If $u \in C^2(\Omega)$ and $(x,y) \in (-1,0)\times(-1,0)$, we have the identity

$$|u(x,y)|^2 = \int_0^1\int_0^1 \partial_s\partial_t (1-s)(1-t)|u(x+s,y+t)|^2 dsdt;$$

by executing the differentiations and applying Schwarz' inequality we find (48). By a density argument the inequality extends to the larger set. □

In the space $H^{(0,n)}(\Omega)$ we define the differential operator S as the restriction of L to the set

(49) $$\mathcal{D}(S^{(n)}) := \Big\{u \in H^{(0,n)}(\Omega) \,|\, \Delta u \in H^{(0,n)}(\Omega), u\big|_{x=\pm 1} = 0 \text{ and } \partial_y^{n+1}u\big|_{y=\pm 1} = 0\Big\};$$

it satisfies:

THEOREM 1.17. *The operator* $S^{(n)}$ *is semibounded from above and has a compact inverse for some* $\lambda \in \mathbb{C}$.

PROOF. Integration by parts yields for any $u \in \mathcal{D}(S^{(n)})$

$$\Big\{\| \partial_y^n S^{(n)}u\|^2 + \| S^{(n)}u\|^2\Big\}^{\frac12}\Big\{\| u\|^2 + \| \partial_y^n u\|\Big\}^{\frac12} \ge$$

$$\ge \Big|Re\,\langle \partial_y^n Lu, \partial_y^n u\rangle + Re\,\langle Lu,u\rangle\Big| \ge$$

$$\ge \Big|A(\partial_y^n u, \partial_y^n u) + \text{inner products containing derivatives of lower order}\Big|,$$

hence straightforward computation shows that $S^{(n)}$ is semi-bounded from above. In order to prove invertibility we consider the special operator

$$S_o^{(n)}u := \Delta u \qquad \text{for all } u \in \mathcal{D}(S^{(n)})$$

and we operate in the same way as in the proof of theorem 1.8. □

1.3. CRITICAL POINTS OF FIRST ORDER PARTIAL DIFFERENTIAL OPERATORS IN THE PLANE

The critical points of the first order partial differential operator in the plane

(50) $\ell := p\partial_x + q\partial_y + r,$

with real C^∞-coefficients, are connected with the singular points of the system of ordinary differential equations

(51) $\frac{dx}{ds} = p(x,y), \quad \frac{dy}{ds} = q(x,y);$

its integral curves are the characteristics of ℓ. The origin is a non-degenerate singular point of (51), if $p(0,0) = q(0,0) = 0$ and if the Jacobian matrix M of (p,q) does not vanish in a neighbourhood of the origin. The type of the singularity is determined by $M(0,0)$; by a linear transformation it takes one of the following standard forms

1. saddle-point: $M(0,0) = \begin{pmatrix} 1 & 0 \\ 0 & -\mu \end{pmatrix}$ with $\mu \in \mathbb{R}^+$,

2. nodes a: $M(0,0) = \pm\begin{pmatrix} 1 & 0 \\ 0 & \mu \end{pmatrix}$ with $\mu \in \mathbb{R}^+$,

   b: $M(0,0) = \pm\begin{pmatrix} 1 & 0 \\ 1 & 1 \end{pmatrix}$,

3. vortices a: $M(0,0) = \pm\begin{pmatrix} 1 & \nu \\ -\nu & 1 \end{pmatrix}$ with $\nu \in \mathbb{R}$, $\nu \neq 0$,

   b: $M(0,0) = \begin{pmatrix} 0 & 1 \\ -1 & 0 \end{pmatrix}$.

Among these non-degenerate singular points we can distinguish three "structurally stable" classes (i.e. the type of a singular point in such a class does not change under small perturbations) namely the "saddles" (type 1), the attracting centers (types 2a and 3a with a plus sign) and the repelling centers (types 2a and 3a with a minus sign).

In most cases, cf. STERNBERG [28], a smooth coordinate transformation (in a neighbourhood of the origin) exists, which transforms equation (51) into a linear differential equation and hence the Jacobian M into a constant matrix. Therefore we shall restrict our analysis to problems in which ℓ belongs to one of the three structurally stable types with a constant Jacobian:

	Node:	$x\partial_x + \mu y\partial_y,$	$\mu \in \mathbb{R}^+,$
(53)	Vortex:	$(x-\nu y)\partial_x + (y+\nu x)\partial_y = r\partial_r + \nu\partial_\phi,$	$\nu \in \mathbb{R},\ \nu \neq 0,$
	Saddle point:	$x\partial_x - \mu y\partial_y,$	$\mu \in \mathbb{R}^+.$

CHAPTER II

PERTURBATIONS OF d/dx.

On the interval [0,1] of the real line we consider the singular perturbation problem

$$(1) \qquad \varepsilon\tau u + u' - \lambda u = f, \qquad u(0) = A, \qquad u(1) = B,$$

in which f is a (smooth) complex valued function; λ and ε are complex parameters; without loss of generality we can assume that the coefficient a(x) of d^2/dx^2 in τ satisfies a(0) = 1. We are interested in the behaviour of the solution of (1) for $|\varepsilon| \to 0$. We prove L^2-convergence of it using a device of KATO [19] ch. 8 and construct asymptotic approximations to it in a manner analogous to [8] and [5]. The aim of this chapter is to illustrate methods to be used later on in a fairly simple case.

2.1. L^2-CONVERGENCE OF THE RESOLVENT OPERATOR

In connection with the boundary value problem (1) we define the family of differential operators T_ε by

$$(2a) \qquad T_\varepsilon u := \varepsilon\tau u + u', \qquad u \in \mathcal{D}(T_\varepsilon) := \{v \in H^2(0,1) \mid v(0) = v(1) = 0\},$$

$$(2b) \qquad T_o u := u', \qquad u \in \mathcal{D}(T_o) := \{v \in H^1(0,1) \mid v(1) = 0\}.$$

The existence and unicity of the solution of (1) with $f \in L^2(0,1)$ and $\varepsilon \neq 0$ and its convergence for $\varepsilon \to 0$ are equivalent to the invertibility of $T_\varepsilon - \lambda$ for $\varepsilon \neq 0$ and the convergence of the inverse for $\varepsilon \to 0$. Let $S_\alpha \subset \mathbb{C}$ be the sector

$$S_\alpha := \{\lambda \in \mathbb{C} \mid |Im\ \lambda| \leq \alpha Re\lambda\}, \qquad \text{with } \alpha \in \mathbb{R}^+,$$

then we are going to prove that $T_\varepsilon - \lambda$ is invertible if $|\varepsilon|$ is small enough, and that $(T_\varepsilon-\lambda)^{-1}$ converges to $(T_o-\lambda)^{-1}$ in (operator-) norm if $\varepsilon \in S_\alpha$ and $\varepsilon \to 0$.

LEMMA 2.1. *If* $\varepsilon \in S_\alpha$ *and sufficiently small, the operator* $T_\varepsilon - \lambda$ *has a bounded inverse, which satisfies (uniformly with respect to* ε*) the inequality*

(3) $$\|(T_\varepsilon-\lambda)^{-1}\| \le e^n(Re\lambda+n-|\varepsilon|K_n)^{-1} \qquad \text{if } Re\lambda + n > |\varepsilon|\, K_n,$$

where $n \in \mathbb{N}_0$ *and* $K_n := \frac{1}{4}(\alpha+1)[a^{-\frac{1}{2}}b - 2na^{\frac{1}{2}}]^2 + [c - nb + n^2a - na']$.

PROOF. For any $u \in \mathcal{D}(T_0)$ we have

$$Re\left\langle u',u\right\rangle = \tfrac{1}{2}\int_0^1 (u'\bar{u}+u\bar{u}')\,dx = -\tfrac{1}{2}\, u(0)\bar{u}(0) < 0,$$

hence if $Re\lambda > 0$ we find

(4a) $$\|T_0u-\lambda u\| \ge |Re\left\langle u'-\lambda u,u\right\rangle|/\|u\| \ge Re\lambda\|u\|.$$

Since $T_0\, e^{-nx}u = e^{-nx}(T_0u-nu)$ and since

$$\|u\| \le \|e^{nx}u\| \le e^n\|u\| \qquad \text{for all } n \in \mathbb{N} \text{ and } u \in L^2(0,1),$$

we find for $Re\lambda > -n$ with $n \in \mathbb{N}$

(4b) $$\|T_0u-\lambda u\| \ge |\; Re\left\langle (T_0-\lambda)e^{-nx}\, e^{nx}u,\; e^{2nx}u\right\rangle\,|\;/\|e^{2nx}u\| \ge$$

$$\ge (Re\lambda+n)\|e^{nx}u\|^2/\|e^{2nx}u\| \ge (Re\lambda+n)e^{-n}\|u\|.$$

This inequality proves that the range of $T_0 - \lambda$ is closed for all $\lambda \in \mathbb{C}$. Since the nullspace of the adjoint $T_0^* - \bar{\lambda}$,

$$T_0^*u = -u' \qquad \text{for all } u \in \mathcal{D}(T_0^*) = \{v \in H^1(0,1) \mid v(0) = 0\},$$

is zero, $T_0 - \lambda$ is invertible for all $\lambda \in \mathbb{C}$.

For any $u \in \mathcal{D}(T_\varepsilon)$ with $\varepsilon \neq 0$ we have the inequality

(5) $$|\left\langle bu',u\right\rangle| \le [a^{-\frac{1}{2}}b]\, \|a^{\frac{1}{2}}u'\|\, \|u\| \le [a^{-\frac{1}{2}}b](\tfrac{1}{4}t\|u\|^2+t^{-1}\left\langle au',u'\right\rangle),$$

valid for all $t \in \mathbb{R}^+$. With the choice $t := (\alpha+1)[a^{-\frac{1}{2}}b]$ we find from (4) and (5) the inequality

$$Re\left\langle \varepsilon\tau u,u\right\rangle = -(Re\,\varepsilon)\left\langle au',u'\right\rangle + Re\left\langle \varepsilon bu' + cu,u\right\rangle \le$$

$$\le \left(|\varepsilon|/(\alpha+1) - Re\,\varepsilon\right)\left\langle au',u'\right\rangle + |\varepsilon|\left(\tfrac{1}{4}(\alpha+1)[a^{-\frac{1}{2}}b]^2+[c]\right)^2\|u\|^2$$

$$\le |\varepsilon|K_o\|u\|^2, \qquad \text{with } K_o := \tfrac{1}{4}(\alpha+1)[a^{-\frac{1}{2}}b]^2 + [c],$$

valid for any $u \in \mathcal{D}(T_\varepsilon)$ with $\varepsilon \in S_\alpha\backslash\{0\}$; analogously we obtain

$$Re\left\langle \varepsilon\tau u,e^{2nx}u\right\rangle = Re\left\langle \varepsilon e^{nx}\tau e^{-nx}e^{nx}u,e^{nx}u\right\rangle =$$

$$= Re\left\langle \varepsilon\left(\frac{d}{dx}\,a\,\frac{d}{dx} + (b-2na)\,\frac{d}{dx} + c + n^2a - na' - nb\right)e^{nx}u,e^{nx}u\right\rangle \le$$

$$\le |\varepsilon|K_n\|\,e^{nx}u\|^2 .$$

Combined with (4) this results in the inequality

$$\text{(6)}\qquad \|\,T_\varepsilon u-\lambda u\| \ge \left|\,Re\left\langle \varepsilon\tau u + u' - \lambda u,e^{2nx}u\right\rangle\right| \,/\, \|\,e^{2nx}u\|$$

$$\ge (Re\lambda+n-|\varepsilon|K_n)e^{-n}\|u\|$$

for all $u \in \mathcal{D}(T_\varepsilon)$ and for all $\varepsilon \in S_\alpha$, $\lambda \in \mathbb{C}$ and $n \in \mathbb{N}_o$ satisfying the relation $Re\lambda + n > |\varepsilon|K_n$. If $\lambda \in \mathbb{R}^+$ is large enough and if $\varepsilon \in S_\alpha$, $T_\varepsilon - \lambda$ is invertible by corollary 1.5, hence by inequality (6) $T_\varepsilon - \lambda$ is invertible for all $\lambda \in \mathbb{C}$, provided $\varepsilon \in S_\alpha$ is small enough, and satisfies (3). □

For later use it is convenient to show here that the following stability property is a simple consequence of this lemma:

COROLLARY 2.2: *If* $u_\varepsilon \in H^2(0,1)$ *satisfies for some* $\nu \in \mathbb{R}$ *the estimates*

$$\|(\varepsilon\tau+d/dx-\lambda)u_\varepsilon\| = \mathcal{O}(\varepsilon^\nu), \qquad u_\varepsilon(0) = \mathcal{O}(\varepsilon^\nu) \quad \textit{and} \quad u_\varepsilon(1) = \mathcal{O}(\varepsilon^\nu)$$

then $\|u_\varepsilon\| = \mathcal{O}(\varepsilon^\nu)$ *for* $\varepsilon \in S_\alpha$ *and* $\varepsilon \to 0$.

PROOF. Since $u_\varepsilon - xu_\varepsilon(1) - (1-x)u_\varepsilon(0) \in \mathcal{D}(T_\varepsilon)$ we have by lemma 2.1

$$\|u_\varepsilon\| = \|u_\varepsilon - xu_\varepsilon(1) - (1-x)u_\varepsilon(0)\| + \mathcal{O}(\varepsilon^\nu) \le$$

$$\le \|(T_\varepsilon-\lambda)^{-1}\|\;\|(\varepsilon\tau+d/dx-\lambda)\left(u_\varepsilon-xu_\varepsilon(1)-(1-x)u_\varepsilon(0)\right)\| + \mathcal{O}(\varepsilon^\nu) =$$

$$= \mathcal{O}(\varepsilon^\nu).$$ □

This property is called the "*inverse stability*" of the family T_ε.

For simplicity of the computations, we now define the special operator Π_ε with $\mathcal{D}(\Pi_\varepsilon) := \mathcal{D}(T_\varepsilon)$ and

$$\Pi_\varepsilon u := \varepsilon(au')' + u', \qquad u \in \mathcal{D}(\Pi_\varepsilon).$$

By lemma 2.1 we know that Π_ε has a bounded inverse if ε is sufficiently small; we can compute the Green's function of Π_ε and determine its asymptotic behaviour. Moreover, Π_ε dominates the difference between Π_ε and T_ε, such that convergence of Π_ε^{-1} implies convergence of T_ε^{-1}. First we shall prove the dominance:

<u>LEMMA 2.3</u>. *For any* $u \in \mathcal{D}(T_\varepsilon)$ *and* $\varepsilon \in S_\alpha$ *the difference* $T_\varepsilon - \Pi_\varepsilon$ *satisfies the inequality*

$$\| T_\varepsilon u - \Pi_\varepsilon u\| \le C_1 |\varepsilon|^{\frac{1}{2}} (\| \Pi_\varepsilon u\| + \|u\|), \tag{7}$$

in which the constant C_1 *does not depend on* ε *and* u.

<u>PROOF</u>. Since $u(0) = u(1) = 0$ we have the identity

$$\langle u',u\rangle + \langle u,u'\rangle = \int_0^1 \frac{d}{dx}(uu)\,dx = 0.$$

Since $Re\varepsilon > 0$ and $|\varepsilon| \le (1+\alpha)Re\varepsilon$, this leads to the inequality

$$\begin{aligned} 0 \le (\varepsilon+\bar{\varepsilon}) \| a^{\frac{1}{2}}u'\|^2 &= -(\varepsilon+\bar{\varepsilon}) \langle (au')',u\rangle - \langle u',u\rangle - \langle u,u'\rangle = \\ &= -\langle \varepsilon(au')' + u',u\rangle - \langle u,\varepsilon(au')' + u'\rangle \le \\ &\le 2\| \Pi_\varepsilon u\| \, \|u\| \end{aligned} \tag{8a}$$

and taking square roots we find

$$\| a^{\frac{1}{2}}u'\| \le \tfrac{1}{2}|\varepsilon|^{-\frac{1}{2}}(1+\alpha)^{\frac{1}{2}}(\| \Pi_\varepsilon u\| + \|u\|) . \tag{8b}$$

This inequality results in the estimate

$$\|\Pi_\varepsilon u - T_\varepsilon u\| \le \tfrac{1}{2}|\varepsilon|^{\frac{1}{2}}(1+\alpha)^{+\frac{1}{2}}[a^{-\frac{1}{2}}b]\,(\|\Pi_\varepsilon u\|+\|u\|) + |\varepsilon|[c]\,\|u\|. \quad \square$$

<u>LEMMA 2.4</u>. *A constant* C_2 *exists, such that*

(9) $$\|\Pi_\varepsilon^{-1} - T_o^{-1}\| \le C_2|\varepsilon|^{\frac{1}{2}}, \qquad (\varepsilon \in S_\alpha \text{ and sufficiently small})$$

i.e. Π_ε^{-1} *converges to* T_o^{-1} *in the uniform operator topology for* $\varepsilon \to 0$.

<u>PROOF</u>. The Green's function of Π_ε is

$$G_\varepsilon(x,t) := \begin{cases} (\exp \frac{A(t)}{\varepsilon} - 1)\{\exp(-\frac{A(1)}{\varepsilon}) - \exp(-\frac{A(x)}{\varepsilon})\}/(1-\exp(-\frac{A(1)}{\varepsilon})) & \text{if } t < x, \\ (\exp(-\frac{A(x)}{\varepsilon}) - 1)(1-\exp\frac{A(t)-A(1)}{\varepsilon})/(1-\exp(-\frac{A(1)}{\varepsilon})) & \text{if } t > x, \end{cases}$$

where $A(x) = \int_0^x \frac{ds}{a(s)}$; for each $h \in L^2(0,1)$ we find

$$\Pi_\varepsilon^{-1}h = \int_0^1 G_\varepsilon(\cdot,t)h(t)dt \quad \text{and} \quad T_o^{-1}h = -\int_x^1 h(t)dt.$$

Since A satisfies the inequality $p(x-y) \le A(x) - A(y) \le q(x-y)$ with $p := 1/[a]$ and $q := [1/a]$ if $x \ge y$, we find

$$|G_\varepsilon(x,t)| \le \exp\frac{A(t)-A(x)}{Re\varepsilon} \le \exp\frac{pt-px}{Re\varepsilon}, \quad \text{if } t \le x,$$

and

$$|G_\varepsilon(x,t)+1| \le \exp(-\frac{A(x)}{Re\varepsilon})/(1-\exp(-\frac{A(1)}{Re\varepsilon})) + \exp\frac{A(t)-A(1)}{Re\varepsilon} \le$$

$$\le \exp(-\frac{px}{Re\varepsilon})/(1-\exp(-\frac{p}{Re\varepsilon})) + \exp(\frac{pt-p}{Re\varepsilon}), \quad \text{if } x \le t.$$

By straightforward computation we find a constant C_2, such that

$$\|\Pi_\varepsilon^{-1}h - T_o^{-1}h\|^2 = \|\int_0^x G_\varepsilon(x,t)h(t)dt + \int_x^1 (G_\varepsilon(x,t)+1)h(t)dt\|^2 \le$$

$$\le \|h\|^2\{\int_0^1\int_0^x |G_\varepsilon(x,t)|^2 dtdx + \int_0^1\int_x^1 |G_\varepsilon(x,t)+1|^2 dtdx\} \le$$

$$\le |\varepsilon| C_2^2 \|h\|^2. \qquad \square$$

Now we are able to prove the convergence of $(T_\varepsilon-\lambda)^{-1}$:

<u>THEOREM 2.5</u>. *For each* $\lambda \in \mathbb{C}$ *there exist positive numbers* ε_λ *and* C_λ, *such that the resolvent* $(T_\varepsilon-\lambda)^{-1}$ *of* T_ε *satisfies the inequality*

$$(10) \qquad \| (T_\varepsilon-\lambda)^{-1} - (T_0-\lambda)^{-1} \| \le |\varepsilon|^{\frac{1}{2}} C_\lambda \qquad \textit{for all } \varepsilon \in S_\alpha \textit{ with } |\varepsilon| \le \varepsilon_\lambda;$$

i.e. $(T_\varepsilon-\lambda)^{-1}$ *converges to* $(T_0-\lambda)^{-1}$ *in the uniform operator topology for all* $\lambda \in \mathbb{C}$.

<u>PROOF</u>. By lemma 2.3 and theorem 1.4 (formula (1.2)) we find:

$$(11) \qquad \| T_\varepsilon^{-1} - \Pi_\varepsilon^{-1} \| \le \frac{C_1 |\varepsilon|^{\frac{1}{2}} \|\Pi_\varepsilon^{-1}\| (1+\|\Pi_\varepsilon^{-1}\|)}{1-C_1|\varepsilon|^{\frac{1}{2}}(1+\|\Pi_\varepsilon^{-1}\|)} \quad .$$

This inequality together with lemma 2.4 proves formula (10) for $\lambda = 0$. Since $\|(T_\varepsilon-\lambda)^{-1}\|$ is uniformly bounded with respect to $\varepsilon \in S_\alpha$, provided $|\varepsilon|$ is sufficiently small, by lemma 2.1, we can prove (10) for all $\lambda \in \mathbb{C}$ by analytic continuation. Consider the Neumann series

$$(12) \qquad (T_\varepsilon-\lambda)^{-1} = \sum_{k=0}^{\infty} (\lambda-\mu)^k (T_\varepsilon-\mu)^{-k-1},$$

which converges in (operator-) norm if $|\lambda-\mu| \le \|(T_\varepsilon-\mu)^{-1}\|^{-1}$. If $(T_\varepsilon-\mu)^{-1}$ converges in norm for $\varepsilon \to 0$ to $(T_0-\mu)^{-1}$, then $(T_\varepsilon-\mu)^{-k}$ converges to $(T_0-\mu)^{-k}$ for all $k \in \mathbb{N}$, hence the infinite sum converges for all λ within the radius of convergence; since (10) is true for $\lambda = 0$, this proves (10) for all $\lambda \in \mathbb{C}$. □

2.2. ASYMPTOTIC EXPANSIONS

The approximation $(T_0-\lambda)^{-1}f$ of $(T_\varepsilon-\lambda)^{-1}f$, which we deduced in the previous section is of order $\mathcal{O}(\varepsilon^{\frac{1}{2}}\|f\|)$ in L^2-sense for all $f \in L^2(0,1)$. Following more or less the lines of [8] and [5], we construct higher order approximations of $(T_\varepsilon-\lambda)^{-1}f$ for a more restricted class of functions. If $f \in H^1(0,1)$, we have

$$\|(\varepsilon\tau+d/dx-\lambda)\{(T_\varepsilon-\lambda)^{-1}f - (T_0-\lambda)^{-1}f\}\| = \|\varepsilon\tau(T_0-\lambda)^{-1}f\| = \mathcal{O}(\varepsilon\|f\|_1)$$

and if in addition $(T_o-\lambda)^{-1}f \in \mathcal{D}(T_\varepsilon)$, we conclude from cor.2.2

$$\|(T_\varepsilon-\lambda)^{-1}f - (T_o-\lambda)^{-1}f\| = \mathcal{O}(\varepsilon\|f\|_1).$$

In general however, $(T_o-\lambda)^{-1}f \notin \mathcal{D}(T_\varepsilon)$, i.e. it does not satisfy the boundary condition of T_ε at $x = 0$, so our first objective will be to find a correction term $v \in H^2(0,1)$ such that we can apply corollary 2.2 to $v + (T_o-\lambda)^{-1}f$.

Let us now fix the function $f \in H^1(0,1)$ and the parameter $\lambda \in \mathbb{C}$ and introduce the notation $u_\varepsilon := (T_\varepsilon-\lambda)^{-1}f$ and $u_o := (T_o-\lambda)^{-1}f$. The correction term v which we are looking for, has to satisfy

$$\|\varepsilon\tau v + v' - \lambda v\| = \mathcal{O}(\varepsilon), \tag{13}$$

$$v(0) = -u(0) + \mathcal{O}(\varepsilon) \quad \text{and} \quad v(1) = \mathcal{O}(\varepsilon), \tag{14}$$

for this implies by corollary 2.2

$$\|u_\varepsilon - u_o - v\| = \mathcal{O}(\varepsilon), \quad (\varepsilon\to 0).$$

This correction term v is of order unity at $x = 0$, but $\|v\|$ is of order $\mathcal{O}(\sqrt{\varepsilon})$ at most, since $\|u_\varepsilon - u_o\| = \mathcal{O}(\sqrt{\varepsilon})$ by theorem 2.5, hence v is of order unity only on a set of measure $\mathcal{O}(\varepsilon)$, which has to contain a (right-) neighbourhood of the boundary point $x = 0$.

For a closer look in a neighbourhood of the point $x = 0$, we stretch the x-variable. We define $\xi := x/|\varepsilon|$ and the substitution operator $s_\varepsilon: L^2(0,1) \longrightarrow L^2(0,1/|\varepsilon|)$ by $(s_\varepsilon f)(\xi) := f(|\varepsilon|\xi)$. The norms in both spaces satisfy the relation

$$\|h\|_{(0,1)} = |\varepsilon|^{\frac{1}{2}}\|s_\varepsilon h\|_{(0,1/|\varepsilon|)}, \quad h \in L^2(0,1). \tag{15}$$

This substitution induces on $H^2(0,1/|\varepsilon|)$ the formal operator $s_\varepsilon(\varepsilon\tau+d/dx)s_\varepsilon^{-1}$; since we are interested only in a neighbourhood of the origin, we expand its coefficients into a power series in $|\varepsilon|\xi$ and define the formal operators ρ_k $(k\in\mathbb{N}_o)$ by

$$\rho_o := \gamma\frac{d^2}{d\xi^2} + \frac{d}{d\xi}, \qquad \text{(note that } a(0) = 1)$$

$$\rho_1 := \gamma\xi a'(0)\frac{d^2}{d\xi^2} + \gamma\big(a'(0) + b(0)\big)\frac{d}{d\xi},$$

$$\rho_k := \gamma a^{(k)}(0)\frac{\xi^k}{k!}\frac{d^2}{d\xi^2} + \gamma\big(a^{(k)}(0) + b^{(k-1)}(0)\big)\frac{\xi^{k-1}}{(k-1)!}\frac{d}{d\xi} +$$

$$+ \gamma c^{(k-2)}(0)\frac{\xi^{k-2}}{(k-2)!}, \qquad k \geq 2,$$

where $\gamma := \varepsilon/|\varepsilon|$; we define the k-th order remainder operator $\rho_k^{\#}$ by

$$|\varepsilon|^n \rho_k^{\#} := s_\varepsilon(\varepsilon\tau + \frac{d}{dx})s_\varepsilon^{-1} - \sum_{j=0}^{k} |\varepsilon|^{j-1}\rho_j .$$

Clearly there is a constant r_k depending on the remainders in the Taylor expansions of a, b and c, such that for each $h \in H^2(0,1)$

(16) $$\|\rho_k^{\#}h\|_{(0,1/|\varepsilon|)} \leq r_k \|\xi^{k+1}h\|_{2,(0,1/|\varepsilon|)} .$$

In the equation $\varepsilon\tau v + v' - \lambda v = \mathcal{O}(\varepsilon)$ we substitute $x = |\varepsilon|\xi$, we expand operator and solution formally into powers of ε and ignore all but the terms of lowest order (with respect to ε); for the resulting equation $\rho_o v = 0$ we seek a solution v_o in $H^2(0,\infty)$ (this space contains $H^2(0,1/|\varepsilon|)$ for all ε), which satisfies the boundary condition $v_o(0) = -u_o(0)$. We find

$$v_o(\xi) = -u_o(0)\exp(-\xi).$$

In view of (15) and (16) this solution satisfies

(17a) $$\|(\varepsilon\tau + d/dx - \lambda)s_\varepsilon^{-1}v_o\| = \mathcal{O}(\varepsilon^{1/2}u_o(0)),$$

(17b) $$v_o(0) = -u_o(0) \quad \text{and} \quad v_o(1/\varepsilon) = \mathcal{O}(e^{-1/\varepsilon}u_o(0)),$$

provided $\varepsilon \in S_\alpha$ and $|\varepsilon| \to 0$, hence we find

$$\|u_\varepsilon - u_o - s_\varepsilon^{-1}v_o\| = \mathcal{O}(\varepsilon^{1/2}(\|f\|_1 + |u_o(0)|)) .$$

Although we have not increased the order of approximation, we have now developed all the machinery for obtaining approximations of higher order. Let $\tilde{v}_1 \in H^2(0,\infty)$ be the solution of the equation $\rho_o\tilde{v}_1 = \lambda v_o - \rho_1 v_o$ satisfying the boundary condition $\tilde{v}_1(0) = 0$, i.e.

$$\tilde{v}_1(\xi) := \int_0^\infty k(\xi,t)(\lambda-\rho_1)v_o(t)dt$$

where the kernel k is defined by

$$k(\xi,t) = \begin{cases} e^{-\xi/\gamma} - e^{(t-\xi)/\gamma} & \text{if } \xi > t, \\ e^{-\xi/\gamma} - 1 & \text{if } \xi < t. \end{cases}$$

The function $v_o + |\varepsilon|\tilde{v}_1$ satisfies

(18a) $$\|(\varepsilon\tau+d/dx-\lambda)s_\varepsilon^{-1}(v_o+|\varepsilon|\tilde{v}_1)\| = \mathcal{O}(\varepsilon^{3/2}u_o(0))$$

(18b) $$v_o(0) + \varepsilon\tilde{v}_1(0) = -u_o(0) \text{ and } v_o(1/\varepsilon) + \varepsilon\tilde{v}_1(1/\varepsilon) = \mathcal{O}(e^{-1/\varepsilon}u_o(0)),$$

hence in the same way as above we find by corollary 2.2

(18c) $$\| u_\varepsilon - u_o - s_\varepsilon^{-1}(v_o+|\varepsilon|\tilde{v}_1)\| = \mathcal{O}(\varepsilon(\|f\|_1 + |u_o(0)|).$$

In order to remove the term $u_o(0)$ from the order estimate, we prove the following lemma:

LEMMA 2.6. (Sobolev): *All functions* $u \in H^1(0,1)$ *satisfy*

(19) $$[u]^2 \le 2\|u\|^2 + 2\|u\| \, \|u'\|$$

PROOF. Consider the integral

$$|u(x)|^2 = -\int_0^{\frac{1}{2}} \frac{d}{dt}\{(1-2t)|u(x\pm t)|^2\}dt,$$

in which the plus sign is chosen if $x \le \frac{1}{2}$ and the minus sign otherwise. Hence

$$|u(x)|^2 \le 2\int_0^{\frac{1}{2}} |u(x\pm t)|^2 dt + 2\int_0^{\frac{1}{2}} |u(x\pm t)u'(x\pm t)|dt \le$$

$$\le 2\|u\|^2 + 2\|u\| \, \|u'\|$$

by Schwarz's inequality. □

From this lemma and inequality (4a) we easily find a constant C such that

$$|u_o(0)|^2 \le 2\|u_o\|(\|u_o'\|+\|u_o\|) \le 2\|u_o\|((|\lambda|+1)\|u_o\|+\|f\|) \le C\|f\|^2, \tag{20}$$

hence from (18c) we find

$$\|u_\varepsilon - u_o - s_\varepsilon^{-1}(v_o+|\varepsilon|\tilde{v}_1)\| = \mathcal{O}(\varepsilon\|f\|_1).$$

This approximation can still be improved without additional assumptions on f. By (18a) and (20) we have

$$\|(\varepsilon\tau+\frac{d}{dx}-\lambda)(u_\varepsilon-u_o+(T_\varepsilon-\lambda)^{-1}\varepsilon\tau u_o - s_\varepsilon^{-1}(v_o+|\varepsilon|\tilde{v}_1))\| = \mathcal{O}(\varepsilon^{3/2}\|f\|),$$

so we find from (18b), lemma 2.1 and theorem 2.5:

$$\|u_\varepsilon - u_o + \varepsilon(T_o-\lambda)^{-1}\tau u_o - s_\varepsilon^{-1}(v_o+|\varepsilon|\tilde{v}_1)\| = \mathcal{O}(\varepsilon^{3/2}\|f\|_1). \tag{21}$$

If f is an element of $H^2(0,1)$, the approximation obtained in (21) is in $H^2(0,1)$ too and we see that the difference $u_\varepsilon^\#$ between u_ε and the approximation satisfies the equation

$$(\varepsilon\tau+\frac{d}{dx}-\lambda)u_\varepsilon^\# = \varepsilon^2\tau(T_o-\lambda)^{-1}\tau u - s_\varepsilon^{-1}\{\varepsilon\rho_2 v_o + \varepsilon(\rho_1-\lambda)\tilde{v}_1 + \varepsilon^2(\rho_2^\# v_o+\rho_1^\#\tilde{v}_1)\},$$

where the remainder by (15), (16) and (20) satisfies

$$\|\varepsilon^2(\rho_2^\# v_o+\rho_1^\# v_1)\| = \mathcal{O}(\varepsilon^{5/2}\|f\|) \qquad \text{if } \varepsilon\in S_\alpha \text{ and } \varepsilon\to 0.$$

Furthermore $u_\varepsilon^\#$ satisfies the boundary condition

$$u_\varepsilon^\#(0) = \varepsilon(T_o-\lambda)^{-1}\tau u_o\Big|_{x=0} \qquad\text{and}\qquad u_\varepsilon^\#(1) = \mathcal{O}(e^{-1/|\varepsilon|}\|f\|).$$

We see that on $\mathcal{O}(\varepsilon)$ - level we can repeat the procedure in order to obtain an approximation, which is of order $\mathcal{O}(\varepsilon^{5/2})$ in L^2-norm. If f is sufficiently smooth, we can proceed to an arbitrarily high order of ε. If $f\in H^n(0,1)$ with $n\in\mathbb{N}$ we define u_n, v_n and $\tilde{v}_n$ by

$$u_n := -(T_o-\lambda)^{-1}\tau u_{n-1}, \tag{22a}$$

(22b) $$\tilde{v}_n(\xi) := \int_0^\infty k(\xi,t)\Big(\lambda v_{n-1}(t) - \sum_{j=0}^{n-1} \rho_{n-j} v_j(t)\Big)dt,$$

(22c) $$v_n(\xi) := \tilde{v}_n(\xi) - \gamma u_n(0) e^{-\xi/\gamma},$$

and we find:

THEOREM 2.7. *If* $f \in H^n(0,1)$ *and* $\varepsilon \to 0$ *within* S_α, $(T_\varepsilon-\lambda)^{-1}f$ *admits the asymptotic expansion*

(23) $$\| (T_\varepsilon-\lambda)^{-1}f - \sum_{j=0}^{n} \varepsilon^j u_j - s_\varepsilon^{-1}\big(|\varepsilon|^n \tilde{v}_n + \sum_{j=0}^{n-1} |\varepsilon|^j v_j\big)\| = O(\varepsilon^{n+\frac{1}{2}}\| f \|_n).$$

The constant in the order term depends on λ, *on* α *and on the coefficients of* τ, *but not on* ε *and* f.

PROOF. Define

$$A_n := \sum_{j=0}^{n-1} \varepsilon^j u_j + s_\varepsilon^{-1}\big(|\varepsilon|^n \tilde{v}_n + \sum_{j=0}^{n-1} |\varepsilon|^j v_j\big),$$

then by definition we have $A_n(0) = 0$. Since the operator ρ_0 has constant coefficients and the coefficients of ρ_k are ξ^k, ξ^{k-1} and ξ^{k-2}, each function v_k and $\tilde{v}_k$ is a polynomial in ξ of degree 2k multiplied by $e^{-\xi/\gamma}$; moreover, the coefficients in these polynomials depend linearly on $u_0(0),\ldots,u_{k-1}(0)$. Since

$$\| \tau(T_0-\lambda)^{-1}u\| \le C \|u \|_1, \qquad u \in H^1(0,1),$$

for some constant C, we find by iteration of this rule constants C_k such that

$$\|u_k \| = \| (T_0-\lambda)^{-1}(\tau(T_0-\lambda)^{-1})^k f\| \le C_k\| f \|_k$$

and analogously to (20) this yields constants $\tilde{C}_j$ so that

$$|u_j(0)| \le \tilde{C}_j\| f \|_j .$$

We infer from these facts

(24) $$A_n(1) = O(\varepsilon^{-n} e^{-1/\varepsilon} \| f \|_{n-1}) \qquad (\varepsilon\in S_\alpha, \varepsilon\to 0)$$

and

$$(25)\qquad \| (\varepsilon\tau + \frac{d}{dx} - \lambda)\{(T_\varepsilon-\lambda)^{-1}f + \varepsilon^n (T_\varepsilon-\lambda)^{-1}\tau u_{n-1} - A_n\}\| =$$

$$= \| (|\varepsilon|^n \rho_n^{\#} + \sum_{p=0}^{n} |\varepsilon|^{p-1}\rho_p)(|\varepsilon|^n \tilde{v}_n + \sum_{j=0}^{n-1} |\varepsilon|^j v_j)\| =$$

$$= |\varepsilon|^n \|\{\rho_1^{\#}\tilde{v}_n + \sum_{j=2}^{n} \rho_j^{\#} v_{n-j}\}\|_{(0,\infty)} =$$

$$= \mathcal{O}(\varepsilon^n \|\xi^{2n+1} e^{-\xi/\gamma}\|_{(0,\infty)} \|f\|_{n-1}) = \mathcal{O}(\varepsilon^{n+\frac{1}{2}} \|f\|_{n-1}) .$$

By corollary 2.2 this results in

$$\|(T_\varepsilon-\lambda)^{-1}(f+\varepsilon^n \tau u_{n-1}) - A_n\| = \mathcal{O}(|\varepsilon|^{n+\frac{1}{2}} \|f\|_{n-1})$$

and by theorem 2.5 and estimate (24) we find

$$\|u_n + (T_\varepsilon-\lambda)^{-1}\tau u_{n-1}\| = \mathcal{O}(\varepsilon^{\frac{1}{2}} \|\tau u_{n-1}\|) = \mathcal{O}(\varepsilon^{\frac{1}{2}} \|f\|_n),$$

hence (23) is a simple consequence of these estimates. □

By Sobolev's lemma we can prove regularity of the approximation constructed above, i.e. we can prove that the approximation converges in the maximum norm too.

<u>THEOREM 2.8</u>. *If* $f \in H^n(0,1)$ *then* A_n *is a uniform asymptotic approximation to* $(T_\varepsilon-\lambda)^{-1}f$ *and*

$$(26)\qquad [(T_\varepsilon-\lambda)^{-1}f - A_n] = \mathcal{O}(\varepsilon^{n-\frac{1}{4}} \|f\|_n) \qquad \textit{for } \varepsilon \in S_\alpha \textit{ and } \varepsilon \to 0.$$

<u>PROOF</u>. By lemma 2.6 any $u \in H^1(0,1)$ satisfies

$$[u]^2 \le 2\|u\|(\|u\|+\|u'\|),$$

hence if $u \in \mathcal{D}(T_\varepsilon)$ we find by (8a) a constant C such that

$$(27)\qquad [u]^2 \le 2\|u\|^2 + C\varepsilon^{-\frac{1}{2}}\|u\|^{3/2}\|T_\varepsilon u\|^{\frac{1}{2}} \le$$

$$\le 2\|u\|^2 + C\varepsilon^{-\frac{1}{2}}\|u\|^{3/2}(\|T_\varepsilon u - \lambda u\| + |\lambda|\|u\|)^{\frac{1}{2}}.$$

Since $A_n - xA_n(1) \in \mathcal{D}(T_\varepsilon)$ and since

$$\| (T_\varepsilon-\lambda)\{(T_\varepsilon-\lambda)^{-1}f - A_n + xA_n(1)\}\| = \| \varepsilon^n \tau u_{n-1} \| + \mathcal{O}(\varepsilon^{n+\frac{1}{2}} \| f \|_{n-1}) =$$

$$= \mathcal{O}(\varepsilon^n \| f \|_n)$$

by (25), we find from cor. 2.2

$$\| (T_\varepsilon-\lambda)^{-1}f - A_n + xA_n(1)\| = \mathcal{O}(\varepsilon^n \| f \|_n);$$

Substituting this in (27) and using the estimate (24) we prove formula (26). □

<u>REMARK</u>. The results on approximations of the solution of problem (1) are stated for homogeneous boundary conditions, since inhomogeneous boundary conditions can easily be transformed into homogeneous ones.

2.3. DISCUSSION OF THE RESULTS

a. *The restriction on* ε, that it should tend to zero within the sector S_α, is essential in all lemmas and theorems we proved in this chapter. If we choose ε in the sector $-S_\alpha$ we find in a completely analogous way that $(T_\varepsilon-\lambda)^{-1}$ converges to $(\tilde{T}_0-\lambda)^{-1}$ for $\varepsilon \to 0$, where

$$\mathcal{D}(\tilde{T}_0) := \{u \in H^1(0,1) \mid u(0) = 0\} \quad \text{and} \quad \tilde{T}_0 u := u'.$$

We see that the boundary condition at x = 0 is lost if $\varepsilon \to 0$ within S_α while the boundary condition at x = 1 is lost if $\varepsilon \to 0$ within $-S_\alpha$. Moreover, the spectrum of T_ε disappears at infinity if $\varepsilon \to 0$; if $\varepsilon \in S_\alpha$ it moves away to the left and if $\varepsilon \in -S_\alpha$ it vanishes at the right-hand side of the complex plane. In the asymptotic expansion of $(T_\varepsilon-\lambda)^{-1}f$ for $\varepsilon \in -S_\alpha$ and $\varepsilon \to 0$ the boundary layer is located at x = 1; the boundary layer terms in the expansion are computed in the same way as before after substitution of the local coordinate $\eta := (1-x)/\varepsilon$.

If ε tends to zero via the imaginary axes, convergence cannot be expected. Let us consider for example the special case $\Pi_\varepsilon u := \varepsilon u'' + iu'$ for $u \in \mathcal{D}(T_\varepsilon)$ and $\varepsilon \in \mathbb{R}^+$ (we multiplied the operator by i in order to make it selfadjoint). Its spectrum is the set $\sigma(\Pi_\varepsilon) := \{\frac{1}{4\varepsilon} - \varepsilon k^2\pi^2 \mid k \in \mathbb{N}\}$. Every eigenvalue tends to $+\infty$ if $\varepsilon \to +0$, but the spectrum as a whole does not vanish for $\varepsilon \to +0$, since it extends from $1/4\varepsilon$ to $-\infty$ for each $\varepsilon > 0$.

This means that for each real λ we can find a sequence ε_n ($n\in\mathbb{N}$) with $\lim_{n\to\infty}\varepsilon_n = 0$, such that $\Pi_{\varepsilon_n} - \lambda$ does not have an inverse for any $n \in \mathbb{N}$, and so convergence of $(\Pi_\varepsilon-\lambda)^{-1}$ for $\varepsilon \to +0$ and λ real is out of the question. If λ is non-real we have at least

$$\|\Pi_\varepsilon u - \lambda u\| \geq |Im\lambda|\,\|u\|,$$

such that $(\Pi_\varepsilon-\lambda)^{-1}$ exists and is uniformly bounded with respect to $\varepsilon \in \mathbb{R}^+$. However, $(\Pi_\varepsilon-\lambda)^{-1}$ does not converge for non-real λ either, as we can see by the choice $\lambda = i + \varepsilon$. We find

$$(\Pi_\varepsilon-i-\varepsilon)^{-1}(px+q) = -(px+q)/(i+\varepsilon) - ip/(i+\varepsilon)^2 +$$

$$+ \{(Ae^{-1-i/\varepsilon}-B)e^x + (B-Ae)e^{-x-ix/\varepsilon}\}/(e-e^{-1-i/\varepsilon}),$$

where $A := q/(i+\varepsilon) + ip/(i+\varepsilon)^2$ and $B := p/(i+\varepsilon) + A$. It is clear that this expression does not converge if $\varepsilon \in \mathbb{R}^+$ and $\varepsilon \to +0$.

b. *Dependence on boundary conditions*. The asymptotic behaviour of any restriction of the formal operator $\varepsilon\tau + d/dx$ depends heavily on the boundary conditions we impose on its domain. When we take for instance periodic boundary conditions (instead of the Dirichlet-boundary conditions used before) and define

$$U_\varepsilon u := \varepsilon u'' + iu' \quad \text{for} \quad u \in \mathcal{D}(U_\varepsilon) := \{v \in H^2(0,1) \mid v(0) = v(1) \ \&\ v'(0) = v'(1)\},$$

$$U_o u := iu' \quad \text{for} \quad u \in \mathcal{D}(U_o) := \{v \in H^1(0,1) \mid v(0) = v(1)\},$$

we see at once that $U_\varepsilon = -\varepsilon U_o^2 + U_o$. Since the eigenvalues of U_o are the numbers $2k\pi$ ($k\in\mathbb{Z}$) with the eigenfunction $e^{-2ik\pi x}$, we find by the spectral mapping theorem that the eigenvalues of U_ε are the numbers $2k\pi - 4\varepsilon k^2\pi^2$ with the same eigenfunction. The set of eigenfunctions of U_o is complete, so we have for any $f \in L^2(0,1)$

$$f(x) = \sum_{k\in\mathbb{Z}} f_k e^{-2ki\pi x}, \quad \text{with } f_k := \left\langle f, e^{-2k\pi i x}\right\rangle \text{ and } \|f\|^2 = \sum_k |f_k|^2.$$

If $\lambda \notin \sigma(U_\varepsilon)$ the resolvent satisfies

$$(U_\varepsilon-\lambda)^{-1}f = \sum_{k\in\mathbb{Z}} f_k e^{-2ki\pi x}/(2k\pi-4\varepsilon k^2\pi^2-\lambda)$$

and if $\lambda \notin \sigma(U_\varepsilon) \cup \sigma(U_o)$ we find the estimate

$$\|(U_\varepsilon-\lambda)^{-1}f - (U_o-\lambda)^{-1}f\|^2 = \sum_{k\in\mathbb{Z}} |f_k|^2 |(2k\pi-4\varepsilon k^2\pi^2-\lambda)^{-1}-(2k\pi-\lambda)^{-1}|^2 \leq$$

$$\leq |\varepsilon|^2 \sum_{k\in\mathbb{Z}} |4k^2\pi^2 f_k|^2 |2k\pi - 4\varepsilon k^2\pi^2 - \lambda|^{-2} |2k\pi - \lambda|^{-2} \leq$$

$$\leq |\varepsilon|^2 \|f\|^2 (\mathrm{dist}(\lambda,\sigma(U_\varepsilon)))^{-2} \ (\mathrm{dist}(\lambda,\sigma(U_o)))^{-2}.$$

We see that $(U_\varepsilon-\lambda)^{-1}$ converges in norm to $(U_o-\lambda)^{-1}$ for $\varepsilon \to 0$ and that the convergence is of order $\mathcal{O}(\varepsilon)$, if the path in the ε-λ-plane is chosen in such a way that $\mathrm{dist}(\lambda,\sigma(U_\varepsilon) \cup \sigma(U_o))$ is bounded away from zero uniformly.

c. *Generalizations and related work*. We constructed in this chapter approximations to the solution of problem (1) and proved their convergence in L^2-sense; only at the end we showed that uniform convergence is a simple consequence of L^2-convergence. The essential points in the proofs are the inverse stability (lemma 2.1) of the family of operators T_ε and the estimate (8a) of $\|u'\|$ by $\|u\|$ and $\|T_\varepsilon u\|$. It does not seem difficult to extend these methods to ordinary and (elliptic) partial differential operators for which we can prove the inverse stability.

The method explained here has advantages over the maximum principle method as it was used by ECKHAUS & DE JAGER [8] since it admits generalizations to operators of (even) order higher than two and since it remains valid for complex values of the parameters ε and λ and of the coefficients of τ (provided $\varepsilon a \in S_\alpha$ and $\mathcal{Re}\, a$ strictly positive). Furthermore it is simpler than the method of BESJES [5], who uses Hölder norms, since the presence of an inner product in L^2 makes estimates of type (8a) much easier and since the inverse stability in L^2-norm is a direct consequence of Gårdings inequality.

Generalizations to elliptic operators on a bounded domain $\Omega \subset \mathbb{R}^n$ with $n \geq 2$ are possible. In [21] ch. 5 Lions proves weak L^2-convergence of the inverse operator and it does not seem difficult to prove strong convergence. Uniform L^2-convergence of the inverse is probably not true in general, except in case $\partial\Omega$ is nowhere tangent to the characteristics of the first order operator. But even then it seems difficult to extend the proof of §2.1, since this proof uses full knowledge of the Green's function of the main part of the operator; the construction of §2.2 can easily be extended in the non-tangency case, cf. §4.3.

CHAPTER III

PERTURBATIONS OF xd/dx

On the interval [-1,1] of the real line we consider the singular perturbation problems

$$(1\pm) \qquad \varepsilon\tau u \pm xu' - \lambda u = f, \qquad u(\pm 1) = A \pm B,$$

in which f is a (smooth) complex valued function; λ is a complex "spectral" parameter and ε is now chosen in $\mathbb{R}^+$. We are interested in the behaviour of its solution for $\varepsilon \longrightarrow +0$. First we study a special example; we observe that in this case the spectrum does not vanish and converges to $-\mathbb{N}$ (or $-\mathbb{N}_0$) and we generalize this property to all problems of type (1). Next we prove that the solution of (1) converges to a definite solution of the reduced equation if λ is not a limit point of the spectrum, and we give some order estimates of the difference between the solution of (1) and the approximation.

3.1. EXAMPLES

Consider the boundary value problem

$$(2) \qquad \varepsilon u'' + xu' - \lambda u = 0, \qquad u(\pm 1) = A \pm B.$$

By the transformation $x^2 = -2\varepsilon t$ the equation is transformed into the confluent hypergeometric equation

$$t\ddot{u} + (\tfrac{1}{2}-t)\dot{u} + \tfrac{1}{2}\lambda u = 0, \qquad (\dot{u}=du/dt),$$

hence the solution of (2) is

$$(3) \qquad u(x;\lambda,\varepsilon) := \frac{AF(-\frac{1}{2}\lambda;\frac{1}{2};-x^2/2\varepsilon)}{F(-\frac{1}{2}\lambda;\frac{1}{2};-1/2\varepsilon)} + \frac{BxF(\frac{1}{2}-\frac{1}{2}\lambda;3/2;-x^2/2\varepsilon)}{F(\frac{1}{2}-\frac{1}{2}\lambda;3/2;-1/2\varepsilon)},$$

provided none of the denominators vanishes, i.e. provided λ is not an eigenvalue of (2); in (3) $F(\cdot;\cdot;\cdot)$ denotes the confluent hypergeometric (or Kummer's) function, cf. SLATER [27]. This function has for complex p,q and t and for $|t| \to \infty$ the asymptotic behaviour

$$(4a) \qquad F(p;q;t) = \left\{\frac{\Gamma(q)}{\Gamma(p)} e^t t^{p-q} + e^{ip\pi} \frac{\Gamma(q)}{\Gamma(q-p)} t^{-p}\right\}(1 + \mathcal{O}(1/t))$$

provided $|arg\,t| < 3\pi/2$; the order term depends continuously on t, cf. [27] ch. 4.1.1. From this formula we find that the solution of (2) has the asymptotic behaviour.

$$u(x;\lambda,\varepsilon) = |x|^{\lambda-1}(A|x|+Bx)(1+\mathcal{O}(\varepsilon/x^2)) \qquad (\varepsilon\to+0), \tag{4b}$$

provided $\lambda \notin -\mathbb{N}$. We see that the solution of (2) converges on (0,1] to the solution of $xu' = \lambda u$ which satisfies the boundary condition at $x = 1$, and on [-1,0) to the solution of $xu' = \lambda u$ which satisfies the boundary condition at -1; clearly the boundary value problem is torn in two in the limit for $\varepsilon \to +0$ and the breaking point is $x = 0$. This agrees with the results of the previous chapter; the restriction of (2) to $[\rho,1]$ with $\rho > 0$ is of type (2.1), hence the limit of its solution satisfies the boundary condition at $x = 1$, just as the restriction of the limit does. However, the points $\lambda \in -\mathbb{N}$ have to be excluded, since at these points a phenomenon occurs which we did not observe in the previous chapter, namely these points are the limits of eigenvalues of (2) and at these points the solution of (2) and any approximation of it do not depend continuously on λ.

Let us first prove the persistence of the spectrum. Define the operator Π_ε by

$$\Pi_\varepsilon u := \varepsilon u'' + xu' \quad \text{for all } u \in \mathcal{D}(\Pi_\varepsilon) := \{v \in H^2(-1,1) \mid v(\pm 1) = 0\}. \tag{5}$$

It satisfies:

THEOREM 3.1. *Let* $\sigma(\Pi_\varepsilon)$ *be the set* $\{\lambda_k(\varepsilon) \mid k \in \mathbb{N}\}$, *where the eigenvalues are arranged in such a way that* $\lambda_k > \lambda_{k+1}$ *for all* $k \in \mathbb{N}$, *then the* k-th *eigenvalue satisfies the asymptotic formula*

$$\lambda_k(\varepsilon) = -k + \mathcal{O}(e^{-1/2\varepsilon}\varepsilon^{-k-\frac{1}{2}}/k!) \qquad \textit{for } \varepsilon \to +0. \tag{6}$$

PROOF. First we observe that for each $\varepsilon \in \mathbb{R}^+$ the spectrum of Π_ε consists of isolated eigenvalues only. The function u is an eigenfunction of Π_ε iff the function $v(t) := e^{\frac{1}{4}t^2}u(\varepsilon^{\frac{1}{2}}t)$ is an eigenfunction of the boundary value problem on $(-\varepsilon^{-\frac{1}{2}},\varepsilon^{-\frac{1}{2}})$:

$$v'' - \tfrac{1}{4}t^2 v - (\lambda+\tfrac{1}{2})v = 0, \qquad v(\pm\varepsilon^{-\frac{1}{2}}) = 0. \tag{7}$$

Since this boundary value problem is of *limit point type* for $\varepsilon \to +0$, all its eigenvalues converge for $\varepsilon \to +0$ to the eigenvalues of the well-known Hermite-operator, cf. [6] ch. 9.5 example 2, hence $\lim_{\varepsilon\to+0} \lambda_k(\varepsilon) = -k$.

From (3) it is clear that the eigenvalues are given by the equations

$$F(-\tfrac{1}{2}\lambda;\tfrac{1}{2};-1/2\varepsilon) = 0 \quad \text{and} \quad F(\tfrac{1}{2}-\tfrac{1}{2}\lambda;3/2;-1/2\varepsilon) = 0.$$

When we insert (4a) in these equations disregarding the (multiplicative) $(1+\mathcal{O}(\cdot))$-term and equating the main term to zero, we find (6) by straightforward computation. □

In order to show that the limit of the solution $u(x;\lambda,\varepsilon)$ of (2) does not depend continuously on λ for $\varepsilon \to +0$ at the negative integers, we insert (4a) in (3) with $\lambda = -2n$ and with $\lambda = -2n + \varepsilon$, $n \in \mathbb{N}$; in the first case the coefficient of $x|x|^{\lambda-1}$ in the approximation of the odd part of u vanishes, hence we get

$$(8) \qquad u(x;-2n,\varepsilon) = \{Ax^{-2n} + Bx^{2n-1}\exp(\frac{1-x^2}{2\varepsilon})\}(1+\mathcal{O}(\varepsilon/x^2)), \qquad \varepsilon \to +0,$$

while in the second case formula (4b) remains valid!

3.2. CONVERGENCE OF THE SPECTRUM

Define the operator T_ε by

$$(9a) \qquad T_\varepsilon u := \varepsilon\tau u + xu' \quad \text{for all } u \in \mathcal{D}(T_\varepsilon) := \{u \in H^2(-1,1) \mid u(\pm 1) = 0\};$$

it is connected with the boundary value problem (1+) and its adjoint, $T_\varepsilon^* u = \varepsilon\tau^* - xu' - u$, is connected with (1-). It is our aim to prove by comparison of the operators T_ε and Π_ε that the limiting set of $\sigma(T_\varepsilon)$ for $\varepsilon \to +0$ equals the limiting set of $\sigma(\Pi_\varepsilon)$. As before we observe that the spectra of T_ε and of Π_ε consist of isolated eigenvalues and that u is an eigenfunction of Π_ε iff $u(x)\exp(x^2/4\varepsilon)$ is an eigenfunction of the operator $\tilde{\Pi}_\varepsilon$, cf. (7),

$$(9b) \qquad \tilde{\Pi}_\varepsilon v := \exp(x^2/4\varepsilon)\Pi_\varepsilon(\exp(-x^2/4\varepsilon)v) = \varepsilon v'' - (\tfrac{1}{2}+x^2/4\varepsilon)v.$$

Analogously u is an eigenfunction of T_ε iff $u(x)\ \exp\{\tfrac{1}{2}\int_0^x sds/\varepsilon a(s)\}$ is an eigenfunction of the operator $\tilde{T}_\varepsilon$,

$$\text{(9c)}\qquad (\tilde{T}_\varepsilon v)(x) := \exp\{\tfrac{1}{2}\int_0^x sds/\varepsilon a(s)\}T_\varepsilon\big(v(x)\exp\{-\tfrac{1}{2}\int_0^x sds/\varepsilon a(s)\}\big) = (\varepsilon\tau - xb/2a - x^2/4\varepsilon a - \tfrac{1}{2})\,v(x).$$

We remark that $\mathcal{D}(\tilde{\Pi}_\varepsilon) = \mathcal{D}(\tilde{T}_\varepsilon) = \mathcal{D}(T_\varepsilon)$ and that $\sigma(\tilde{T}_\varepsilon) = \sigma(T_\varepsilon)$ and $\sigma(\tilde{\Pi}_\varepsilon) = \sigma(\Pi_\varepsilon)$ by definition; we defined $\tilde{\tilde{T}}_\varepsilon$ in this way in order that it should be equal to a selfadjoint operator plus a small non-selfadjoint perturbation thereof, such that we can estimate the norm of its resolvent by the distance to the spectrum (cf. theorem 1.2). We define R_ε as the main part of $\tilde{T}_\varepsilon$,

$$R_\varepsilon u := \varepsilon(au')' - x^2u/4\varepsilon a - \tfrac{1}{2}u, \qquad \mathcal{D}(R_\varepsilon) := \mathcal{D}(\tilde{T}_\varepsilon)$$

and connect it to $\tilde{\Pi}_\varepsilon$ by the continuous chain

$$R_{\varepsilon,t} := (1-t)\tilde{\Pi}_\varepsilon + tR_\varepsilon, \qquad t \in [0,1].$$

We observe that $R_{\varepsilon,t}$ is selfadjoint for all ε and t.

The limiting set for $\varepsilon \to +0$ of $\sigma(R_{\varepsilon,o})$ is known and we will prove that it does not change, when t increases from zero to one. The continuous dependence of the eigenvalues of $R_{\varepsilon,t}$ on $\varepsilon \in \mathbb{R}^+$ and $t \in [0,1]$ is a consequence of theorem 1.6 and the following lemma:

LEMMA 3.2. *Constants* C_i $(i = 1,\ldots,6)$ *exist such that the inequalities*

$$\text{(10a)}\qquad \| R_{\varepsilon,t}u - R_{\varepsilon,s}u\| \le |s - t|\,(C_1\|R_{\varepsilon,t}u\| + C_2\|u\|),$$

$$\text{(10b)}\qquad \| R_{\varepsilon,t}u - R_{\delta,t}u\| \le \varepsilon^{-1}|\varepsilon - \delta|\,(C_3\|R_{\varepsilon,t}u\| + C_4\|u\|),$$

$$\text{(10c)}\qquad \| \tilde{T}_\varepsilon u - R_{\varepsilon,1}u\| \le \varepsilon^{\frac{1}{2}}(C_5\|R_{\varepsilon,t}u\| + C_6\|u\|),$$

are satisfied for all $u \in \mathcal{D}(R_{\varepsilon,t})$, s *and* $t \in [0,1]$ *and* ε *and* $\delta \in \mathbb{R}^+$.

PROOF. Let $u \in \mathcal{D}(R_{\varepsilon,t})$ and let p and q be positive C^∞-functions, then integrating by parts twice we find

$$\|\varepsilon(pu')' - x^2qu/\varepsilon\|^2 = \|\varepsilon(pu')'\|^2 + \|x^2qu/\varepsilon\|^2 - 2Re\left\langle (pu')', x^2qu\right\rangle =$$

$$= \|\varepsilon(pu')'\|^2 + \|x^2qu/\varepsilon\|^2 + \|p^{\frac{1}{2}}q^{\frac{1}{2}}xu'\|^2 - Re\left\langle (p(x^2q)')'u, u\right\rangle \geq$$

$$\geq \|\varepsilon(pu')'\|^2 + \|x^2qu/\varepsilon\|^2 + \|p^{\frac{1}{2}}q^{\frac{1}{2}}xu'\|^2 - [(p(x^2q)')']\,\|u\|^2$$

and taking the square root we obtain

$$\text{(11)} \qquad \|\varepsilon(pu')'\| + \|x^2qu/\varepsilon\| + [(p(x^2q)')']^{\frac{1}{2}}\,\|u\| \geq$$

$$\geq \|\varepsilon(pu')' - x^2qu/\varepsilon\| + [(p(x^2q)')']^{\frac{1}{2}}\,\|u\| \geq$$

$$\geq \tfrac{1}{2}\,\|\varepsilon(pu')'\| + \tfrac{1}{2}\,\|x^2qu/\varepsilon\|;$$

furthermore, we find

$$\text{(12)} \qquad \|\varepsilon bu'\| \leq \varepsilon^{\frac{1}{2}}[p^{-\frac{1}{2}}b]\left\langle \varepsilon pu', u'\right\rangle^{\frac{1}{2}} = \varepsilon^{\frac{1}{2}}[p^{-\frac{1}{2}}b]\,\left|\left\langle \varepsilon(pu')', u\right\rangle\right|^{\frac{1}{2}} \leq$$

$$\leq \tfrac{1}{2}\,\varepsilon^{\frac{1}{2}}[p^{-\frac{1}{2}}b](\|\varepsilon(pu')'\| + \|u\|)$$

and, if in addition r is a continuous function,

$$\text{(13)} \qquad \|xru\| \leq \varepsilon^{\frac{1}{2}}[q^{-\frac{1}{2}}r]\left\langle x^2qu/\varepsilon, u\right\rangle \leq \tfrac{1}{2}\,\varepsilon^{\frac{1}{2}}[q^{-\frac{1}{2}}r](\|x^2qu/\varepsilon\| + \|u\|).$$

By substituting $p_t := 1 - t + ta$ for p and $q_t := 1 - t + t/a$ for q and with the aid of the estimates $p_t - p_s = \mathcal{O}(s-t)$ and $q_t - q_s = \mathcal{O}(s-t)$ we prove the inequalities (10a-b) from (11). Inequality (10c) is a direct consequence of (11), (12) and (13) when we substitute a for p and q and tb/2a for r. □

Further information on the spectrum of $R_{\varepsilon,t}$ is obtained from the eigenfunctions χ_n of the operator $\varepsilon d^2/dx^2 - \frac{1}{4}x^2/\varepsilon$ with domain $H^2(\mathbb{R})$,

$$\text{(14)} \qquad \chi_n(x;\varepsilon) := \exp(-x^2/4\varepsilon)H_n(x/\sqrt{2\varepsilon}), \quad \tilde{\chi}_n := \chi_n/\|\chi_n\|,$$

where H_n is the n-th Hermite polynomial. These functions appear to be approximate eigenfunctions of $R_{\varepsilon,t}$ for all $t \in [0,1]$ and for $\varepsilon \in \mathbb{R}^+$, provided ε is sufficiently small.

LEMMA 3.3. *The functions* χ_n *satisfy the order estimate*

$$\| (R_{\varepsilon,t} + n)\tilde{\chi}_{n-1} \| = O(\varepsilon^{\frac{1}{2}} n^{3/2}), \qquad (\varepsilon \to +0) \tag{15}$$

uniformly for all $n \in \mathbb{N}$ *and* $t \in [0,1]$.

PROOF. From the well-known relations for the Hermite polynomials we obtain

$$x\chi_n = (2\varepsilon)^{\frac{1}{2}}(n\chi_{n-1} + \tfrac{1}{2}\chi_{n+1}), \tag{16a}$$

$$\chi_n' = (2\varepsilon)^{-\frac{1}{2}}(n\chi_{n-1} - \tfrac{1}{2}\chi_{n+1}), \tag{16b}$$

$$\| \chi_n \|^2 = (2\varepsilon)^{\frac{1}{2}} \int_{-1/\sqrt{2\varepsilon}}^{1/\sqrt{2\varepsilon}} \exp(-x^2) H_n^2(x)\,dx \le (2\pi\varepsilon)^{\frac{1}{2}} 2^n n! \tag{16c}$$

and from the integral we find

$$\| \chi_n \| = (2\pi\varepsilon)^{\frac{1}{4}} 2^{\frac{1}{2}n} (n!)^{\frac{1}{2}} (1 + O(e^{-1/2\varepsilon}\varepsilon^{-n})), \qquad (\varepsilon \to +0). \tag{16d}$$

Since $a \in C^\infty$ and $a(0) = 1$, the functions $(a-1)/x$, $(p_t-1)/x$ and $(q_t-1)/x^2$ are bounded and since χ_n is a solution of the equation $\varepsilon u'' + (n+\frac{1}{2}-x^2/4\varepsilon)u = 0$, we can find constants C_k such that

$$\| (R_{\varepsilon,t}+n+1)\chi_n \| = \| \varepsilon((p_t-1)\chi_n')' - x^2(q_t-1)\chi_n/4\varepsilon + \varepsilon t(b\chi_n'+c\chi_n) \| \le$$

$$\le \varepsilon C_1 \|x\chi_n''\| + C_2 \|x^3\chi_n/\varepsilon\| + \varepsilon t C_3 \|\chi_n'\| + \varepsilon C_4 \| \chi_n \| ;$$

in conjunction with the relations (16) this proves (15). □

REMARK. Strictly speaking, the functions χ_n are not elements of $\mathcal{D}(R_{\varepsilon,t})$ since $\chi_n(\pm 1;\varepsilon) \neq 0$; this is easily amended by subtracting from χ_n the constant function $\chi_n(1;\varepsilon)$ if n is even and the linear function $x\chi_n(1;\varepsilon)$ if n is odd. When doing this we add to χ_n an exponentially small (for $\varepsilon \to +0$) term, which can be disregarded in all computations.

Now we are able to prove the convergence of the eigenvalues of T_ε for $\varepsilon \to +0$. Let $\{\lambda_k(\varepsilon,t) \mid k \in \mathbb{N}\}$ be the set of eigenvalues of $R_{\varepsilon,t}$, arranged in such a way that $\lambda_{k+1} < \lambda_k$, and let $\{\mu_k(\varepsilon) \mid k \in \mathbb{N}\}$ with $Re\mu_{k+1} < Re\mu_k$ be the spectrum of T_ε.

THEOREM 3.4. *The eigenvalues of* T_ε *and* $R_{\varepsilon,t}$ *satisfy the asymptotic estimates*

(17a) $$\lambda_k(\varepsilon,t) = -k + O(\varepsilon^{\frac{1}{2}}k^{3/2}),$$

(17b) $$\mu_k(\varepsilon) = -k + O(\varepsilon^{\frac{1}{2}}k^{3/2}),$$

for $\varepsilon \to +0$ *and for all* $k \in \mathbb{N}$ *and* $t \in [0,1]$

PROOF. Let $D(z,r)$ be the open disk with center z and radius r and let $W_k(r)$ be the set

$$W_k(r) := \{z \in \mathbb{C} \mid |z| \geq k+1-r\} \cup \bigcup_{j=1}^{k} D(-j,r).$$

Let $\lambda \in \sigma(R_{\varepsilon,s})$ and let u be the eigenfunction at λ then we have by (10a) and by the selfadjointness of $R_{\varepsilon,t}$

$$0 = \|R_{\varepsilon,s}u - \lambda u\| \geq \|R_{\varepsilon,t}u - \lambda u\| - \|R_{\varepsilon,s}u - R_{\varepsilon,t}u\| \geq$$

$$\geq \|u\| \operatorname{dist}(\sigma(R_{\varepsilon,t}),\lambda) - |s-t|(C_1|\lambda|+C_2)\},$$

hence for all $k \in \mathbb{N}$ we have

(18) $$\operatorname{dist}(\lambda_k(\varepsilon,s),\sigma(R_{\varepsilon,t})) \leq (C_1|\lambda_k(\varepsilon,s)| + C_2)|s-t|,$$

Define the number $t_n := 1/((3m+4)C_1+3C_2)$; then we find from (18) that, if $\sigma(R_{\varepsilon,t}) \subset W_n(\frac{1}{6})$, then $\sigma(R_{\varepsilon,s}) \subset W_n(\frac{1}{2})$ and $\partial W_n(\frac{1}{2}) \subset \rho(R_{\varepsilon,s})$ for all $s \in [t-t_n, t+t_n]$.

Let $n \in \mathbb{N}$ be fixed and let $m \in \mathbb{N}$ be such that $\sum_{j=n+1}^{n+m} t_j \geq 1$. From theorem 3.1 we can find an ε_o such that $\sigma(R_{\varepsilon,o}) = \sigma(\Pi_\varepsilon) \subset W_{n+m}(\frac{1}{6})$ for all $\varepsilon \in (0,\varepsilon_o]$ and by what is shown above we have $\sigma(R_{\varepsilon,t}) \subset W_{n+m}(\frac{1}{2})$ for all $\varepsilon \in (0,\varepsilon_o]$ and $t \in [0,t_{n+m}]$; furthermore, since $D(-k,\frac{1}{6}) \cap \sigma(R_{\varepsilon,o}) = \{\lambda_k(\varepsilon,0)\}$ for $1 \leq k \leq n+m$ and since the eigenvalues depend continuously on t and $\partial W_{n+m}(\frac{1}{2}) \subset \rho(R_{\varepsilon,t})$, each disk $D(-k,\frac{1}{2})$ can contain only the eigenvalue $\lambda_k(\varepsilon,t)$ for $t \in [0,t_{n+m}]$. Let $P_{\varepsilon,t,k}$ be the projection

$$P_{\varepsilon,t,k} := \frac{1}{2\pi i}\int_{\partial D(-k,\frac{1}{2})} (R_{\varepsilon,t}-\lambda)^{-1}d\lambda, \quad \text{with } k \leq n+m$$

on the eigenfunction belonging to the eigenvalue of $R_{\varepsilon,t}$ contained in $D(-k,\frac{1}{2})$; it is orthogonal and it commutes with $R_{\varepsilon,t}$ (thm.1.3) and hence we have

$$\text{(19a)}\qquad \|(R_{\varepsilon,t}+k)\tilde{\chi}_{k-1}\|^2 = |\lambda_k(\varepsilon,t)+k|^2\|P_{\varepsilon,t,k}\tilde{\chi}_{k-1}\|^2 + \\ + \|(R_{\varepsilon,t}+k)(1-P_{\varepsilon,t,k})\tilde{\chi}_{k-1}\|^2 .$$

Since $\operatorname{dist}\left(-k,\sigma(R_{\varepsilon,t}|_{\mathcal{R}(1-P_{\varepsilon,t,k})})\right) \ge \frac{1}{2}$, we have

$$\text{(19b)}\qquad \|(R_{\varepsilon,t}+k)(1-P_{\varepsilon,t,k})\tilde{\chi}_k\| \ge \tfrac{1}{2}\|(1-P_{\varepsilon,t,k})\tilde{\chi}_k\| .$$

From the inequalities (15) and (19b), we infer that $\|(1-P_{\varepsilon,t,k})\tilde{\chi}_n\| \to 0$ and hence with (19a) we find that $\|P_{\varepsilon,t,k}\tilde{\chi}_n\| \to 1$ and

$$\text{(20)}\qquad \lambda_k(\varepsilon,t) = -k + \mathcal{O}(\varepsilon^{\frac{1}{2}}k^{3/2}) \qquad (\varepsilon\to+0)$$

for $1 \le k \le n+m$ and for all $t \in [0,t_{n+m}]$. Since the unbounded component of $W_{n+m}(\frac{1}{2})$ is contained in $W_{n+m-1}(\frac{1}{6})$, we can by (20) find a number $\varepsilon_1 \in (0,\varepsilon_o]$ such that $\sigma(R_{\varepsilon,t}) \subset W_{n+m-1}(\frac{1}{6})$ for all $t \in [0,t_{n+m}]$. By definition of t_{n+m-1} we now have $\sigma(R_{\varepsilon,t}) \subset W_{n+m-1}(\frac{1}{2})$ for all $t \in [t_{n+m},t_{n+m}+t_{n+m-1}]$ and we can prove (20) for $1 \le k \le n+m-1$ as before. After m steps we find that (20) is true for $1 \le k \le n$ and for $t \in [0,\sum_{k=n+1}^{n+m} t_k] \supset [0,1]$. This proves (17a).

If $\lambda \in \sigma(\tilde{T}_\varepsilon)$ and if u is the eigenfunction belonging to λ, then we find by (10c)

$$0 = \|T_\varepsilon u - \lambda u\| \ge \|R_{\varepsilon,1}u - \lambda u\| - \|T_\varepsilon u - R_{\varepsilon,1}u\| \ge \\ \ge \{(1-C_5\varepsilon^{\frac{1}{2}})\operatorname{dist}(\lambda,\sigma(R_{\varepsilon,1})) - C_6\varepsilon^{\frac{1}{2}}\}\|u\| .$$

From this it follows that

$$\operatorname{dist}(\lambda,\sigma(R_{\varepsilon,1})) \le C_6\varepsilon^{\frac{1}{2}}/(1-C_5\varepsilon^{\frac{1}{2}});$$

in conjunction with (17a) this proves (17b). □

REMARKS. 1. Up to now we considered only problem (1+), in which the term xu' is preceded by a plus sign. In connection with the minus sign case we define the operator U_ε with $\mathcal{D}(U_\varepsilon) := \mathcal{D}(T_\varepsilon)$ and

$$U_\varepsilon u := \varepsilon\tau u - xu' \qquad \text{for all } u \in \mathcal{D}(U_\varepsilon). \tag{21a}$$

It is easily seen that its adjoint U_ε^*,

$$U_\varepsilon^* u := \varepsilon\tau^* u + xu' + u \qquad \text{for } u \in \mathcal{D}(U_\varepsilon^*) = \mathcal{D}(U_\varepsilon) \tag{21b}$$

satisfies all conditions of theorem 3.4, hence if $\sigma(U_\varepsilon) = \{\nu_k(\varepsilon) \mid k \in \mathbb{N}\}$ with $Re\nu_{k+1} < Re\nu_k$, then

$$\nu_k(\varepsilon) = -k + 1 + \mathcal{O}(\varepsilon^{\frac{1}{2}}k^{3/2}) \qquad (\varepsilon \to +0). \tag{21c}$$

2. The functions χ_n, defined in (14), are approximate eigenfunctions of $\tilde{T}_\varepsilon$, hence the functions $\hat{\chi}_n := \exp(-x^2/4\varepsilon)\chi_n$ are approximate eigenfunctions of T_ε. By the Rodrigues relation for H_n (cf. [2] ch. 22.11) we find

$$\hat{\chi}_n(x;\varepsilon) = \exp(-x^2/2\varepsilon)H_n(x/\sqrt{2\varepsilon}) = (-1)^n(2\varepsilon)^{\frac{1}{2}n}\frac{d^n}{dx^n}\exp(-x^2/2\varepsilon).$$

Since $(2\varepsilon\pi)^{-\frac{1}{2}}\exp(-x^2/2\varepsilon)$ converges to the Dirac δ-distribution for $\varepsilon \to +0$, the n-th (approximate) eigenfunction $\hat{\chi}_n$ of T_n converges after suitable renormalization to the n-th derivative of δ.

3.3. STRONG L^2-CONVERGENCE OF THE RESOLVENT IN THE PLUS SIGN CASE

The inverse stability of $T_\varepsilon - \lambda$ in a part of the complex plane results from the following lemma:

<u>LEMMA 3.5</u>. *If $\varepsilon \in \mathbb{R}^+$ and sufficiently small and if $\lambda \in \mathbb{C}$ with $Re\lambda > -\frac{1}{2}$, the operator $T_\varepsilon - \lambda$ has a bounded inverse, which satisfies (uniformly with respect to ε) the inequality*

$$\|(T_\varepsilon-\lambda)^{-1}\| \le (\tfrac{1}{2} + Re\lambda - K\varepsilon)^{-1} \tag{22}$$

with $K := \frac{1}{4}[b^2/a] + [c]$.

PROOF. Any $u \in \mathcal{D}(T_\varepsilon)$ satisfies

$$\|\varepsilon(au')' + xu' - \lambda u\| \, \|u\| \geq \left|Re\left\langle \varepsilon(au')' + xu' - \lambda u, u\right\rangle\right| =$$

$$= \left|-\varepsilon\left\langle au', u'\right\rangle - \tfrac{1}{2}\left\langle u, u\right\rangle - Re\lambda\left\langle u, u\right\rangle\right| =$$

$$= \varepsilon\left\langle au', u'\right\rangle + (Re\lambda + \tfrac{1}{2})\|u\|^2 \qquad \text{if } Re\lambda > -\tfrac{1}{2},$$

since $Re\left\langle xu', u\right\rangle = \frac{1}{2}\int_{-1}^{1} x(u\bar{u})'dx = -\frac{1}{2}\left\langle u, u\right\rangle$, and

$$\left|\left\langle \varepsilon bu', u\right\rangle\right| \leq \varepsilon\|a^{\frac{1}{2}}u'\| \, \|a^{-\frac{1}{2}}bu\| \leq \varepsilon\left\langle au', u'\right\rangle + \tfrac{1}{4}[b^2/a]\|u\|^2.$$

From these inequalities we find

$$\|T_\varepsilon u - \lambda u\| \geq \left|Re\left\langle \varepsilon\tau u + xu' - \lambda u, u\right\rangle\right| / \|u\| \geq (Re\lambda + \tfrac{1}{2} - K\varepsilon)\|u\|,$$

provided $Re\lambda > -\frac{1}{2} + K\varepsilon$. Since by theorem 3.4 $T_\varepsilon - \lambda$ is invertible if $Re\lambda > -\frac{1}{2}$ and if ε is small enough, this inequality proves formula (22). □

Guided by the idea that the limit of the solution of (2) still satisfies both boundary conditions of (2), we define the presumed limit operator T_o by

$$T_o u := xu' \qquad \text{for all } u \in \mathcal{D}(T_o) := \{v \in L^2(-1,1) \,|\, xv' \in L^2(-1,1) \,\&\, v(\pm 1) = 0\};$$

we stipulate that we can impose two boundary conditions on the domain of T_o since this domain contains functions that are discontinuous at $x = 0$.

LEMMA 3.6. $\rho(T_o) = \{\lambda \in \mathbb{C} \mid Re\lambda > -\frac{1}{2}\}$ *and* $\|(T_o - \lambda)^{-1}\| \leq (\frac{1}{2} + Re\lambda)^{-1}$ *if* $\lambda \in \rho(T_o)$.

PROOF. Any $u \in \mathcal{D}(T_o)$ satisfies

$$\|T_o u - \lambda u\| \geq \left|Re\left\langle T_o u - \lambda u, u\right\rangle\right| / \|u\| = \left|\tfrac{1}{2} + Re\lambda\right| \|u\|,$$

hence $\mathcal{R}(T_o - \lambda)$ is closed if $Re\lambda \neq \frac{1}{2}$. The adjoint of T_o is T_o^*,

$$T_o^* u = -xu' - u \qquad \text{for all } u \in \mathcal{D}(T_o^*) = \{v \in L^2(-1,1) \,|\, xv' \in L^2(-1,1)\};$$

it has no boundary conditions. The solutions of the equation $T_o^* u - \lambda u = 0$, i.e. of $xu' + u + \lambda u = 0$, are $\alpha|x|^{-\lambda-1} + \beta x|x|^{-\lambda-2}$; those are square integrable iff $Re\lambda < -\frac{1}{2}$. This proves that $N(T_o^*) = \{0\}$ iff $Re\lambda > -\frac{1}{2}$ and the assertion of the lemma follows from theorem 1.1. □

<u>THEOREM 3.7</u>. *If* $Re\lambda > -\frac{1}{2}$ *the resolvent* $(T_\varepsilon-\lambda)^{-1}$ *converges in* $L^2(-1,1)$ *strongly to* $(T_o-\lambda)^{-1}$ *for* $\varepsilon \to +0$; *if, moreover,* $f \in H^2(-1,1)$ *and* $Re\lambda > 3/2$, *then*

$$\|(T_\varepsilon-\lambda)^{-1}f - (T_o-\lambda)^{-1}f\| = O(\varepsilon\|f\|_2/(Re\lambda-\tfrac{3}{2})) \qquad (\varepsilon\to+0).$$

<u>PROOF</u>. First we prove the $O(\varepsilon)$ estimate and thereafter we show that it implies strong convergence for all $\lambda \in \rho(T_o)$ in the same way as in the proof of theorem 2.5.

If $f \in H^1(-1,1)$, we find that $\frac{d}{dx}(T_o-\lambda)^{-1}f$ is the solution of the equation $xu' - (\lambda-1)u = f'$, $u'(\pm 1) = f(\pm 1)$; hence we find by the lemma's 2.6 and 3.6

$$\text{(23a)} \qquad \left\|\frac{d}{dx}((T_o-\lambda)^{-1}f)\right\| = \|(T_o-\lambda+1)^{-1}f' + f(1)Y(x)x^{\lambda-1} + f(-1)Y(-x)|x|^{\lambda-1}\| \le$$

$$\le (Re\lambda-\tfrac{1}{2})^{-1}\|f'\| + |2\lambda-1|^{-\frac{1}{2}}(|f(1)| + |f(-1)|) \le$$

$$\le K\|f\|_1/(Re\lambda-\tfrac{1}{2}), \qquad \text{if } Re\lambda > \tfrac{1}{2},$$

where Y is the unit step (or Heaviside's) function, $Y(x) = 1$ if $x > 0$ and $Y(x) = 0$ otherwise, and K is a constant not depending on λ. In the same way we prove

$$\text{(23b)} \qquad \left\|\frac{d^2}{dx^2}((T_o-\lambda)^{-1}f)\right\| \le K'\|f\|_2/(Re\lambda-3/2)$$

provided $Re\lambda > 3/2$ and $f \in H^2(-1,1)$. This shows that $(T_o-\lambda)^{-1}f \in D(T_\varepsilon)$ if $f \in H^2(-1,1)$ and if $Re\lambda > 3/2$, and that a constant K'' exists, such that

$$\text{(23c)} \qquad \|(T_\varepsilon-\lambda)\{(T_\varepsilon-\lambda)^{-1}f - (T_o-\lambda)^{-1}f\}\| = \varepsilon\|\tau(T_o-\lambda)^{-1}f\| \le$$

$$\le \varepsilon K''\|f\|_2/(Re\lambda-3/2).$$

Hence by lemma 3.5 we find

$$\|(T_\varepsilon-\lambda)^{-1}f - (T_0-\lambda)^{-1}f\| \le \varepsilon K''\|f\|_2/(Re\lambda-3/2) \qquad \text{if } Re\lambda > 3/2.$$

Since $H^2(-1,1)$ is dense in $L^2(-1,1)$, $(T_\varepsilon-\lambda)^{-1}$ converges to $(T_0-\lambda)^{-1}$ strongly for $\varepsilon \to +0$, i.e. $\|(T_\varepsilon-\lambda)^{-1}f - (T_0-\lambda)^{-1}f\| \to 0$ for all $f \in L^2(-1,1)$, provided $Re\lambda > 3/2$.

We extend this result to all $\lambda \in \rho(T_0)$ by analytic continuation. Consider the Neumann-series

$$(T_\varepsilon-\mu)^{-1} = \sum_{k=0}^{\infty} (\mu-\lambda)^k (T_\varepsilon-\lambda)^{-k-1},$$

which is uniformly convergent (with respect to the infinite summation) if $|\mu - \lambda| < Re\lambda + \frac{1}{2} - K\varepsilon$ by lemma 3.5. If $(T_\varepsilon-\lambda)^{-1}$ converges strongly for $\varepsilon \to +0$, all its powers converge strongly too, hence $(T_\varepsilon-\mu)^{-1}$ converges strongly for $\varepsilon \to +0$ and for all μ within the radius of convergence of the infinite sum. Since $(T_\varepsilon-\lambda)^{-1}$ converges strongly for $Re\lambda > 3/2$, this proves the theorem. □

<u>COROLLARY 3.8</u>. *If* $f \in L^2(-1,1)$ *and* $Re\lambda > -\frac{1}{2}$ *and if* u_ε *and* u_0 *are the solutions of the boundary value problems*

(24a) $$(\varepsilon\tau + xd/dx-\lambda)u_\varepsilon = f, \qquad u_\varepsilon(\pm1) = A \pm B,$$

(24b) $$(xd/dx-\lambda)u_0 = f, \qquad u_0(\pm1) = A \pm B,$$

then $\lim_{\varepsilon\to+0}\|u_\varepsilon - u_0\| = 0$. *If moreover* $f \in H^2(-1,1)$ *and* $Re\lambda > 3/2$, *then*

(25a) $$\|u_\varepsilon - u_0\| = \mathcal{O}(\varepsilon(|A|+|B|+\|f\|_2)/(Re\lambda-3/2)), \qquad (\varepsilon\to+0).$$

<u>PROOF</u>. The function $v_\varepsilon(x) := u_\varepsilon(x) - A - Bx$ is an element of $\mathcal{D}(T_\varepsilon)$ and $(\varepsilon\tau+xd/dx-\lambda)v_\varepsilon(x)$ converges to $f + \lambda A + (\lambda-1)B$ for $\varepsilon \to +0$; since $\|(T_\varepsilon-\lambda)^{-1}\|$ is uniformly bounded if ε is in some closed set $[0,\varepsilon_\lambda]$ and if $Re\lambda > -\frac{1}{2}$ by lemma 3.6, the function v_ε converges to the same limit as $(T_\varepsilon-\lambda)^{-1}(f+\lambda A+(\lambda-1)B)$ does and we find that v_ε converges to

$$A|x|^\lambda - A + Bx|x|^{\lambda-1} - Bx + \int_{x/|x|}^{x} f(t)\left(\frac{x}{t}\right)^\lambda \frac{dt}{t};$$

this proves the first assertion. If $f \in H^2(-1,1)$ and $Re\lambda > \frac{3}{2}$ then $u_\varepsilon - u_o \in \mathcal{D}(T_\varepsilon)$ and

$$\|(T_\varepsilon-\lambda)(u_\varepsilon-u_o)\| = \|\varepsilon\tau u_o\| = O(\varepsilon(|A|+|B|+\|f\|_2)/(Re\lambda-3/2)) \tag{25b}$$

by (23), hence (25a) is a consequence of lemma 3.5. □

<u>REMARK</u>. The convergence $(T_\varepsilon-\lambda)^{-1} \longrightarrow (T_o-\lambda)^{-1}$ cannot be uniform i.e. $\|(T_\varepsilon-\lambda)^{-1} - (T_o-\lambda)^{-1}\|$ does not converge to zero for $\varepsilon \to +0$, as the following example shows. Let h be the function

$$h(x) := 1 \quad \text{if} \quad |x| < \delta \quad \text{and} \quad h(x) = 0 \quad \text{otherwise};$$

then the solution $u_\varepsilon := -\Pi_\varepsilon^{-1}h$ of the equation $\varepsilon u'' + xu' = -h$, $u(\pm 1) = 0$ is

$$u_\varepsilon(x) := \frac{1}{\varepsilon}\int_x^1\int_0^t h(s)\exp((s^2-t^2)/2\varepsilon)\,ds\,dt.$$

It is even and positive, hence

$$0 \le u_\varepsilon(x) \le \frac{1}{\varepsilon}\int_0^\infty\int_0^t h(s)\exp((s^2-t^2)/2\varepsilon)\,ds\,dt \le$$

$$\le \frac{1}{\varepsilon}\int_0^\infty\int_s^\infty h(s)\exp((s^2-t^2)/2\varepsilon)\,dt\,ds.$$

By the inequality (cf. [2] formula 7.1.13)

$$\frac{1}{x+(x^2+1)^{\frac{1}{2}}} \le e^{x^2}\int_x^\infty e^{-t^2}\,dt \le \frac{1}{x+(x^2+4/\pi)^{\frac{1}{2}}}$$

we find

$$0 \le u_\varepsilon(x) \le 2\int_0^\delta \frac{ds}{s+\sqrt{(s^2+8\varepsilon/\pi)}} \le \delta(\pi/2\varepsilon)^{\frac{1}{2}}, \qquad \text{if } |x| < \delta.$$

On the other hand the solution $u_o := -T_o^{-1}h$ of $xu' = 0$, $u(\pm 1) = 0$ is

$$u_o(x) = \begin{cases} \log\delta - \log|x|, & \text{if } 0 < |x| \le \delta, \\ 0, & \text{if } |x| \ge \delta. \end{cases}$$

Choose $\delta = \varepsilon$, then $|u_o(x)| > \log 2$ if $|x| \le \frac{1}{2}\varepsilon$ and $|u_\varepsilon| < \sqrt{\frac{1}{2}\pi\varepsilon}$, hence

$$\|u_o - u_\varepsilon\| \ge \|u_o - u_\varepsilon\|_{(-\frac{1}{2}\varepsilon,\frac{1}{2}\varepsilon)} \ge \varepsilon^{\frac{1}{2}}(\log 2-\sqrt{\tfrac{1}{2}\pi\varepsilon})^{\frac{1}{2}}.$$

Furthermore $\|h\| = \sqrt{2\varepsilon}$, so we have

$$\|\Pi_\varepsilon^{-1} - T_o^{-1}h\|/\|h\| \ge (\log 2-\sqrt{\tfrac{1}{2}\pi\varepsilon})^{\frac{1}{2}},$$

which disproves uniform convergence of $(T_\varepsilon-\lambda)^{-1}$ for any $\lambda \in \rho(T_o)$.

3.4. STRONG CONVERGENCE IN $H^{-n}(-1,1)$.

We proved in theorem 3.4 that the spectrum of T_ε converges if $\varepsilon \to +0$, but from lemma 3.6 we see that the limit of the spectrum is not equal to the spectrum of the limit-operator; the latter set is much larger. This means that $(T_\varepsilon-\lambda)^{-1}f$ exists and is an element of $L^2(-1,1)$ if $\lambda \notin \sigma(T_\varepsilon)$ but it need not have a limit in $L^2(-1,1)$ for $\varepsilon \to +0$ if $\lambda \in \sigma(T_o)$. In order to answer the question whether we can assign to the sequence $(T_\varepsilon-\lambda)^{-1}f$ a limit in some weaker sense, we enlarge the space in which the formal operator $\varepsilon\tau + xd/dx$ acts, in such a way that it contains distributions. This is motivated by the fact that the approximate eigenfunctions converge in (Schwartz-) distributional sense to the derivatives of δ and by the fact that the non-square-integrable solutions of the "limit"-equation $xu' = \lambda u$ can be interpreted as distributions of finite order. The solutions of $xu' = \lambda u$ are linear combinations of the distributions

$$\text{(26a)}\qquad X_\lambda := \begin{cases} 2^{-\lambda}\, Pf.(|x|^\lambda)/\Gamma(\frac{1}{2}\lambda+\frac{1}{2}) & \text{if } \lambda \neq 1-2j \\ (-1)^j 2\pi^{\frac{1}{2}}\delta^{(2j-2)}/\Gamma(j+\frac{1}{2}) & \text{if } \lambda = 1-2j \end{cases}, \qquad j \in \mathbb{N},$$

and

$$\text{(26b)}\qquad Z_\lambda := \begin{cases} 2^{-\lambda}\, Pf.(x|x|^{\lambda-1})/\Gamma(\frac{1}{2}\lambda+1) & \text{if } \lambda \neq 2j \\ (-1)^j 2\pi^{\frac{1}{2}}\delta^{(2j-1)}/\Gamma(j+\frac{1}{2}) & \text{if } \lambda = -2j \end{cases}, \qquad j \in \mathbb{N};$$

with respect to λ they are non-vanishing holomorphic distributions on all of $\mathbb{C}$, cf. SCHWARTZ [26] ch. 5.6; 18. The symbol *Pf.* denotes the "*pseudofunction*", cf. [26] 2 §2 example 2. These distributions can be identified with square integrable functions iff $Re\lambda > -\frac{1}{2}$; they are elements of $H_o^{-k}(-1,1)$ iff $Re\lambda > -k-\frac{1}{2}$.

We reformulate the boundary value problem (1+) in $H^{-n}(-1,1)$ by imposing suitable restrictions on the domain H^{-n+2} of $\varepsilon\tau + xd/dx$; since the functionals $u \mapsto u(\pm 1)$ are not continuous on H^{-n+2} we replace them by the functionals $u \mapsto (J_n u)(\pm 1)$, cf. (1.5) and theorem 1.7. We define the restrictions $T_{\varepsilon,n}$ of $\varepsilon\tau + xd/dx$ and $T_{o,n}$ of xd/dx by

(27a) $$T_{\varepsilon,n}u := \varepsilon\tau u + xu'$$

$$\text{for all } u \in \mathcal{D}(T_{\varepsilon,n}) := \{v \in H^{-n+2}(-1,1) \mid (J_n v)(\pm 1) = 0\},$$

and

(27b) $$T_{o,n}u := xu' \qquad \text{for all } u \in \mathcal{D}(T_{o,n}),$$

$$\mathcal{D}(T_{o,n}) := \{v \in H^{-n}(-1,1) \mid xv' \in H^{-n}(-1,1) \;\&\; (J_n v)(\pm 1) = 0\}.$$

They satisfy the analogues of the lemma's 3.5 and 3.6:

<u>LEMMA 3.9</u>. *A positive constant* K_n *exists such that for all* $\varepsilon \in [0,1]$ *the operator* $T_{\varepsilon,n} - \lambda$ *is invertible if* $Re\lambda > -\frac{1}{2} - n + K_n\varepsilon$, *and satisfies*

(28) $$|(T_{\varepsilon,n}-\lambda)^{-1}|_{-n} \le (Re\lambda+n+\tfrac{1}{2}-K_n\varepsilon)^{-1}.$$

<u>PROOF</u>. If $u \in \mathcal{D}(T_{o,n})$, then by (1.8a) and (1.10) we find

(29) $$|T_{o,n}u - \lambda u|_{-n}|u|_{-n} \ge \left|Re\left\langle J_n(xu'),J_n u\right\rangle - Re\lambda|u|_{-n}^2\right| =$$

$$= \left|Re\left\langle x(J_n u)',J_n u\right\rangle - (Re\lambda+n)|u|_{-n}^2\right|$$

$$\ge \left|\tfrac{1}{2} + n + Re\lambda\right| \; |u|_{-n}^2.$$

The H^{-n}-adjoint of $T_{o,n}$ is the operator $T^*_{o,n}$,

$$T^*_{o,n}u = -xu' - (2n+1)u$$

$$\text{for all } u \in \mathcal{D}(T^*_o) = \{v \in H^{-n}(-1,1) \mid xv' \in H^{-n}(-1,1)\}.$$

By (26) we see that the solutions of $T^*_{o,n}u = \lambda u$ are in $H^{-n}(-1,1)$ iff $Re\lambda < -n - \frac{1}{2}$, hence by theorem 1.1 we find $\rho(T_{o,n}) = \{\lambda \in \mathbb{C} \mid Re\lambda > -n - \frac{1}{2}\}$ and (28) follows from (29) in case $\varepsilon = 0$.

If $\varepsilon \neq 0$, $T_\varepsilon = \varepsilon S + xd/dx$ in which S is defined by (1.9); from (1.14) and (29) we find for any $u \in \mathcal{D}(T_{\varepsilon,n})$

$$|T_{\varepsilon,n}u - \lambda u|_{-n} \geq |Re\langle \varepsilon\tau u + xu' - \lambda u, u\rangle_{-n}|/|u|_{-n}$$

$$\geq (Re\lambda + n + \tfrac{1}{2} - C_n\varepsilon)|u|_{-n} \quad \text{if } Re\lambda + u + \tfrac{1}{2} - C_n\varepsilon > 0.$$

Since T_ε satisfies the conditions on the operator S in theorem 1.7, and since therefore $T_\varepsilon - \lambda$ is invertible if λ is sufficiently large positive, this inequality proves (28) in case $\varepsilon > 0$. □

Analogously to theorem 3.7 we find:

<u>THEOREM 3.10</u>. *If* $n \in \mathbb{N}_o$ *and* $Re\lambda > -n - \frac{1}{2}$, *the resolvent* $(T_{\varepsilon,n}-\lambda)^{-1}$ *converges strongly to* $(T_{o,n}-\lambda)^{-1}$ *for* $\varepsilon \to +0$. *If, moreover,* $f'' \in H^{-n}(-1,1)$, *then*

$$(30) \qquad |(T_{\varepsilon,n}-\lambda)^{-1}f - (T_{o,n}-\lambda)^{-1}f|_{-n} = \mathcal{O}(\varepsilon(|f|_{-n}+|f''|_{-n})/(Re\lambda+n-3/2))$$

for $\varepsilon \to +0$ *uniformly for all* λ *contained in a bounded subset of* $\{\lambda \in \mathbb{C} \mid Re\lambda > -n + 3/2\}$.

<u>PROOF</u>. If $u \in \mathcal{D}(T_o)$ and $\langle u, x^j\rangle = 0$ for some $j \in \mathbb{N}_o$, then we find by integration by parts

$$\langle xu', x^j\rangle = -(j+1)\langle u, x^j\rangle = 0.$$

Since P_n is the orthogonal projection on the span of $\{1, x, \ldots, x^{n-1}\}$ and since $P_nJ_n = 0$ this implies that $P_n x(J_nu)' = 0$ for all $u \in \mathcal{D}(T_{o,n})$. By the identity $(-d/dx)^n J_nu = u$ and the formulae (1.7) and (1.10) we find for any $u \in \mathcal{D}(T_{o,n})$

$$(31)\qquad J_n xu' = (-1)^n J_n\{(\tfrac{d}{dx})^n (x(J_n u)'-nJ_n u)\} =$$

$$= (1-\mathcal{P}_n)\{x(J_n u)' - nJ_n u\} = x(J_n u)' - nJ_n u.$$

So we find that $u \in \mathcal{D}(T_{o,n})$ satisfies the equation $xu' - \lambda u = f$ if and only if $J_n u$ satisfies $xv' - \lambda v - nv = J_n f$, hence

$$(32)\qquad J_n(T_{o,n}-\lambda)^{-1}f = (T_o-\lambda-n)^{-1}J_n f$$

for all $f \in H^{-n}(-1,1)$. By (23) this implies

$$|(T_{\varepsilon,n}-\lambda)\{(T_{\varepsilon,n}-\lambda)^{-1}f - (T_{o,n}-\lambda)^{-1}f\}|_{-n} = |\varepsilon\tau(T_{o,n}-\lambda)^{-1}f|_{-n} =$$

$$= \mathcal{O}(\varepsilon(|f|_{-n}+|f|_{-n+2})/(Re\lambda+n-3/2)),$$

which proves (30). The strong convergence is obtained by analytic continuation as in theorem 3.7. □

<u>COROLLARY 3.11</u>. *If* $n \in \mathbb{N}_o$, $f \in H^{-n}(-1,1)$ *and* $Re\lambda > -n-\frac{1}{2}$ *and if* $u_{\varepsilon,n}$ *and* $u_{o,n}$ *are the solutions of the boundary value problems*

$$(33a)\qquad (\varepsilon\tau+xd/dx-\lambda)u_{\varepsilon,n} = f, \qquad (J_n u_{\varepsilon,n})(\pm 1) = A_n \pm B_n$$

$$(33b)\qquad (xd/dx-\lambda)u_{o,n} = f, \qquad (J_n u_{o,n})(\pm 1) = A_n \pm B_n$$

then

$$\lim_{\varepsilon\to+0} |u_{\varepsilon,n} - u_{o,n}|_{-n} = 0.$$

If moreover $f'' \in H^{-n}(-1,1)$ *and* $Re\lambda > -n+3/2$ *then for* $\varepsilon \to +0$ *we have*

$$(34)\qquad |u_{\varepsilon,n} - u_{o,n}|_{-n} = \mathcal{O}\big(\varepsilon(|A_n|+|B_n|+|f|_{-n}+|f''|_{-n})/(Re\lambda+n-3/2)\big).$$

The proof is analogous to the one of cor. 3.8.

3.5. ESTIMATES OF ORDER $\mathcal{O}(\varepsilon)$ IN WEIGHTED NORMS

If the right-hand sides of (24) and (33) are smooth functions, the solutions of the equations are smooth too; as often occurs in differential equations, convergence in distributional sense together with regularity of the solutions induces convergence in stronger norms also in this case (in casu convergence in a weighted uniform norm). In this section we will prove that the solution of (24a) converges to the solution of (24b) in the norms $u \mapsto \|x^{n+2}u\|$ and $u \mapsto [x^{n+5/2}u]$, if $f \in H^2(-1,1)$, $Re\lambda > -n-\frac{1}{2}$ and $n \in \mathbb{N}_o$, and that the appoximation is of order $\mathcal{O}(\varepsilon)$. We remark that this type of norms disregards the non-uniformity of the solutions near the point $x = 0$.

We can extend the limit-operator $T_{o,o}$ to the space $\mathcal{B}_k$ of measurable functions u on (-1,1) for which $\|x^k u\| < \infty$ with $k \in \mathbb{N}$; $\mathcal{B}_k$ is a Hilbert space with respect to the inner product $\{u,v\} \mapsto \langle x^k u, x^k v\rangle$. In this space we define the extension E_k of $T_{o,o}$ by

(35a) $$E_k u := xu' \quad \text{for all } u \in \mathcal{D}(E_k) := \{u \in \mathcal{B}_k \mid xu' \in \mathcal{B}_k \ \& \ u(\pm 1) = 0\}.$$

In a way analogous to lemma 3.6 we prove

<u>LEMMA 3.12</u>. *The resolvent set of* E_k *is the set*

$$\rho(E_k) := \{\lambda \in \mathbb{C} \mid Re\lambda > -n-\tfrac{1}{2}\}$$

and for all $\lambda \in \rho(E_k)$ *and* $f \in \mathcal{B}_k$ *the resolvent satisfies the inequality*

(35b) $$\|x^k(E_k-\lambda)^{-1}f\| \le \|x^k f\|/(Re\lambda+k+\tfrac{1}{2}).$$

<u>PROOF</u>. For any $u \in \mathcal{D}(E_k)$ we have

$$\|x^k(E_k-\lambda)u\| \ge \left| Re\langle x^{k+1}u', x^k u\rangle/\|x^k u\| - Re\lambda\|x^k u\| \right|$$

$$\ge (Re\lambda+k+\tfrac{1}{2})\|u\|.$$

Since the null-space of the adjoint is zero for $Re\lambda > -k-\frac{1}{2}$, this proves the lemma. □

If $f \in L^2(-1,1)$ and if $Re\lambda > -k + \frac{1}{2}$, the solution of equation (33b) with $n = 0$ (or of (24b)) is

$$(36)\qquad u_{o,o}(x,\lambda) := (E_k-\lambda)^{-1}f + A_o|x|^\lambda + B_o x|x|^{\lambda-1} =$$

$$= \int_{x/|x|}^{x} f(t)\left(\frac{x}{t}\right)^\lambda \frac{dt}{t} + A_o|x|^\lambda + B_o x|x|^{\lambda-1}, \qquad (x \neq 0).$$

If $Re\lambda > -1$, $u_{o,o}$ is certainly in $H^{-k}(-1,1)$ for all $k \in \mathbb{N}$ and is a solution of the equation $xu' - \lambda u = f$ in that space. If $Re\lambda \le -1$, we rewrite (36) and find

$$(37)\qquad u_{o,o}(x,\lambda) = \int_0^x f(t)\left(\frac{x}{t}\right)^\lambda \frac{dt}{t} + |x|^\lambda\{A_o - \tfrac{1}{2}\int_0^1 (f(t)+f(-t))t^{-\lambda-1}dt\} +$$

$$+ x|x|^{\lambda-1}\{B_o - \tfrac{1}{2}\int_0^1 (f(t) - f(-t))t^{-\lambda-1}dt\}.$$

The first integral in the right-hand side of (37) is in $L^2(-1,1)$ and hence certainly in $H^{-k}(-1,1)$ for $k \in \mathbb{N}$. The linear combinations of $|x|^\lambda$ and $x|x|^{\lambda-1}$ are in $H^{-k}(-1,1)$ in case $Re\lambda > -k - \frac{1}{2}$, if we consider them as "pseudo functions", cf. (26); however, in the space $H^{-k}(-1,1)$ they are solutions of the equation $xu' = \lambda u$ iff $\lambda \notin -\mathbb{N}$. We conclude that $Pf(u_{o,o}(\cdot,\lambda))$ is in $H^{-k}(-1,1)$ and is a solution of $xu' - \lambda u = f$ in that space for all $f \in L^2(-1,1)$ iff $Re\lambda > -k - \frac{1}{2}$ and $\lambda \notin -\mathbb{N}$.

Since by theorem 3.4, the solution $u_{\varepsilon,o}$ of (33a) is in $L^2(-1,1)$ if $\lambda \notin \sigma(T_{\varepsilon,o})$, $f \in L^2(-1,1)$ and $\varepsilon \neq 0$, we can consider the convergence of $|u_{\varepsilon,o} - Pf(u_{o,o})|_{-k}$ for $Re\lambda > -k - \frac{1}{2}$ and $\lambda \notin -\mathbb{N}$; we will prove convergence of this expression by comparing it to $|u_{\varepsilon,k} - u_{o,k}|_{-k}$. The solutions $u_{\varepsilon,o}$ and $u_{\varepsilon,k}$ differ by a solution of the homogeneous equation, so we will first examine the convergence of solutions of the homogeneous equation $\varepsilon\tau u + xu' = \lambda u$ and then prove convergence in the inhomogeneous case. We begin with a fundamental estimate:

<u>LEMMA 3.13</u>. *For each* $k \in \mathbb{N}_o$ *constants* C_k *and* $\varepsilon_k \in \mathbb{R}^+$ *exist, such that*

$$\left.\begin{array}{ll}(38a) & \|x^k v\| \\ (38b) & \|x^{k+1}v'\|\end{array}\right\} \le 4\|x^k(\varepsilon\tau v + xv' - \lambda v)\| + C_k(\lambda)|v|_{-k}$$

for all $\varepsilon \in (0,\varepsilon_k]$, $\lambda \in \mathbb{C}$ *and* $v \in H^{-k}(-1,1)$ *for which* $\|x^k v''\| < \infty$.

PROOF. We have the inequality

$$(39)\qquad \| \varepsilon x^k (av')' + x^{k+1} v' \|^2 =$$

$$= \| \varepsilon x^k (av')' \|^2 + \| x^{k+1} v' \|^2 + \varepsilon \int_{-1}^{1} x^{2k+1} \left(v'(a\bar{v}')' + (av')'\bar{v}' \right) dx =$$

$$= \| \varepsilon x^k (av')' \|^2 + \| x^{k+1} v' \|^2 + \varepsilon \int_{-1}^{1} x^{2k} \left(xa' - (2k+1)a \right) v'\bar{v}' dx + $$

$$+ \varepsilon a x^{2k+1} v'\bar{v}' \Big|_{x=-1}^{x=1} \geq$$

$$\geq \| \varepsilon x^k (av')' \|^2 + \| x^{k+1} v' \|^2 - \varepsilon [xa' - (2k+1)a] \| x^k v' \|^2 .$$

We estimate the term $\|x^k v'\|$ as follows; if $w \in H^1_o(-1,1)$, then

$$(40a)\qquad \| x^{k+1} w' \| \geq \left| \tfrac{1}{2} \int_{-1}^{1} x^{2k+1} (w'\bar{w} + \bar{w}'w) dx \right| / \| x^k w \| = (k+\tfrac{1}{2}) \| x^k w \|$$

and since $(1-x^2)av' \in H^1_o(-1,1)$ we obtain from this the inequality

$$(40b)\qquad \| x^{k-1} av' \| \leq \| x^{k+1} av' \| + \| x^{k-1} (1-x^2) av' \| \leq$$

$$\leq \| x^{k+1} av' \| + \| x^k ((1-x^2)av')' \| / (k-\tfrac{1}{2}) \leq$$

$$\leq [a](1+2/(k-\tfrac{1}{2})) \| x^{k+1} v' \| + \| x^k (av')' \| / (k-\tfrac{1}{2}) .$$

This inequality implies

$$(41)\qquad \| x^k v' \|^2 \leq \| x^{k+1} v' \|^2 + [1/a] \int_{-1}^{1} x^{2k} (1-x^2) av'\bar{v}' dx =$$

$$= \| x^{k+1} v' \|^2 - [1/a] \int_{-1}^{1} (x^{2k} (1-x^2) av')' \bar{v} dx \leq$$

$$\leq \| x^{k+1} v' \|^2 + [1/a] \; \| x^k v \| \Big\{ [1-x^2] \| x^k (av')' \| + $$

$$+ [2k-(2k+2)x^2] \| x^{k-1} av' \| \Big\} \leq$$

$$\leq \| x^{k+1} v' \|^2 + \frac{[1/a]}{k-\tfrac{1}{2}} \| x^k v \| \Big\{ (3k-\tfrac{1}{2}) \| x^k (av')' \| + $$

$$+ k(2k+3)[a] \| x^{k+1} v' \| \Big\} .$$

From (39) we now conclude that we can find constants $\tilde{C}_k$ and ε_k in $\mathbb{R}^+$ such that the inequality

$$\| \varepsilon x^k (av')' \| + \| x^{k+1} v' \| \le 2 \| x^k (\varepsilon (av')' + xv') \| + \tilde{C}_k \| x^k v \|$$

holds for all v, for which $\| x^2 v'' \| < \infty$ and for all $\varepsilon \in (0, \varepsilon_k]$. With little additional effort we find in the same way a constant $\hat{C}_k$, such that

(42) $$\| \varepsilon x^k (av')' \| + \| x^{k+1} v' \| \le 2 \| x^k (\varepsilon \tau v + xv' - \lambda v) \| + (\hat{C}_k + 2|\lambda|) \| x^k v \|$$

for all $\varepsilon \in (0, \varepsilon_k]$. Now we can find a constant K_k, such that

(43a) $$\| x^k v \| \le t \| x^{k+1} v' \| + t^{-k} K_k |v|_{-k}$$

for all $t \in (0,1]$. In conjunction with (42) this proves (38).

In order to prove (43a) we set $w := J_k v$ and find the equivalent statement

(43b) $$\| x^k w^{(k)} \| \le t \| x^{k+1} w^{(k+1)} \| + K_k t^{-k} \| w \|$$

and since $x^k w^{(k)} = (x \frac{d}{dx} - k+1) x^{k-1} w^{(k-1)}$, it suffices to prove the existence of constants c_j, such that

(43c) $$\| xw' - jw \| \le t \| (x \frac{d}{dx} - j-1)(x \frac{d}{dx} - j) w \| + c_j t^{-1} \| w \|$$

for all $t \in (0,1]$, $j \in \mathbb{Z}$ and $w \in L^2(-1,1)$ with $\| x^2 w'' \| < \infty$. By integration by parts we find

(43d) $$\| xw' - jw \|^2 = Re\Big\{ - \Big\langle w, (x \frac{d}{dx} - j-1)(xw' - jw) \Big\rangle + \\ - (2j+2) \Big\langle w, xw' - jw \Big\rangle + \Big[xw(x\bar{w}' - j\bar{w}) \Big]_{-1}^{1} \Big\} \le$$

$$\le Re\Big\{ - \Big\langle w, (x \frac{d}{dx} - j-1)(xw' - jw) \Big\rangle + \Big[x\bar{w}(xw' - jw) - (j+1) x |w|^2 \Big]_{-1}^{1} \Big\} + \\ + (j+1)(2j+1) \| w \|^2 .$$

For the boundary term we find

$$|w(1)|^2 + |w(-1)|^2 = \int_{-1}^{1} \frac{d}{dx}(xw\overline{w})\,dx =$$

$$= \int_{-1}^{1} \{(xw'-jw)\overline{w} + (x\overline{w}'-j\overline{w})w + (2j+1)|w|^2\}dx$$

$$\leq 2\|xw' - jw\|\,\|w\| + (2j+1)\|w\|^2$$

and analogously

$$\left[x|xw' - jw|^2\right]_{-1}^{1} \leq 2\|(x\frac{d}{dx} - j-1)(xw'-jw)\|\,\|xw'-jw\| +$$

$$+ (2j+3)\|xw' - jw\|^2 ;$$

hence by Young's inequality we find a constant $\hat{c}_j$ such that

$$\left[xw(x\overline{w}'-jw) - (j+1)x|w|^2\right]_{-1}^{1} \leq$$

$$\leq \left[(j+1)x|w|^2\right]_{-1}^{1} + \left\{\left[x|w|^2\right]_{-1}^{1}\left[x|xw' - jw|^2\right]_{-1}^{1}\right\}^{\frac{1}{2}}$$

$$\leq t\|(x\frac{d}{dx} - j-1)(xw'-jw)\|^2 + \tfrac{1}{2}\|xw'-jw\|^2 + t^{-1}\hat{c}_j\|w\|^2$$

for all $t \in (0,1]$. In conjunction with (43d) this proves (43c). □

<u>REMARK</u>. The essential point in the proof of this lemma is the fact that the boundary terms due to the integration by parts of the cross product in (39) are non-negative and can be skipped in the estimate from below. This means that the estimate (38) holds for the operator $\varepsilon\tau - xd/dx$ only if u satisfies $u'(\pm 1) = 0$.

Define the (pseudo-)functions $p_{\varepsilon,n}(\cdot,\lambda)$ and $q_{\varepsilon,n}(\cdot,\lambda)$ as the (distributional) solutions of the equation $\varepsilon\tau u + xu' = \lambda u$ for all $\varepsilon \geq 0$, which satisfy the (generalized) boundary conditions

$$(J_n p_{\varepsilon,n})(1) = (-1)^n (J_n p_{\varepsilon,n})(-1) = (J_n q_{\varepsilon,n})(1) =$$

$$= (-1)^{n+1}(J_n q_{\varepsilon,n})(-1) = 1.$$

We observe that we write down $p_{\varepsilon,n}$ and $q_{\varepsilon,n}$ as if they were only functions and not distributions; in fact they are equivalent to C^{∞}-functions if $\varepsilon \neq 0$ or if $x \neq 0$. Since J_n preserves or inverts symmetry if n is even or odd, i.e.

(44) $$(J_n f)(x) = \pm(-1)^n (J_n f)(-x) \quad \text{if} \quad f(x) = \pm f(-x),$$

we find that $p_{o,n}$ and $q_{o,n}$ are constant multiples of X_λ and Z_λ, cf. (26),

(45) $$p_{o,n}(\cdot,\lambda) = \alpha_n(\lambda) X_\lambda \quad \text{and} \quad q_{o,n}(\cdot,\lambda) = \beta_n(\lambda) Z_\lambda;$$

the functions $\alpha_n(\lambda)$ and $\beta_n(\lambda)$ are meromorphic functions of λ which cannot have poles or zeros in the resolvent set of $T_{o,n}$.

With the aid of the functions $p_{o,n}$ and $q_{o,n}$ we can express $(T_{o,n}-\lambda)^{-1}f$ with $f \in L^2(-1,1)$ in terms of the better accessible function $(E_k-\lambda)^{-1}f$ for $Re\lambda > -k-\frac{1}{2}$. As we argued at the beginning of this section, cf. (36) and (37), $Pf((E_k-\lambda)^{-1}f)$ is an element of $H^{-k}(-1,1)$ if $Re\lambda > -k-\frac{1}{2}$ and $f \in L^2(-1,1)$. Define the numbers μ_n and ν_n

$$\mu_n \pm \nu_n := (J_n Pf.((E_k-\lambda)^{-1}f))(\pm 1);$$

since any $u \in H^1(-1,1)$ satisfies

(46) $$|u(1)|^2 + |u(-1)|^2 = \int_{-1}^{1} (xu\bar{u})'dx \le \|u\|^2 + \|u\| \, \|xu'\|$$

and any $v \in H^{-n+1}(-1,1)$ satisfies

(47) $$\| x(J_n v)' \| = |nv + xv'|_{-n},$$

we infer from (36) - (37) that μ_n and ν_n are bounded by $C\|f\|/(Re\lambda+n+\frac{1}{2})$ if $Re\lambda > -n-\frac{1}{2}$ for some constant $C > 0$. So we find

(48) $$(T_{o,n}-\lambda)^{-1}f = Pf((E_k-\lambda)^{-1}f) + \mu_n p_{o,n}(\cdot,\lambda) + \nu_n q_{o,n}(\cdot,\lambda)$$

if $f \in L^2(-1,1)$ and $Re\lambda > -k-\frac{1}{2} \ge -n-\frac{1}{2}$; we remark that the only reason for the restriction $Re\lambda > -k-\frac{1}{2}$ is that $E_k - \lambda$ is not invertible for other values of λ.

If the right-hand side f of (33) is chosen in a more restricted class of functions, we can prove the much stronger result:

LEMMA 3.14. *If* $n \in \mathbb{N}$, $Re\lambda > -n + 3/2$ *and* $f \in H^1(-1,1)$, *then the solutions* $u_{\varepsilon,n}$ *of* (33a) *and* $u_{o,n}$ *of* (33b) *satisfy*

$$\left.\begin{array}{ll}(49a) & \| x^n(u_{\varepsilon,n}-u_{o,n}) \| = \\ (49b) & [\,|x|^{n+\frac{1}{2}}(u_{\varepsilon,n}-u_{o,n})] = \end{array}\right\} O(\varepsilon(|A_n| + |B_n| + \|f\|_1)/(Re\lambda+n-3/2)), \quad (\varepsilon \to +0).$$

PROOF. In case n = 1 we find from (48)

$$xu''_{o,1} = (xu'_{o,1}-u_{o,1})' = (\lambda-1)\left\{\frac{d}{dx}(Pf.(T_{o,o}-\lambda)^{-1}f) + (A_1+\mu_1)p'_{o,1} + (B_1+\nu_1)q'_{o,1}\right\} + f'.$$

By (23a) this results in the estimate

$$(50) \qquad \| xu''_{o,1} \| = O(\| f\|_1).$$

If n ≥ 2 we find from (48)

$$x^n u''_{o,n} = x^{n-1}f' + \lambda x^{n-2}f + \lambda(\lambda-1)x^{n-2}\{Pf.(E_{n-2}-\lambda)^{-1}f + (A_n+\mu_n)p_{o,n} + (B_n+\nu_n)q_{o,n}\}.$$

Since $x^k Pf.(|x|^\lambda) = x^k|x|^\lambda \in L^2(-1,1)$ if $Re\lambda > -k - \frac{1}{2}$, we find by lemma 3.12

$$\| x^{n-2}Pf.(E_{n-2}-\lambda)^{-1}f \| \le \| x^{n-2}f \| /(Re\lambda+n-3/2),$$

hence we have the estimate

$$(51) \qquad \| x^n u''_{o,n} \| = O((|A_n| + |B_n| + \| f\|_1)/(Re\lambda+n-3/2)).$$

The estimates (50) and (51) imply for n ≥ 1

$$(52) \qquad \| x^n(\varepsilon\tau+xd/dx-\lambda)(u_{\varepsilon,n}-u_{\varepsilon,o}) \| = \varepsilon\| x^n \tau u_{o,n} \| = O(\varepsilon(|A_n| + |B_n| + \| f\|_1)/(Re\lambda+n-3/2)).$$

In conjunction with cor. 3.11 and lemma 3.13 this estimate proves (49a).

By analogy to Sobolev's inequality (2.19) we derive from the identity

$$|x^{2k+1}w^2(x)| = -\int_0^1 \frac{d}{dt}\{(1-t)(x-tx/|x|)^{2k+1}|w(x-tx/|x|)|^2 dt,$$

valid for all $w \in H^1(-1,1)$, the inequality

$$(53) \qquad [|x|^{k+\frac{1}{2}}w(x)]^2 \leq (2k+2)\|x^k w\|^2 + 2\|x^k w\|\,\|x^{k+1}w'\|.$$

Formula (49b) is a consequence of (38), (49a), (52) and (53). □

Now we can prove our final result on the convergence of $(T_{\varepsilon,o}-\lambda)^{-1}f$:

THEOREM 3.15. *If* $n \in \mathbb{N}_o$, $\lambda \in \mathbb{C}\setminus(-\mathbb{N})$ *and* $Re\lambda > -n+3/2$ *and if* $f \in H^2(-1,1)$ *for* $n = 0$ *and* $f \in H^1(-1,1)$ *for* $n \neq 0$, *the solution* $u_\varepsilon(\cdot,\lambda)$ *of the boundary value problem*

$$\varepsilon\tau u + xu' - \lambda u = f, \qquad u(\pm 1) = A \pm B$$

satisfies for $\varepsilon \to +0$ *the asymptotic estimates*

$$\left.\begin{array}{ll} (54a) & \|x^n(u_\varepsilon(\cdot,\lambda) - u_o(\cdot,\lambda))\| = \\ (54b) & [|x|^{n+\frac{1}{2}}(u_\varepsilon(\cdot,\lambda) - u_o(\cdot,\lambda))] = \end{array}\right\} O(\varepsilon(|A|+|B|+\|f\|_s)\Gamma(\lambda+1)/(Re\lambda+n-3/2))$$

where $s = 2$ *if* $n = 0$ *and* $s = 1$ *otherwise and where* u_o *is defined by*

$$u_o(x,\lambda) := A|x|^\lambda + Bx|x|^{\lambda-1} + \int_{x/|x|}^{x} f(t)\left(\frac{x}{t}\right)^\lambda \frac{dt}{t}.$$

PROOF. If $n = 0$, (54a) is proved in corollary 3.8 and (54b) is a consequence of (25a-b) and (53). If $n > 0$ we define the matrix $M_{\varepsilon,n}(\lambda)$ by

$$M_{\varepsilon,n}(\lambda) := \begin{pmatrix} p_{\varepsilon,n}(1,\lambda) & p_{\varepsilon,n}(-1,\lambda) \\ q_{\varepsilon,n}(1,\lambda) & q_{\varepsilon,n}(-1,\lambda) \end{pmatrix}.$$

By the previous lemma it depends continuously on ε if $\varepsilon \geq 0$ and $Re\lambda > -n+3/2$ and the differences between the entries of $M_{\varepsilon,n}(\lambda)$ and $M_{o,n}(\lambda)$ are of order $O(\varepsilon/(Re\lambda+n+3/2))$. By (26) and (45) we find

$$M_{o,n}(\lambda) = \begin{pmatrix} 2^{-\lambda}\alpha_n(\lambda)/\Gamma(\tfrac{1}{2}\lambda+\tfrac{1}{2}) & 2^{-\lambda}\alpha_n(\lambda)/\Gamma(\tfrac{1}{2}\lambda+\tfrac{1}{2}) \\ 2^{-\lambda}\beta_n(\lambda)/\Gamma(\tfrac{1}{2}\lambda+1) & -2^{-\lambda}\beta_n(\lambda)/\Gamma(\tfrac{1}{2}\lambda+1) \end{pmatrix} \quad ;$$

since $\alpha_n(\lambda)$ and $\beta_n(\lambda)$ do not have zeros or poles if $Re\lambda > -n-\tfrac{1}{2}$, $M_{o,n}(\lambda)$ has an inverse, whose norm is of order $\mathcal{O}(\Gamma(\lambda+1))$ (near the poles of the Γ-function). So we can find a number $\varepsilon_\lambda \in \mathbb{R}^+$, $\varepsilon_\lambda = \mathcal{O}(1/\Gamma(\lambda+1))$, such that $M_{\varepsilon,n}(\lambda)$ is invertible for all $\varepsilon \in [0,\varepsilon_\lambda]$ and (cf. thm.1.4)

$$\text{(55)} \qquad \| M^{-1}_{\varepsilon,n}(\lambda) - M^{-1}_{o,n}(\lambda) \| \le \varepsilon \| M^{-1}_{o,n}(\lambda) \| / (1-\varepsilon \| M^{-1}_{o,n}(\lambda) \|) =$$

$$= \mathcal{O}(\varepsilon\Gamma(\lambda+1))$$

where $\|\cdot\|$ denotes in this case the L^2-norm on the 2×2 matrices.

The solutions of (33a) are related to $u_{\varepsilon,o}$ as follows:

$$\text{(56)} \qquad u_{\varepsilon,o}(x,\lambda) = u_{\varepsilon,n}(x,\lambda) + {}^t\begin{pmatrix} A_o+B_o-u_{\varepsilon,n}(1,\lambda) \\ A_o-B_o-u_{\varepsilon,n}(-1,\lambda) \end{pmatrix} M^{-1}_{\varepsilon,n}(\lambda) \begin{pmatrix} p_{\varepsilon,n}(x,\lambda) \\ q_{\varepsilon,n}(x,\lambda) \end{pmatrix}$$

and we see that the assertions of the theorem are a consequence of (55) and the previous lemma. □

<u>REMARK</u>. From the proof of lemma 3.13 we can obtain a third inequality:

$$\varepsilon \| x^k v'' \| \le 4 \| x^k(\varepsilon\tau v + xv' - \lambda v) \| + C_k(\lambda) |v|_{-k}$$

and in the same manner as in (53) we can derive the inequality

$$[x^k w]^2 = \mathcal{O}(\| x^k w \|^2 + \| x^k w \|^{3/2} \| x^k w'' \|^{\frac{1}{2}}).$$

By analogy to (49b) and (54b) this results in the estimate

$$\text{(54c)} \qquad [x^n(u_\varepsilon(\cdot,\lambda) - u_o(\cdot,\lambda))] = \mathcal{O}(\varepsilon^{\frac{3}{4}}(.....)),$$

where the remainder of the order term is as in (54b).

3.6. THE MINUS SIGN CASE: ESTIMATES IN A UNIFORM NORM

In ch. 2 we observed that the boundary layer jumps from one endpoint of the interval to the other, when we change the sign of the "reduced" formal operator d/dx (or equivalently when we change the sign of $Re\varepsilon$). The change of the sign of xd/dx in problem (1+) has the same effect: the (major part of the) nonuniformity at x = 0 is displaced to the boundary points x = ±1 when we go over to problem (1-). If the right-hand side f of (1) is identically equal to zero, we can show this in the following way. Define the function $\omega(x)$ by

$$\omega(x) := -\int_{-1}^{x} s\, ds/a(s).$$

and assume that $\omega(1) = 0$; later on we will deal with the case $\omega(1) \neq 0$. Let u_ε be the solution of

$$(57) \qquad \varepsilon\tau u - xu' - \lambda u = 0, \qquad u(\pm 1) = A \pm B,$$

then $v(x) := u(x)\exp(\omega(x)/2\varepsilon)$ satisfies, cf. (9b),

$$(58) \qquad \varepsilon\tau v + xbv/2a - x^2 v/4\varepsilon a - (\lambda - \tfrac{1}{2})v = 0, \qquad v(\pm 1) = A \pm B.$$

As in §3.2 we find that the operator $\tilde{U}_\varepsilon$,

$$\tilde{U}_\varepsilon := \varepsilon\tau + xb/2a - x^2/4\varepsilon a + \tfrac{1}{2} \qquad \text{with } \mathcal{D}(\tilde{U}_\varepsilon) = \mathcal{D}(\tilde{T}_\varepsilon)$$

is "nearly" self-adjoint, i.e.

$$\|\tilde{U}_\varepsilon v - \tilde{U}_\varepsilon^* v\| = \mathcal{O}(\varepsilon^{\frac{1}{2}}\{\|\tilde{U}_\varepsilon v - \lambda v\| + (|\lambda|+1)\|v\|\}),$$

cf. (10c). By this inequality, by formula (21c) and by theorem 1.4 we find constants ε_o and K in $\mathbb{R}^+$ such that

$$(59a) \qquad \|\tilde{U}_\varepsilon v - \lambda v\| \geq \tfrac{1}{2}\text{dist}(\lambda, -\mathbb{N}_o)\|v\|$$

for all $v \in \mathcal{D}(\tilde{U}_\varepsilon)$, $\varepsilon \in (0,\varepsilon_o]$ and $\lambda \in \mathbb{C}$ satisfying

$$(59b) \qquad \text{dist}(\lambda, -\mathbb{N}_o) \geq K\varepsilon^{\frac{1}{2}}(1+|\lambda|^{3/2}).$$

We now construct a formal approximation to the solution of (58) in a manner completely analogous to §2.2. Boundary layers of width $\mathcal{O}(\varepsilon)$ will arise at both endpoints of the interval. We therefore introduce the local variables $\xi^{\pm}:=(1\mp x)/\varepsilon$ and the substitution operators $s_{\varepsilon}^{\pm}:f(x)\mapsto f(\pm\varepsilon\xi\mp 1)$, and we make the formal expansions

$$s_{\varepsilon}^{\pm}(\varepsilon\tau+xb/2a-x^2/4\varepsilon a+\tfrac{1}{2})(s_{\varepsilon}^{\pm})^{-1} = \sum_{j=0}^{k} \varepsilon^{j-1}\rho_j^{\pm} + \varepsilon^k\rho_k^{\pm\#},$$

where $\rho_o^{\pm} = a(\pm 1)(d/d\xi^{\pm})^2 - 1/4a(\pm 1)$. Let $v^{\pm}(\xi) := \sum_j \varepsilon^j v_j^{\pm}$ be the formal expansions of the boundary layer solutions; they satisfy

$$v_o^{\pm}(\xi^{\pm}) = (A\pm B)\exp(-\xi^{\pm}/2a(\pm 1))$$

$$v_j^{\pm}(\xi^{\pm}) = \int_0^{\infty} k^{\pm}(\xi^{\pm},s)\Big(\sum_{m=0}^{j-1}\rho_{j-m}^{\pm}v_m^{\pm}(s) - \lambda v_{j-1}^{\pm}(s)\Big)ds,$$

where the kernels $k^{\pm}$ are defined by

$$k^{\pm}(s,t) := k^{\pm}(t,s) := \tfrac{1}{2}e^{-t/2a(\pm 1)}\big(e^{s/2a(\pm 1)}-e^{-s/2a(\pm 1)}\big)$$

if $0 < s < t$. Since $v_o^{\pm}$ are exponentially decreasing for $\xi\to\infty$, all functions $v_j^{\pm}$ are exponentially decreasing, hence if ψ is a C^{∞}-function satisfying

(60) $$\psi(x) = 1 \text{ if } x > 2/3 \quad\text{and}\quad \psi(x) = 0 \text{ if } x < 1/3,$$

then we find by analogy to (2.18a) and (2.25) that the formal approximation

$$w_{\varepsilon,n}(x) := \sum_{j=0}^{n} \varepsilon^j\{\psi(x)v_j^{+}((1-x)/\varepsilon) + \psi(-x)v_j^{-}((1+x)/\varepsilon)\}$$

satisfies the estimate

(61) $$\|(\varepsilon\tau+xb/2a-x^2/4\varepsilon a-\lambda+\tfrac{1}{2})w_{\varepsilon,n}\| = \mathcal{O}(\varepsilon^{n+\frac{1}{2}}(|A|+|B|)).$$

<u>LEMMA 3.16</u>. *If* $\varepsilon > 0$ *and small enough and if* $\lambda\in\mathbb{C}\backslash(-\mathbb{N}_o)$ *does not depend on* ε, *then the solution* u_ε *of* (57) *satisfies for* $\varepsilon\to +0$

(62) $$u_\varepsilon(x,\lambda) = w_{\varepsilon,n}(x)\exp\{(\omega(x/|x|)-\omega(x))/2\varepsilon\} + \mathcal{O}(\varepsilon^{n+\frac{1}{4}}(|A|+|B|))$$

uniformly with respect to $x \in [-1,1]$. *In particular we have*

$$(63)\qquad u_\varepsilon(x,\lambda) = (A+B)\exp((x-1)/\varepsilon a(1)) + (A-B)\exp(-(x+1)/\varepsilon a(-1)) + \\ + \mathcal{O}(\varepsilon(|A|+|B|)) \qquad (\varepsilon \to +0).$$

PROOF. If $\omega(1) = 0$ we set $v_\varepsilon := u_\varepsilon \exp(\omega/2\varepsilon)$ and we find that v_ε is the solution of (58). The construction of $w_{\varepsilon,n}$ implies $v_\varepsilon - w_{\varepsilon,n} \in \mathcal{D}(\tilde{U}_\varepsilon)$, hence from (59a) and (61) we infer

$$(64a)\qquad \| v_\varepsilon - w_{\varepsilon,n} \| = \mathcal{O}(\varepsilon^{n+\frac{1}{2}}(|A|+|B|)).$$

Since, furthermore, any function $z \in \mathcal{D}(\tilde{U}_\varepsilon)$ satisfies

$$\varepsilon^{\frac{1}{2}}\|z'\| = \mathcal{O}(\|\tilde{U}_\varepsilon z\| + \|z\|),$$

we find from (2.19), (61) and (64a)

$$(64b)\qquad [v_\varepsilon - w_{\varepsilon,n}] = \mathcal{O}(\varepsilon^{n+\frac{1}{4}}(|A|+|B|));$$

multiplication of the functions by $\exp(-\omega(x)/2\varepsilon)$ results in (62), since the exponential with negative exponent does not enlarge the order of the estimate.

If $\omega(1) \neq 0$, we assume $\omega(1) < 0$ (otherwise we invert the interval) and we apply to problem (57) the same transformation as before. This results in the same differential equation as in (58) but the boundary conditions become

$$v(-1) = A - B \quad \text{and} \quad v(+1) = (A+B)\exp(\omega(1)/2\varepsilon).$$

Since the boundary value at $x = 1$ is already exponentially small, we have to construct a boundary layer expansion at $x = -1$ only. By analogy to (64b) we find

$$v_\varepsilon(x) = \sum_{j=0}^{n} \varepsilon^j \psi(-x) v_j^-((1+x)/\varepsilon) + \mathcal{O}(\varepsilon^{n+\frac{1}{4}}|A-B|)$$

uniformly for $x \in [-1,1]$ and hence

$$u_\varepsilon(x) = \exp(-\omega(x)/2\varepsilon)\{\psi(-x)\sum_{j=0}^{n} \varepsilon^j v_j^-((1+x)/\varepsilon) + \mathcal{O}(\varepsilon^{n+\frac{1}{4}}|A-B|)\}.$$

Since $\omega(x)$ is monotonically increasing on $(-1,0)$ and decreasing on $(0,1)$ it has a zero somewhere in $(0,1)$, say at $x = \alpha$; we see that the exponential factor does not destroy the order term on the interval $[-1,\alpha]$. Choose now some $\beta \in (0,\alpha)$ and consider the restriction of (57) to the interval $[\beta,1]$; to this restriction we can apply corollary 2.2, for the coefficient of the reduced operator xd/dx does not have a zero in this interval and $u_\varepsilon(\beta)$ is known to tend to zero exponentially fast. So we can directly verify the validity of (62) on the subinterval $[\beta,1]$ in the same manner as in theorem 2.8. □

The trick used above in the homogeneous case applies also if the right-hand side of (1-) is nonzero but does not contain the point $x = 0$ in its support. Let u_ε now be the solution of (1-) with $f(x) = 0$ if $|x| \le \alpha < 1$ and choose $\beta \in (0,\alpha)$ and $\gamma > 0$ such that $\omega(x) - \gamma \ge 0$ if $|x| < \beta$ and $\omega(x) - \gamma < 0$ if $|x| \ge \alpha$. Making the transformation

$$v_\varepsilon(x) := u_\varepsilon(x)\ \exp((\omega(x)-\gamma)/2\varepsilon)$$

we obtain again the equation

(65a) $$\varepsilon\tau v + xbv/2a - x^2v/4\varepsilon a - \lambda v + \tfrac{1}{2}v = f\ \exp((\omega-\gamma)/2\varepsilon)$$

with boundary conditions

(65b) $$v(\pm 1) = (A\pm B)\ \exp((\omega(\pm 1)-\gamma)/2\varepsilon).$$

Since both the boundary conditions and the right-hand side of (65a) are of order $e^{-\theta/2\varepsilon}$ where $\theta := \min\{\gamma - \omega(\alpha),\ \gamma - \omega(-\alpha)\}$, we immediately find by the above reasoning that the solution v_ε of (65) satisfies for $\lambda \in \mathbb{C}\backslash(-\mathbb{N}_0)$ and for $\varepsilon \to +0$

$$v_\varepsilon(x) = \mathcal{O}(e^{-\theta/2\varepsilon})$$

uniformly with respect to $x \in [-1,1]$. On multiplying by the exponential we find that u_ε is exponentially small in the subinterval $[-\beta,\beta]$, namely

(66) $$u_\varepsilon(x) = \mathcal{O}(\exp\{(\gamma-\theta-\omega(x))/2\varepsilon\}),$$

uniformly with respect to x.

Since the coefficient of the reduced operator xd/dx is bounded away from zero on the intervals $[-1,-\beta]$ and $[\beta,1]$, we can apply theorem 2.8 to the restrictions of the boundary value problem (65) to the subintervals $[-1,-\beta]$ and $[\beta,1]$ with the additional boundary conditions $u(\pm\beta) = \mathcal{O}(e^{-\theta/\varepsilon})$. Defining

$$w(x) := -\int_0^x f(t)\left(\frac{t}{x}\right)^\lambda \frac{dt}{t} \quad \text{and} \quad C^\pm := A \pm B - w(\pm 1)$$

we have in first approximation:

<u>THEOREM 3.17</u>. *If* $\lambda \in \mathbb{C}\backslash(-\mathbb{N}_0)$, $\gamma \in \mathbb{R}^+$ *and* $f \in H^2(-1,1)$ *with* $(-\gamma,\gamma) \cap \mathrm{supp}(f) = \emptyset$, *then the solution* u_ε *of*

(67) $$\varepsilon\tau u - xu' - \lambda u = f, \qquad u(\pm 1) = A \pm B$$

satisfies for $\varepsilon \to +0$ *the asymptotic formula*

(68) $$u_\varepsilon(x) = w(x) + C^+ \exp((x-1)/\varepsilon a(1)) + C^- \exp(-(x+1)/\varepsilon a(-1)) + \\ + \mathcal{O}(\varepsilon(|A|+|B|+\|f\|_2))$$

uniformly with respect to $x \in [-1,1]$.

<u>REMARK</u>. The order term in (68) depends heavily on γ and it will certainly increase beyond bound for $\gamma \to +0$ (if $Re\lambda \le \frac{1}{2}$).

3.7. CONVERGENCE IN $H^n(-1,1)$

If the function f in the right-hand side of (67) is not zero in a neighbourhood of the point $x = 0$, we cannot get any idea of the behaviour of the solution of (67) by using the method used in the previous section. By the dual of the method employed in the plus sign-case we can give a partial answer to this question, namely if f is smooth enough. We define a sequence of operators $U_{\varepsilon,n}$ in the space $H^n(-1,1)$ and prove their inverse stability in the part $Re\lambda > -n + \frac{1}{2}$ of the complex λ-plane. As a dual of the plus-sign case, we now have to impose stronger smoothness conditions in order to enlarge the region of inverse stability. If $\varepsilon > 0$ we define

(69a) $$U_{\varepsilon,n}u := \varepsilon\tau u - xu'$$

$$\text{for all } u \in \mathcal{D}(U_{\varepsilon,n}) := \{v \in H^{n+2}(-1,1) \mid v^{(n+1)}(\pm 1) = 0\}$$

and for $\varepsilon = 0$ we define

(69b) $$U_{o,n}u := -\, xu'$$

$$\text{for all } u \in \mathcal{D}(U_{o,n}) := \{v \in H^{n}(-1,1) \mid xv' \in H^{n}(-1,1)\}.$$

LEMMA 3.18. *The spectrum of* $U_{o,n}$ *is the set*

(70) $$\sigma(U_{o,n}) = \{\mu \in \mathbb{C} \mid Re\mu \le -n + \tfrac{1}{2}\} \cup (-\mathbb{N}_o)$$

and constants C_1 *and* C_2 *exist, such that*

(71) $$\| (U_{\varepsilon,n}-\lambda)u\|_n \ge \{C_1 \operatorname{dist}(\lambda,\sigma(U_{o,n})) - \varepsilon C_2\}\|u\|_n$$

for all $u \in \mathcal{D}(U_{\varepsilon,n})$, *for all* $\lambda \in \mathbb{C}$ *satisfying* $Re\lambda + n + \tfrac{1}{2} \ge \tfrac{1}{2}\,[xa'/a]$ *and for all* $\varepsilon \ge 0$; *if, furthermore,* λ *is such that the right-hand side of* (71) *is positive, then* $U_{\varepsilon,n} - \lambda$ *has a bounded inverse.*

PROOF. We observe that the orthogonal decomposition (1.19) of the Hilbert space $(H^n(-1,1), \langle\cdot,\cdot\rangle_n^{(1)})$ remains invariant under the action of the operator $U_{o,n}$, so let us consider first the restriction $U_{o,n}^{(1)}$ of $U_{o,n}$ to $H_1^n(-1,1)$. For all $u \in H_1^n(-1,1)$ this restriction satisfies:

(72) $$|U_{o,n}^{(1)}u - \lambda u|_n^{(1)} = |U_{o,n}^{(1)}u - \lambda u|_n \ge$$

$$\ge |Re \langle (xu'-\lambda u)^{(n)}, u^{(n)}\rangle| / |u|_n \ge$$

$$\ge (Re\lambda + n - \tfrac{1}{2})\, |u|_n^{(1)} .$$

If $Re\lambda \le -n + \tfrac{1}{2}$, then the solutions $x \mapsto |x|^{-\lambda}$ and $x \mapsto x|x|^{-1-\lambda}$ of $U_{o,n}u = \lambda u$ are in $H_1^n(-1,1)$ and hence λ is in the spectrum of $U_{o,n}$. The adjoint of $U_{o,n}^{(1)}$ is the operator

$$U_{o,n}^{(1)*}u := xu' - (2n-1)u$$

$$\text{for all } u \in \mathcal{D}(U_{o,n}^{(1)*}) := \{u \in \mathcal{D}(U_{o,n}^{(1)}) \,|\, u^{(n)}(\pm 1) = 0\}$$

and we see that $U_{o,n}^{(1)*} - \lambda$ has zero null-space if $Re\lambda > -n + \frac{1}{2}$; hence we find by theorem 1.1 and inequality (72) that $\lambda \in \rho(U_{o,n}^{(1)})$ in that case. Since, furthermore, the monomial $x \longmapsto x^j$ with $j \in \mathbb{N}_o$ is the eigenfunction of $U_{o,n}$ at the eigenvalue $-j$, we find that (70) is true and that any $u \in \mathcal{D}(U_{o,n})$ satisfies

$$(|U_{o,n}u-\lambda u|_n^{(1)})^2 = |U_{o,n}u - \lambda u|_n^2 + \sum_{j=0}^{n-1} |\lambda - j|^2 \, |u^{(j)}(0)|^2 \geq$$

$$\geq \{|u|_n^{(1)} \operatorname{dist}(\lambda,\sigma(U_{o,n}))\}^2.$$

By the equivalence of the norms $\|\cdot\|_n$ and $|\cdot|_n^{(1)}$, cf. (1.18), we find a constant C_1 such that

(73) $$\| U_{o,n}u - \lambda u\|_n \geq C_1 \| u \|_n \operatorname{dist}(\lambda,\sigma(U_{o,n}))$$

which proves (71) for $\varepsilon = 0$.

Integration by parts yields for all $v \in H^2(-1,1)$ the identity

$$2Re\left\langle (au')', xu'+\lambda u\right\rangle = -\left\langle ((\lambda+\bar{\lambda}+1)a+xa')u',u'\right\rangle +$$

$$+ \left[xau'\bar{u}' + 2Re(\lambda a\bar{u}'u)\right]_{-1}^{+1} .$$

This implies the inequality

(74a) $$2\| \varepsilon\tau u-xu'-\lambda u\|^2 \geq \| \varepsilon(au')'-xu'-\lambda u\|^2 -2\varepsilon^2\| bu'+cu\| =$$

$$= \| \varepsilon(au')'\|^2 + \| xu'+\lambda u\|^2 +\varepsilon(\lambda+\bar{\lambda}+1)\| a^{\frac{1}{2}}u'\|^2 +\varepsilon\left\langle xa'u',u'\right\rangle +$$

$$-2\varepsilon^2\| bu'+cu\| + \left[xau'\bar{u}'+2Re(\lambda\bar{u}'u)\right]_{-1}^{+1} .$$

Defining the formal differential operator θ_n of order $n + 1$ by

$$\theta_n := (\tau u)^{(n)} - \frac{d}{dx}(au^{(n+1)})$$

we find from (74a) for all $u \in \mathcal{D}(U_{\varepsilon,n})$, i.e. $u^{(n+1)}(\pm 1) = 0$, the inequality

$$(74b) \qquad 2|\varepsilon\tau u - xu' - \lambda u|_n^2 = 2\| \varepsilon \frac{d}{dx}(au^{(n+1)}) + \theta_n u - xu^{(n+1)} - (\lambda+n)u^{(n)} \|^2 \geq$$
$$\geq |\varepsilon au^{(n+1)}|_1^2 + |xu'+\lambda u|_n^2 - \| \varepsilon\theta_n u\|^2 +$$
$$+ \varepsilon \left\langle \lambda+\bar{\lambda}+2n+1-[xa'/a] \right\rangle \| a^{\frac{1}{2}}u^{(n+1)} \|^2 .$$

Since a constant C_n exists such that

$$\| \theta_n u\|^2 + \| \tau u\|^2 \leq \nu|au^{(n+1)}|_1^2 + C_n\nu^{-1}\|u\|_n$$

for all $\nu \in (0,1]$ and $u \in H^{n+2}(-1,1)$, the inequalities (73) and (74b) imply formula (71).

Since theorem 1.8 implies that $U_{\varepsilon,n} - \lambda$ is invertible for $\varepsilon \neq 0$, provided $Re\lambda$ is large enough, inequality (71) implies that $U_{\varepsilon,n} - \lambda$ is invertible for all $\lambda \in \mathbb{C}$ for which the right-hand side of (71) is positive. □

In a manner analogous to §2.2 we can now construct an asymptotic approximation to $(U_{\varepsilon,n}-\lambda)^{-1}f$ with $f \in H^{n+2}(-1,1)$ for all $\lambda \in \rho(U_{o,n})$ and for $\varepsilon \to +0$; we will give a first order approximation only. Let $\psi \in C^\infty(\mathbb{R})$ be as in (60); then we find that the function w_ε,

$$w_\varepsilon(x,\lambda) := w_o(x,\lambda) + \varepsilon^{n+1}\{\psi(x)w_o^{(n+1)}(1,\lambda)\exp\frac{x-1}{\varepsilon a(1)} +$$
$$+ \psi(-x)w_o^{(n+1)}(-1,\lambda)\exp\frac{-1-x}{a(-1)}\}$$

with

$$w_o(x,\lambda) := (U_{o,n}-\lambda)^{-1}f = -\sum_{j=0}^{n-1}\frac{x^j f^{(j)}(0)}{(\lambda+j)j!} +$$
$$-\int_0^x \{f(t) - \sum_{j=0}^{n-1} t^j f^{(j)}(0)/j!\}\left(\frac{t}{x}\right)^\lambda \frac{dt}{t},$$

is an element of $\mathcal{D}(U_{\varepsilon,n})$, provided $f \in H^{n+2}(-1,1)$ and $\lambda \in \rho(U_{o,n})$, and that it satisfies

$$\| (U_{\varepsilon,n}-\lambda)w_\varepsilon(x,\lambda) - f \|_n = \mathcal{O}(\varepsilon\| f \|_{n+2}) .$$

By lemma 3.18 this implies

$$(75)\qquad \| w_\varepsilon(x,\lambda) - (U_{\varepsilon,n}-\lambda)^{-1}f\|_n = \mathcal{O}(\varepsilon\| f\|_{n+2}) \qquad (\varepsilon\to+0)$$

if $\lambda \in \rho(U_{o,n})$.

Since for all $n \geq 1$ the $\|\cdot\|_n$-norm is stronger than the maximum norm and since $(U_{\varepsilon,n}-\lambda)^{-1}f$ and $(U_{\varepsilon,o}-\lambda)^{-1}f$ differ by a solution of the homogeneous equation (57) with boundary conditions $u(\pm1) = w_o(\pm1,\lambda) + \mathcal{O}(\varepsilon^{n+1})$, we find from the estimates (72) and (75) the result:

THEOREM 3.19. *The solution* u_ε *of the boundary value problem*

$$(76)\qquad \varepsilon\tau u - xu' - \lambda u = f, \qquad u(\pm1) = A \pm B$$

satisfies the asymptotic formula for $\varepsilon \to +0$

$$(77)\qquad u_\varepsilon(x,\lambda) = w_o(x,\lambda) + (A+B-w_o(1,\lambda)) \exp \frac{x-1}{\varepsilon a(1)} +$$

$$+ (A-B-w_o(-1,\lambda))\exp \frac{-x-1}{\varepsilon a(1)} + \mathcal{O}(\varepsilon(|A|+|B|+\| f\|_{n+2}))$$

for all $n \in \mathbb{N}$, $f \in H^{n+2}(-1,1)$ *and* $\lambda \in \mathbb{C}\backslash(-\mathbb{N}_o)$ *with* $Re\lambda > -n + \frac{1}{2}$ *and for all* $x \in [-1,1]$ *uniformly.*

In the transition from (75) to (77) we throw away a considerable amount of information about the convergence of the derivatives of w_ε if n is large. It seems, however, that it is not possible to weaken the smoothness conditions on f at x = 0 if the support of f contains the point zero; the approximation valid up to the line $Re\lambda = \frac{1}{2} - n$ depends explicitly on all the derivatives of f at x = 0 up to the n-th derivative. In our opinion it is not possible to weaken this condition on f in theorem 3.19. In view of the discrepancy between the condition $f \in H^2(-1,1)$ and $0 \notin supp(f)$ (i.e. f is C^∞ in a neighbourhood of x=0) in theorem 3.17 and the condition that f has a locally integrable (n+2)-th derivative everywhere in the interval of theorem 3.19, it seems plausible that in the latter theorem it is sufficient that f can be written as $f_p + f_r$, in which f_p is a polynomial and the remainder f_r is in $H^2(-1,1)$ and satisfies $f(x) = \mathcal{O}(x^n)$ for $x \to 0$. This is further supported by the fact that we can obtain an estimate in $|\cdot|_{-1}$-norm under this condition from the adjoint problem. Since

$$U_\varepsilon^* u - u = \varepsilon\tau^* u + xu' \quad \text{and} \quad \mathcal{D}(U_\varepsilon^*) = \mathcal{D}(T_\varepsilon),$$

theorem 3.15 applies to $U_\varepsilon^* - 1$ too; hence we find

$$\text{(78)} \qquad |(U_\varepsilon - 1 - \lambda)^{-1}\, x^n h - (E_{n-2}^* - \lambda)^{-1}\, x^n h|_{-1} =$$

$$= \sup_{g \in H_o^1(-1,1),\, |g|_1 = 1} |\langle x^n h, (U_\varepsilon^* - 1 - \lambda)^{-1} g - (E_{n-2} - \lambda)^{-1} g\rangle| \le$$

$$\le \sup_{g \in H_o^1(-1,1),\, |g|_1 = 1} \|h\|\ \| x^n\{(U_\varepsilon^* - 1 - \lambda)^{-1} g - (E_{n-2} - \lambda)^{-1} g\}\| =$$

$$= \mathcal{O}(\varepsilon\Gamma(\lambda+1)\|f\|/(\mathrm{Re}\lambda + n - 3/2)) \qquad (\varepsilon \to +0),$$

provided $n \in \mathbb{N}$, $f \in L^2(-1,1)$, $\lambda \in \mathbb{C}\setminus(-\mathbb{N})$ and $\mathrm{Re}\lambda > -n + 3/2$. If we had a good estimate of $(U_\varepsilon - \lambda - 1)^{-1}\, x^n h\big|_{x=\pm 1}$, we could derive from the estimate in $|\cdot|_{-1}$-norm estimates in stronger norms by the analogue of lemma 3.13 for the minus-sign case.

3.8. DISCUSSION OF THE RESULTS

a. The more general looking boundary value problem,

$$\text{(79a)} \qquad \varepsilon(av'' + bv' + cv) \pm xpv' + qv = f$$

on the interval $[\alpha,\beta]$ with $\alpha < 0 < \beta$ and with boundary conditions

$$\text{(79b)} \qquad v(\alpha) = A \quad \text{and} \quad v(\beta) = B,$$

where a, b, c, p and q are C^∞-functions on $[\alpha,\beta]$ with a and p strictly positive, can be transformed into (1±). This is performed by a C^∞-map of $[\alpha,\beta]$ onto $[-1,1]$, which lets the point $x = 0$ invariant, and a transformation of the function v into u by

$$u(x) := v(x)\exp\left\{-\int_0^x \frac{q(t)+\lambda p(t)}{tp(t)}\,dt\right\}$$

with $\lambda := -q(0)/p(0)$.

b. Several authors have already dealt with problems of type (79). ACKERBERG & O'MALLEY [3] discovered that the formal approximation of the solution of problem (79) showed a sudden growth at non-negative integral values of the quotient $q(0)/p(0)$; they called the unexplained phenomenon "resonance". With refined matching methods COOK & ECKHAUS [7] arrived at a better formal approximation of the points where resonance occurs, and computed the coefficient of the $\mathcal{O}(\sqrt{\varepsilon})$-term in this formal expansion. In [14] we conjectured that the phenomenon is caused by a neighbouring eigenvalue of the problem. We proved this conjecture in [15]; the proof is given in §3.2. From a spectral point of view the sudden growth of the solution of (79) near negative (non-positive) integral values of $\lambda(= -q(0)/p(0))$ is caused merely by the neighbouring eigenvalue. As is well-known a boundary value problem like (79) does not have a solution or its solution is not unique if λ is an eigenvalue, and, if λ is in the resolvent set and tends to an eigenvalue, the solution will in general tend to infinity. The problem (79) depends on two parameters, namely λ and ε; for $\varepsilon \to +0$ we proved convergence of its eigenvalues and, provided λ is constant and $\lambda \notin -\mathbb{N}$ (or $\lambda \notin -\mathbb{N}_0$), convergence of its solution. Since $\|(T_{\varepsilon,n}-\lambda)^{-1}\|$ and $M_{\varepsilon,n}(\lambda)$ depend continuously on λ provided $Re\lambda > -n-\frac{1}{2}$ and $\lambda \notin -\mathbb{N}$, the solution of (79) will converge to the same limit if λ depends on ε in such a way that $\lim_{\varepsilon\to+0} \lambda(\varepsilon)$ exists and is not in $-\mathbb{N}$. However, if $\lim_{\varepsilon\to+0} \lambda(\varepsilon)$ is in $-\mathbb{N}$ (or $-\mathbb{N}_0$), convergence of the solution will depend heavily on the path of $(\varepsilon,\lambda(\varepsilon))$ in $\mathbb{R}^+ \times \mathbb{C}$. In the example of §3.1 we see that formula (4b) remains valid when we insert $\lambda = -n + \alpha\varepsilon$ with $\alpha \neq 0$, while from (4a) we infer that the solution (3) is of order $\exp((1-x^2)/2)$ in case $\alpha = 0$.

In [25] RUBENFELD & WILLNER state a proof of convergence of the eigenvalues of problem (1-) and of the solutions of the homogeneous equation. Their proof is totally different from the one stated above. It is based on Langer's approximation methods for turning point problems and it requires an enormous amount of explicit computations.

In [1] ABRAHAMSSON gives a proof of theorem 3.19 for real λ by an a priori-estimate of the form

$$\left[(U_\varepsilon-\lambda)^{-1}f\right] \le K([f^{(n)}]_{(-\delta,\delta)} + \|f\|),$$

provided $-n < \lambda < -n+1$ and $n \in \mathbb{N}$, where δ is a small positive number and λ a positive constant, not depending on ε. The proof of the a priori estimate is based on the fact that we can apply the maximum principle to the n-th derivative of equation (76), thus proving smoothness of the n-th derivative of its solution, and that non-existence of the constant K leads to a contradiction with the Arzela-Ascoli theorem, which is non-constructive.

c. The proofs of convergence of the solutions of (1+) and (1-) are designed especially for nonselfadjoint problems and for those $\lambda \in \mathbb{C}$, for which the associated quadratic forms $\langle T_\varepsilon v - \lambda v, v\rangle$ and $\langle U_\varepsilon v - \lambda v, v\rangle$ have non-definite real parts. The proofs of convergence for the solutions of (1±) are largely contained in [15], but the final result is less general than the results we have obtained in this chapter. In [15] we proved uniform convergence on closed subsets of $[-1,1]$ not containing the point $x = 0$ by a maximum principle, while here we proved by L^2-interpolation convergence with respect to the global norm $u \mapsto [x^{k+\frac{1}{2}}u]$, which smoothes down the nonuniformities at $x = 0$. Only if $Re\lambda > 2$ can we improve estimate (54b) somewhat without having to compute boundary layer terms: by a maximum principle we can show that this estimate is also true in the norm $u \mapsto [u]$, which does not contain the weight factor $|x|^{\frac{1}{2}}$, cf. [14] and [15].

We have not tried to reveal the structure of the nonuniformity in a neighbourhood of $x = 0$ in the plus-sign case, since the solution oscillates faster and faster in this neighbourhood and grows larger, as $-Re\lambda$ grows larger. For instance the solution (3) has n zero's in an $\mathcal{O}(\sqrt{\varepsilon})$-neighbourhood of $x = 0$ if $-n < Re\lambda < -n + 1$, while it has maxima of order $\mathcal{O}(\varepsilon^{Re\lambda})$ in between. In the minus-sign case these oscillations will be present too, but there we do not observe them in the approximations, since they are exponentially small.

In most theorems we merely give estimates of order $\mathcal{O}(\varepsilon)$ in the L^2-norm and in the maximum-norm. Both can be generalized considerably provided the right-hand side of the equations is smooth enough. For expansions of higher order with respect to ε we only have to compute formal expansions of higher order; their validity is proved in the same way as before. Moreover, convergence in stronger norms, e.g. in the norms $u \mapsto \|u\|_2$ or $u \mapsto [u] + [u']$, is not too difficult to achieve. In the plus-sign case we get from (38b) by substitution of v' instead of v

$$(80) \qquad \| x^{k+1}v''\| \leq 4\| \varepsilon\tau v' + xv'' - \lambda v'\| + C_k(\lambda)\,|v|_{-k-1}$$

and we obtain higher order regularity without any loss of order with respect to ε but with a higher exponent in the weight factor x. In the minus sign case we have estimates of the form

$$(81) \qquad \varepsilon^{\frac{1}{2}}\|u'\| = \mathcal{O}(\|\varepsilon\tau u - xu'\| + \|u\|), \qquad (\varepsilon \to +0),$$

valid for all $u \in \mathcal{D}(U_\varepsilon)$ (cf. also 2.8a) and hence

$$\varepsilon\|u''\| = O(\|\varepsilon\tau u - xu'\| + \|xu'\|) = O(\varepsilon^{-\frac{1}{2}}(\|\varepsilon\tau u - xu'\| + \|u\|)). \tag{82}$$

We see that we lose powers of ε in the order estimates in this case, but since the boundary layer structure is known in this case up to any power of ε, we can still compute approximations of any order required.

CHAPTER IV

ELLIPTIC PERTURBATION OF A FIRST ORDER OPERATOR IN $\mathbb{R}^2$ WITH A CRITICAL POINT OF NODAL TYPE

In this chapter we shall study the degeneration of an elliptic operator on a bounded domain $\Omega \subset \mathbb{R}^2$ to a first order operator which has a critical point of nodal type inside Ω. For simplicity we assume that Ω is the open unit disk,

$$\Omega := \{(x,y) \mid x^2 + y^2 < 1\}.$$

On this domain we consider the singular perturbation problems

$$(1\pm) \qquad \varepsilon Lu \pm (x\partial_x u+\mu y\partial_y u) - \lambda u = f, \qquad u_{|\partial\Omega} = g,$$

in which L is a uniformly elliptic (formal) operator of second order,

$$L := a\partial_x^2 + 2b\partial_x\partial_y + c\partial_y^2 + d_1\partial_x + d_2\partial_y + d_3 ,$$

with real C^∞-coefficients satisfying

$$b^2 < ac, \quad a(0,0) = c(0,0) = 1 \quad \text{and} \quad b(0,0) = 0$$

and with the formally selfadjoint principal part L_p,

$$L_p := \partial_x a\partial_x + \partial_x b\partial_y + \partial_y b\partial_x + \partial_y c\partial_y ;$$

moreover, we assume $\varepsilon \in \mathbb{R}^+$, $u \in \mathbb{R}^+$, $\lambda \in \mathbb{C}$, $f \in L^2(\Omega)$ and $g \in L^2(\partial\Omega)$. Without loss of generality we can make the restriction $\mu \le 1$, otherwise we change the roles of x and y and divide by μ.

The problems (1±) have many features in common with the one-dimensional analogues (3.1±) of chapter 3. We shall treat them along the same lines as before; first we shall prove convergence of the eigenvalues of the operators in $L^2(\Omega)$ connected with (1±) and thereafter we study convergence of the solutions of (1±) for $\varepsilon \to +0$.

4.1. CONVERGENCE OF THE SPECTRUM

In connection with the boundary value problem (1+) we define the differential operator T_ε on $L^2(\Omega)$ by

$$(2) \qquad T_\varepsilon u := \varepsilon L u + x\partial_x u + \mu y \partial_y u$$

$$\text{for all } u \in \mathcal{D}(T_\varepsilon) := \{v \in H^2(\Omega) \mid v|_{\partial\Omega} = 0\} .$$

As in chapter 3, we will prove convergence of the eigenvalues of T_ε by comparing T_ε to the special operator in which L in (2) is replaced by Δ. Unlike the one-dimensional case it is, in general, not possible to find a function ω such that the operator $\exp(\omega/\varepsilon)\, T_\varepsilon \exp(-\omega/\varepsilon)$ is equal to a selfadjoint operator plus terms of order $\mathcal{O}(\sqrt{\varepsilon})$ with respect to the main part; compare this with the transition of (3.9a) to (3.9c). In case L = Δ the transformation

$$v(x,y) := u(x,y) \exp\{(x^2+\mu y^2)/4\varepsilon\}$$

works well and produces a selfadjoint operator; we will see that this transformation can be used in the general case too, although slightly more effort is required. We define the operator $\tilde{T}_\varepsilon$ with domain $\mathcal{D}(\tilde{T}_\varepsilon) := \mathcal{D}(T_\varepsilon)$ by

$$(3) \qquad \tilde{T}_\varepsilon v := \exp\big((x^2+\mu y^2)/4\varepsilon\big) T_\varepsilon\{v \exp\big(-(x^2+\mu y^2)/4\varepsilon\big)\} =$$

$$= \varepsilon L v + \omega_1 \partial_x v + \omega_2 \partial_y v - \omega_3 v/\varepsilon - (\tfrac{1}{2}+\tfrac{1}{2}\mu+\omega_4) v$$

in which the coefficients $\omega_1,\dots,\omega_4$ are defined by

$$(4a) \qquad \omega_1(x,y) := x - xa(x,y) - \mu y b(x,y),$$

$$(4b) \qquad \omega_2(x,y) := \mu y - \mu y c(x,y) - x b(x,y),$$

$$(4c) \qquad \omega_3(x,y) := \tfrac{1}{4}\big(2x^2+2\mu^2 y^2 - x^2 a - 2\mu x y b - \mu^2 y^2 c\big),$$

$$(4d) \qquad \omega_4(x,y) := \tfrac{1}{2}\big(a+\mu b-1-\mu+x d_1+\mu y d_2\big) .$$

Since we assume that the principal part of L is equal to Δ at the origin, i.e. $a(0,0) = c(0,0) = 1$ and $b(0,0) = 0$, we find that the functions

$\omega_1,\ldots,\omega_4$ behave near the origin as follows:

$$\left.\begin{aligned} &\text{(5a)} \quad \omega_1(x,y) = \mathcal{O}(x^2+y^2) \\ &\text{(5b)} \quad \omega_2(x,y) = \mathcal{O}(x^2+y^2) \\ &\text{(5c)} \quad \omega_3(x,y) = \tfrac{1}{4}(x^2+y^2) + \mathcal{O}(|x|^3+|y|^3) \\ &\text{(5d)} \quad \omega_4(x,y) = \mathcal{O}(|x|+|y|) \end{aligned}\right\} \quad (x^2+y^2\to 0).$$

In contrast with the one-dimensional case the operator $\tilde{T}_\varepsilon$ now contains a non-selfadjoint term which is not small with respect to the main selfadjoint part. We therefore devide it into its main selfadjoint part R_ε,

(6a) $$R_\varepsilon := \varepsilon\left(\partial_x a\partial_x + \partial_x b\partial_y + \partial_y b\partial_x + \partial_y c\partial_y\right) - \omega_3/\varepsilon ,$$

the large nonselfadjoint term A,

(6b) $$A := \omega_1\partial_x + \omega_2\partial_y ,$$

and the small remainder B,

(6c) $$B := \tilde{T}_\varepsilon - R_\varepsilon - A .$$

Furthermore, we define the special operator S_ε by

(6d) $$S_\varepsilon v := \varepsilon\Delta v - \tfrac{1}{4}\left(x^2+\mu^2y^2\right)v/\varepsilon \qquad \text{for all } v \in \mathcal{D}(S_\varepsilon) := \mathcal{D}(\tilde{T}_\varepsilon)$$

and the continuous chain $R_{\varepsilon,\tau}$ by

(6e) $$R_{\varepsilon,\tau} := (1-\tau)S_\varepsilon + \tau R_\varepsilon, \qquad \tau\in[0,1].$$

Convergence of the eigenvalues of S_ε is a consequence of theorem 3.1 and this is transferred to R_ε by the continuity method of §3.2. Although Au is not small with respect to $\|R_\varepsilon u\| + \|u\|$ uniformly on $\mathcal{D}(\tilde{T}_\varepsilon)$, it has an arbitrarily small R_ε-bound and it is of order $\mathcal{O}(\sqrt{\varepsilon})$ on each joint eigenspace of a finite number of eigenvalues of R_ε; this enables us to prove convergence of the eigenvalues of $R_\varepsilon + A$.

LEMMA 4.1. *Each point of the set* Λ,

$$(7)\qquad \Lambda := \{-n-\mu m \mid (n,m) \in \mathbb{N}^2\},$$

is the limit of an eigenvalue of S_ε *and each eigenvalue converges to an element of* Λ *for* $\varepsilon \to +0$; *the total multiplicity of the eigenvalues which converge to* $\lambda \in \Lambda$ *is equal to* $|\{(n,m) \in \mathbb{N}^2 \mid n+\mu m = \lambda\}|$. *Moreover, if* $\lambda_{n,m}(\varepsilon)$ *is an eigenvalue which converges to* $-n-\mu m$, *it satisfies*

$$(8)\qquad \lambda_{n,m}(\varepsilon) = -n-\mu m + O(e^{-1/2\varepsilon}(\varepsilon^{-n-\frac{1}{2}}+\varepsilon^{-m-\frac{1}{2}})), \qquad (\varepsilon\to+0).$$

PROOF. Let D be an open bounded domain in $\mathbb{R}^2$ with a piecewise smooth boundary and let S^D_ε be the restriction of $\varepsilon\Delta - (x^2+\mu^2y^2)/4\varepsilon$ to the domain $\mathcal{D}(S^D_\varepsilon) := \{u \in H^2(D) \mid u_{|\partial\Omega} = 0\}$, then S^D_ε is selfadjoint and has a compact inverse and the associated quadratic form $u \mapsto \langle S^D_\varepsilon u,u\rangle_D$ is non-positive. We can thus arrange its eigenvalues in a non-increasing sequence such that

$$\sigma(S^D_\varepsilon) = \left\{\ell^D_j \mid j \in \mathbb{N}_o\right\} \quad\text{with}\quad \ell^D_{j+1} \le \ell^D_j$$

and such that the eigenvalues are counted according to their multiplicity. The eigenvalues are characterized by the minimax equation, cf. [10] ch. 11,

$$(9)\qquad \ell^D_n = \inf_{V\subset L^2(D),\,\dim V\le n}\ \sup_{\substack{u\in V^\perp\cap C^\infty_o(D)\\ \|u\|_D=1}} \langle S^D_\varepsilon u,u\rangle_D\,,$$

in which V is a linear subspace and $V^\perp$ its orthocomplement in $L^2(D)$. If $E \subset D$ is another domain and if we take the supremum over the smaller set $V^\perp \cap C^\infty_o(E)$ we obtain ℓ^E_n, hence $\ell^E_n \le \ell^D_n$. With the specific choices $D = [-1,1]\times[-1,1]$ and $E = [-\frac{1}{2},\frac{1}{2}]\times[-\frac{1}{2},\frac{1}{2}]$ we find $\sigma(S^D_\varepsilon) = \sigma(\tilde{\Pi}_\varepsilon \otimes \mu\tilde{\Pi}_{\varepsilon/\mu}) = \sigma(\tilde{\Pi}_\varepsilon) + \sigma(\mu\tilde{\Pi}_{\varepsilon/\mu})$ and by using the coordinate stretching $(\xi,\eta) = (2x,2y)$ in E we find $\sigma(S^E_\varepsilon) = \sigma(\tilde{\Pi}_{\frac{1}{4}\varepsilon}\otimes\mu\tilde{\Pi}_{\frac{1}{4}\varepsilon/\mu})$; here $\tilde{\Pi}_\varepsilon$ is the operator defined in (3.9b). In conjunction with theorem 3.1 this proves the lemma. □

LEMMA 4.2. *Constants* C_i, $i = 1,\dots,6$, *exist such that any* $u \in \mathcal{D}(\tilde{T}_\varepsilon)$ *satisfies the inequalities*

$$\text{(10a)}\qquad \| R_{\varepsilon,\nu}u - R_{\varepsilon,\tau}u\| \le |\tau-\nu|(C_1\| R_{\varepsilon,\tau}u\| + C_2\|u\|), \qquad \tau,\nu \in [0,1],$$

$$\left.\begin{aligned} &\text{(10b)}\qquad \|Au\| \le \nu C_3\| R_{\varepsilon,1}u\| + C_4\|u\|/\nu,\\ &\text{(10c)}\qquad \|Bu\| \le \sqrt{\varepsilon}(\nu C_5\| R_{\varepsilon,1}u\| + C_6\|u\|/\nu),\end{aligned}\right\}\quad 0 < \nu \le 1.$$

The proof is completely analogous to the proof of lemma 3.2 and will be omitted. □

As approximate eigenfunctions we use appropriate products of the functions χ_n, defined in (3.14),

$$\text{(11)}\qquad \chi_{n,m}(x,y;\varepsilon) := k_{nm}\chi_n(x;\varepsilon)\chi_m(y;\varepsilon/\mu)$$

in which k_{nm} is a normalization factor, such that $\|\chi_{n,m}\| = 1$.

<u>LEMMA 4.3</u>. *The functions* $\chi_{n,m}$ *satisfy the order estimates*

$$\left.\begin{aligned} &\text{(12a)}\qquad \|(R_{\varepsilon,\tau}+n+\mu m)\chi_{n-1,m-1}\| = O(\varepsilon^{1/2}(n+m)^{3/2})\\ &\text{(12b)}\qquad \|A\chi_{n-1,m-1}\| = O(\varepsilon^{\frac{1}{2}}(n+m))\end{aligned}\right\}\quad (\varepsilon\to+0)$$

uniformly for all n, m ∈ $\mathbb{N}$ *and* τ ∈ [0,1]. *Furthermore, if* ε *is small enough, each finite number of these functions is linearly independent on* Ω *and "approximately orthogonal".*

<u>PROOF</u>. Since $\langle\chi_{n,m},\chi_{k,j}\rangle_{\mathbb{R}^2} = 0$ if n ≠ k or m ≠ j we find, cf. (3.16c),

$$\text{(13)}\qquad \langle\chi_{n,m},\chi_{i,j}\rangle_{\Omega} = \langle\chi_{n,m},\chi_{i,j}\rangle_{\mathbb{R}^2\setminus\Omega} =$$

$$= 2\varepsilon k_{nm}k_{ij}\iint_{x^2+y^2>1/2\varepsilon} \exp(-x^2-\mu y^2)H_n(x)H_i(x)H_m(y\sqrt{\mu})H_j(y\sqrt{\mu})\,dxdy =$$

$$= O(e^{-\mu/2\varepsilon}\varepsilon^{-\frac{1}{2}(n+m+i+j+1)}), \qquad (\varepsilon\to+0).$$

This approximate orthogonality implies the linear independence. The proof of the estimates (12) is completely analogous to lemma 3.3 and will be omitted. □

LEMMA 4.4. *The eigenvalues of the operator* $R_{\varepsilon,\tau}$ *with* $\tau \in [0,1]$ *can be numbered in such a way that*

(14) $$\sigma(R_{\varepsilon,\tau}) = \left\{\lambda_{n,m}(\varepsilon,\tau) \mid (n,m) \in \mathbb{N}^2\right\}$$

and such that they satisfy for $\varepsilon \to +0$

(15) $$\lambda_{n,m}(\varepsilon,\tau) = -n - \mu m + O(\varepsilon^{\frac{1}{2}}(n^{3/2}+m^{3/2}))$$

uniformly with respect $\tau \in [0,1]$.

PROOF. The proof follows the same lines as the proof of thm. 3.4, but differences arise because of the spacing of the points of Λ and because the multiplicity of an eigenvalue can be larger than one.

Arrange the elements of Λ in descending order such that

$$\Lambda = \{\ell_j \mid j \in \mathbb{N}\}, \qquad \text{with } \ell_{j+1} < \ell_j \text{ for all } j \in \mathbb{N},$$

and define the numbers $\alpha_j := \frac{1}{4}(\ell_{j+1}-\ell_j)$. If $R_{\varepsilon,\theta}$ satisfies the lemma for some $\theta \in [0,1]$, an $\varepsilon_j \in \mathbb{R}^+$ exists such that the inclusion

$$D(0,|\ell_j|+3\alpha_j)\backslash D(0,|\ell_j|+\alpha_j) \subset \rho(R_{\varepsilon,\theta})$$

is true for all $\varepsilon \in (0,\varepsilon_j]$. Since $R_{\varepsilon,\tau}$ is selfadjoint for all $\tau \in [0,1]$, we find by lemma 4.2 and theorem 1.4 that the inclusion

$$\partial D(0,|\ell_j|+2\alpha_j) \subset \rho(R_{\varepsilon,\tau})$$

is true for all $\varepsilon \in (0,\varepsilon_j]$ and $\tau \in [\theta - \theta_j, \theta + \theta_j]$ with $\theta_j := \alpha_j/(C_2+C_1|\ell_{j+1}|)$, hence for this ε-τ-range we can define the orthogonal projection

(16) $$P_{\varepsilon,\tau,j} := \frac{1}{2\pi i} \int_{\partial D(0,|\ell_j|+2\alpha_j)} (R_{\varepsilon,\tau}-\lambda)^{-1} d\lambda$$

on the joint eigenspace of all eigenvalues of $R_{\varepsilon,\tau}$ contained in $D(0,|\ell_j|+2\alpha_j)$. Since we have assumed that $R_{\varepsilon,\theta}$ satisfies the lemma and since the eigenvalues of $R_{\varepsilon,\tau}$ depend continuously on ε and τ, the rank of $P_{\varepsilon,\tau,j}$ is equal to the number of elements of the set

$$\left\{(n,m) \in \mathbb{N}^2 \mid -n-\mu m \geq \ell_j\right\}$$

for all $\tau \in [\theta - \theta_j, \theta + \theta_j]$. If $-n - \mu m \geq \ell_j$, then

(17) $$\|(R_{\varepsilon,\tau}+n+\mu m)\chi_{n-1,m-1}\|^2 =$$

$$= \|(R_{\varepsilon,\tau}+n+\mu m)P_{\varepsilon,\tau,j}\chi_{n-1,m-1}\|^2 + \|(R_{\varepsilon,\tau}+n+\mu m)(1-P_{\varepsilon,\tau,j})\chi_{n-1,m-1}\|^2.$$

Since the restriction of $R_{\varepsilon,\tau}$ to $\mathcal{R}(1-P_{\varepsilon,\tau,j})$ has no eigenvalues in $D(0,|\ell_j|+2\alpha_j)$, (12a) and (17) yield

(18) $$\|(1-P_{\varepsilon,\tau,j})\chi_{n-1,m-1}\| \leq$$

$$\leq \|(R_{\varepsilon,\tau}+n+\mu m)(1-P_{\varepsilon,\tau,j})\chi_{n-1,m-1}\| / (2\alpha_j - \ell_j + n + \mu m) =$$

$$= \mathcal{O}(\varepsilon^{\frac{1}{2}}(n^{3/2}+m^{3/2})), \qquad (\varepsilon \to +0)$$

and with the equation $1 = \|P\chi\|^2 + \|(1-P)\chi\|^2$ this results in

(19) $$\|P_{\varepsilon,\tau,j}\chi_{n-1,m-1}\| = 1 + \mathcal{O}(\varepsilon(n^3+m^3)), \qquad (\varepsilon \to +0).$$

Lemma 4.3 and the formulae (18) and (19) imply that the elements of the set

(20) $$\left\{P_{\varepsilon,\tau,j}\chi_{n-1,m-1} \mid -n-\mu m \geq \ell_j \text{ and } (n,m) \in \mathbb{N}^2\right\}$$

are linearly independent; since their number is equal to the rank of $P_{\varepsilon,\tau,j}$, they form a basis in $\mathcal{R}(P_{\varepsilon,\tau,j})$. By (17) we now find

(21) $$\|(R_{\varepsilon,\tau}+n+\mu m)P_{\varepsilon,\tau,j}\chi_{n-1,m-1}\| = \mathcal{O}(\varepsilon^{\frac{1}{2}}(n^{3/2}+m^{3/2})), \qquad (\varepsilon \to +0).$$

Hence in the matrix-representation of the restriction of $R_{\varepsilon,\tau}$ to $\mathcal{R}(P_{\varepsilon,\tau,j})$ with respect to the basis (20) all elements of the main diagonal are of the form $-n-\mu m + \mathcal{O}(\sqrt{\varepsilon})$ and all off-diagonal elements are of order $\mathcal{O}(\sqrt{\varepsilon})$. Gerschgorin's theorem (cf. [31] ch. 2.13) implies that (15) is true for all eigenvalues of $R_{\varepsilon,\tau}$ in the disk $D(0,|\ell_j|+2\alpha_j)$ and for all $\tau \in [\theta-\theta_j, \theta+\theta_j]$, provided (15) is true for all eigenvalues of $R_{\varepsilon,\theta}$ in the larger disk

$D(0,|\ell_{j+1}|+2\alpha_{j+1})$.

In order to prove the assertion of the lemma for $\tau = 1$ and for all pairs $(n,m) \in \mathbb{N}^2$ with $-n-\mu m \geq \ell_j$, we choose a number $k_j \in \mathbb{N}$ such that

$$\sum_{i=j+1}^{j+k_j} \theta_i \geq 1$$

as in the proof of theorem 3.4 and we start at $\tau = 0$, where convergence of all eigenvalues of $R_{\varepsilon,0}$ contained in $D(0,|\ell_{j+k}|+3\alpha_{j+k})$ is a consequence of lemma 4.1. By applying the above argument k times by diminishing in the i-th step the radius of the disk with $3\alpha_{j+k-i+1} + \alpha_{j+k-i}$ we finally prove the estimate

$$\lambda_{n,m}(\varepsilon,\tau) = -n-\mu m + \mathcal{O}(\sqrt{\varepsilon}), \qquad (\varepsilon \to +0),$$

valid for all $\tau \in [0,1]$ and for all $(n,m) \in \mathbb{N}^2$ with $-n-\mu m > \ell_j$. For each $j \in \mathbb{N}$ a number k_j as defined above exists, since the elements of the set

$$\{\alpha_i \mid i \text{ such that } \lambda - 1 < \ell_i \leq \lambda\}$$

add up to $\frac{1}{4}$ for all $\lambda \in \Lambda$.

In order to prove the n-m-dependence of the $\mathcal{O}$-term, we consider the projection

$$\text{(22a)} \qquad Q_{\varepsilon,\tau,k} := \frac{1}{2\pi i} \int_{\partial D(\ell_k, 2\min(\alpha_k,\alpha_{k-1}))} (R_{\varepsilon,\tau}-\lambda)^{-1} d\lambda .$$

Analogously to (19) and (21) we now find

$$\text{(22b)} \qquad \| Q_{\varepsilon,\tau,k}\chi_{n,m} \| \to 1 \quad \text{and}$$

$$\| (R_{\varepsilon,\tau,k}-\ell_k)Q_{\varepsilon,\tau,k}\chi_{n,m} \| = \mathcal{O}(\varepsilon^{\frac{1}{2}}(n^{3/2}+m^{3/2}))$$

for $\varepsilon \to +0$ if $\ell_k = -n-\mu m-\mu-1$; this proves (15). □

THEOREM 4.5. *The eigenvalues of the operator* $\tilde{T}_\varepsilon$ *(and hence of* T_ε*) can be numbered in such a way that*

$$\text{(23a)} \qquad \sigma(\tilde{T}_\varepsilon) = \left\{\kappa_{n,m}(\varepsilon) \mid (n,m) \in \mathbb{N}^2\right\}$$

and such that they satisfy for $\varepsilon \to +0$

(23b) $$\kappa_{n,m}(\varepsilon) = -n - \mu m + \mathcal{O}(\varepsilon^{\frac{1}{2}}(n^{3/2}+m^{3/2})).$$

PROOF. Let ε_j be such that $\partial D(0,|\ell_j|+2\alpha_j) \subset \rho(R_\varepsilon)$ for all $\varepsilon \in (0,\varepsilon_j]$, then we have by (10b) for any $u \in \mathcal{D}(T_\varepsilon)$

(24) $$\| Au\| \le \frac{1}{8}\| (R_\varepsilon-\lambda)u\| + (8C_3C_4+ \frac{1}{8}|Re\lambda|)\| u\|$$

and hence

(25) $$\| (R_\varepsilon+A-\lambda)u\|^2 \ge \tfrac{1}{2}\| (R_\varepsilon-\lambda)u\|^2 - 2\| AP_{\varepsilon,1,j}u\|^2 - 2\| A(1-P_{\varepsilon,1,j})u\|^2 \ge$$

$$\ge \tfrac{1}{2}\| (R_\varepsilon-\lambda)P_{\varepsilon,1,j}u\|^2 - 2\| AP_{\varepsilon,1,j}u\| \; +$$

$$+ \frac{7}{16}\| (R_\varepsilon-\lambda)(1-P_{\varepsilon,1,j})u\|^2 - 2(8C_3C_4+ \frac{1}{8}|\lambda|)^2\| (1-P_{\varepsilon,1,j}) u\|^2$$

Since the restriction of R_ε to $\mathcal{R}(1-P_{\varepsilon,1,j})$ has no eigenvalues larger than ℓ_{j+1} we have, if $Re\lambda > \ell_{j+1}$,

$$\| (R_\varepsilon-\lambda)(1-P_{\varepsilon,1,j})u\| \ge (|Im\lambda|+Re\lambda-\ell_{j+1})\| (1-P_{\varepsilon,1,j})u\| ,$$

hence we can certainly find a number $J \in \mathbb{N}$, such that the third line of (25) can be estimated from below by $\frac{5}{16}\| (R_\varepsilon-\lambda)(1-P_{\varepsilon,1,j})u\|^2$ for all $j \ge J$ and for all λ with $|Re\lambda| \le \frac{1}{2}|\ell_j|$.

In order to estimate the second line of (25) from below, we consider the basis, given in (20). We observe that its elements are nearly orthogonal if ε is small enough, for by (13) and (18) we have

(26) $$\left\langle P_{\varepsilon,1,j}\chi_{n,m}, P_{\varepsilon,1,j}\chi_{i,k}\right\rangle =$$

$$= \left\langle \chi_{n,m}, \chi_{i,k}\right\rangle + \left\langle (1-P_{\varepsilon,1,j})\chi_{n,m}, (1-P_{\varepsilon,1,j})\chi_{i,k}\right\rangle =$$

$$= \mathcal{O}(\varepsilon(n^{3/2}+m^{3/2})(i^{3/2}+j^{3/2})), \qquad (\varepsilon\to+0),$$

provided $n \neq i$ or $m \neq k$ and $n + \mu m + \mu + 1 \le -\ell_j$ and $i + k\mu + \mu + 1 \le -\ell_j$. This implies

(27) $$P_{\varepsilon,1,j}u = \sum_{n+\mu m+\mu+1\le -\ell_j} \alpha_{n,m}(\varepsilon)P_{\varepsilon,1,j}\chi_{n,m}\ , \qquad (n,m)\in \mathbb{N}_o^2,$$

where $\sum_{n,m} |\alpha_{n,m}|^2 < 2\| P_{\varepsilon,1,j}u\|^2$ if ε is sufficiently small. Since we have, furthermore, by (10b), (12b) and (18)

$$\| AP_{\varepsilon,1,j}\chi_{n,m}\| \le \| A\chi_{n,m}\| + \| A(1-P_{\varepsilon,1,j})\chi_{n,m}\| =$$

$$= \mathcal{O}(\varepsilon^{\frac12}(n+m+1)) + \mathcal{O}(\| (R_\varepsilon+n+\mu m+\mu+1)\chi_{n,m}\| + \| (1-P_{\varepsilon,1,j})\chi_{n,m}\| =$$

$$= \mathcal{O}(\varepsilon^{\frac12}(n^{3/2}+m^{3/2}+1)), \qquad (\varepsilon\to+0),$$

if $n + \mu m + \mu + 1 \le -\ell_j$, $(n,m)\in \mathbb{N}_o^2$, formula (27) implies

$$\| AP_{\varepsilon,1,j}u\| = \mathcal{O}(\varepsilon^{\frac12}|\ell_j|^{3/2}\| P_{\varepsilon,1,j}u\|), \qquad (\varepsilon\to+0)$$

and from formula (25) we find a constant $\tilde{K} > 0$ such that

(28a) $$\| (R_\varepsilon+A-\lambda)u\| \ge \tfrac14\sqrt5\| (R_\varepsilon-\lambda)u\| - \varepsilon^{\frac12}\tilde{K}|\ell_j|^{3/2}\|u\|$$

for all $j \ge J$, $|Re\lambda| \le \frac12|\ell_j|$ and ε sufficiently small.
Estimate (10c) implies the existence of a constant $K \ge \tilde{K}$, such that

(28b) $$\| (\tilde{T}_\varepsilon-\lambda)u\| \ge \tfrac12\| (R_\varepsilon-\lambda)u\| - \varepsilon^{\frac12}|\ell_j|^{3/2}K\|u\| \ge$$

$$\ge \|u\|\left\{\tfrac12\ \mathrm{dist}(\lambda,\sigma(R_\varepsilon)) - 2\varepsilon^{\frac12}K|\ell_j|^{3/2}\right\}$$

for all $j \ge J$, $|Re\lambda| \le \frac12|\ell_j|$ and ε sufficiently small. In conjunction with lemma 4.4 this proves the theorem. □

<u>REMARKS</u>. 1. Another useful version of the statements (23b) and (28b) is

(29) $$\| \tilde{T}_\varepsilon u - \lambda u\| \ge \tfrac12\|u\|\left\{|\lambda - \ell(\lambda)| - 4\varepsilon^{\frac12}K|\ell(\lambda)|^{3/2}\right\}$$

for all $\lambda\in\mathbb{C}$ and all sufficiently small ε; here $\ell(\lambda)$ denotes the point of Λ that is nearest to λ.

2. The operator U_ε associated with problem (1-),

(30) $$U_\varepsilon u := \varepsilon I\!\!\Delta u - x\partial_x u - \mu y\partial_y u \qquad \text{for all } u\in \mathcal{D}(U_\varepsilon) := \mathcal{D}(T_\varepsilon)$$

satisfies the analogue of (29); defining

$$\tilde{U}_\varepsilon := \exp(-(x^2+\mu y^2)/4\varepsilon)U_\varepsilon \exp((x^2+\mu y^2)/4\varepsilon)$$

we find that a constant K > 0 exists, such that

$$(31) \qquad \|(\tilde{U}_\varepsilon-\lambda)v\| \ge \tfrac{1}{2}\|v\|\left\{|\lambda - \ell(\lambda)| - 4\varepsilon^{\frac{1}{2}}K|\ell(\lambda)|^{3/2}\right\}$$

for every $\lambda \in \mathbb{C}$ if ε is sufficiently small; here $\ell(\lambda)$ denotes the point of the limiting set Λ^*, that is nearest to λ;

$$(32) \qquad \Lambda^* := \left\{ -n-\mu m \mid (n,m) \in \mathbb{N}_o^2 \right\}.$$

4.2. STRONG CONVERGENCE OF THE RESOLVENT IN THE CASE OF AN ATTRACTING NODE

As in §3.3 we can prove the inverse stability of $T_\varepsilon - \lambda$ in a part of the complex plane and use it to prove strong convergence of $(T_\varepsilon-\lambda)^{-1}$ in L^2-sense. Here we refine the argument; we prove strong convergence in L^p-sense and we show that this yields uniform convergence of the approximation without recourse to Sobolev's inequality or the maximum principle.

We extend T_ε to an operator on $L^p(\Omega)$ with $1 < p \le \infty$ and on $C^o(\Omega)$ by defining its domain in $L^p(\Omega)$ by

$$(33a) \qquad \mathcal{D}(T_\varepsilon) := \left\{u \in L^p(\Omega) \mid \Delta u \in L^p(\Omega) \ \& \ u|_{\partial\Omega} = 0\right\}$$

and in $C^o(\Omega)$ by $\mathcal{D}(T_\varepsilon) := C^2(\Omega) \cap C^o_o(\Omega)$. Moreover, we define the presumed limit operator T_o as the restriction of $x\partial_x + \mu y\partial_y$ to the sets

$$(33b) \qquad \mathcal{D}(T_o) := \begin{cases} \{u \in L^p(\Omega) \mid x\partial_x u + \mu y\partial_y u \in L^p(\Omega) \ \& \ u|_{\partial\Omega} = 0\} \\ \{u \in C^o(\Omega) \mid x\partial_x u + \mu y\partial_y u \in C^o(\Omega) \ \& \ u|_{\partial\Omega} = 0\} \end{cases}$$

in $L^p(\Omega)$ and $C^o(\Omega)$ respectively. In some part of the complex plane these operators are bounded from below:

<u>LEMMA 4.6</u>. *A constant* $K \in \mathbb{R}$ *exists such that* T_ε *satisfies the inequality*

$$(34) \qquad |T_\varepsilon u - \lambda u|_{o,p} \ge (\mathrm{Re}\lambda+(1+\mu)/p-\varepsilon K)|u|_{o,p}$$

for all $p \geq 1$ ($p=\infty$ *included*), $u \in \mathcal{D}(T_\varepsilon)$, $\varepsilon \geq 0$ *and* $\lambda \in \mathbb{C}$.

PROOF. Let p and the conjugated number q be finite ($1/p + 1/q = 1$); if $u \in L^p$, then $u|u|^{p-2} \in L^q$ and $|u|^p_{o,p} = |u|u|^{p-2}|^q_{o,q}$. For all $u \in \mathcal{D}(T_\varepsilon)$ with $|u|_{o,p} = 1$ we find the inequality

$$(35)\qquad |T_\varepsilon u - \lambda u|_{o,p} = \sup_{v\in L^q(\Omega),\,|v|_{o,q}=1} |\langle T_\varepsilon u - \lambda u, v\rangle| \geq$$

$$\geq |Re\,\langle T_\varepsilon u - \lambda u,\ u|u|^{p-2}\rangle|.$$

In connection with the (symmetric) principal part L_p of L we define in $\mathbb{C}^2$ the Hermitian sesquilinear form A,

$$(36)\qquad A(\alpha,\beta) := a\alpha_1\overline{\beta}_1 + b\alpha_1\overline{\beta}_2 + b\alpha_2\overline{\beta}_1 + c\alpha_2\overline{\beta}_2,\quad \alpha := (\alpha_1,\alpha_2),\ \beta := (\beta_1,\beta_2).$$

Since L is uniformly elliptic on Ω, the associated quadratic form $A(\alpha,\alpha)$ is positive and non-degenerated on $\mathbb{C}^2$; by Schwarz' inequality it satisfies $A(\alpha,\alpha) \geq |Re A(\alpha,\overline{\alpha})|$. Hence we find by integration by parts that L_p satisfies

$$(37a)\qquad -Re\,\langle L_p u,\ u|u|^{p-2}\rangle =$$

$$= \tfrac{1}{2}\iint_\Omega \left\{pA(u\nabla u, u\nabla u) - (p-2)Re A(\overline{u}\nabla u, u\nabla\overline{u})\,|u|^{p-4}\right\}dxdy \geq$$

$$\geq \tfrac{1}{2}(p-|p-2|)\iint_\Omega A(\nabla u,\nabla u)\,|u|^{p-2}\,dxdy.$$

For a term of $T_\varepsilon u$ containing a first order derivative, e.g. $\tilde{d}\partial_x u$, we find by integration by parts

$$(37b)\qquad Re\,\langle \tilde{d}\partial_x u,\ u|u|^{p-2}\rangle = \frac{1}{p}\iint_\Omega \tilde{d}\partial_x |u|^p\,dxdy = -\frac{1}{p}\iint_\Omega |u|^p(\partial_x\tilde{d})\,dxdy;$$

since $|u|_{o,p} = 1$ we find in particular

$$(37c)\qquad Re\,\langle x\partial_x u + \mu y\partial_y u,\ u|u|^{p-2}\rangle = -(1+\mu)/p$$

and

$$\text{(37d)}\qquad |Re\left\langle (L-L_p)u,\ u|u|^{p-2}\right\rangle| =$$

$$= \left| \frac{1}{p} \iint_\Omega |u|^p (pd_3+\partial_x^2 a+2\partial_x\partial_y b+\partial_y^2 c-\partial_x d_1-\partial_y d_2)\,dxdy\right| \le$$

$$\le \left[d_3 + p^{-1}(\partial_x^2 a+2\partial_x\partial_y b+\partial_y^2 c-\partial_x d_1-\partial_y d_2)\right].$$

In conjunction with (35) this proves the estimate (34) for all $p \in (1,\infty)$. Since the constant K in (34) can be chosen independently of p, we can take the limits $p \to \infty$ and $p \to 1$ at both sides of the $\ge$-sign thus proving (34) for all $p \in [1,\infty]$. □

REMARK. If $u \in C^2(\Omega)$ we can replace the L^∞-norm in (34) by the maximum norm, since

$$\text{(37e)}\qquad \lim_{p\to\infty} |v|_{o,p} = |v|_{o,\infty} = [v] \qquad \text{for all } v \in C^o(\Omega).$$

The reduced equation $x\partial_x u + \mu y\partial_y u - \lambda u = f$ of (1+) can be solved explicitly. Its characteristics are all curves parametrized by

$$x = \alpha t,\quad y = \beta t^\mu \qquad \text{with } \alpha,\beta \in \mathbb{R} \text{ and } t \in \mathbb{R}^+$$

and along a characteristic the solution is determined by the equation $t\,\frac{du}{dt} - \lambda u = f(x(t),y(t))$. We introduce the characteristic coordinates $(t,\psi) \in (0,1) \times (\mathbb{R}\ mod\ 2\pi)$ by

$$\text{(38a)}\qquad (x,y) = (t\cos\psi,\ t^\mu \sin\psi),$$

then we find $\frac{\partial(x,y)}{\partial(t,\psi)} = t^\mu(\cos^2\psi+\mu\sin^2\psi)$ and

$$\text{(38b)}\qquad \begin{pmatrix}\partial_x\\ \partial_y\end{pmatrix} = \frac{1}{\cos^2\psi+\mu\sin^2\psi}\begin{pmatrix}\cos\psi & -\mu t^{-1}\sin\psi\\ t^{1-\mu}\sin\psi & t^{-\mu}\cos\psi\end{pmatrix}\begin{pmatrix}\partial_t\\ \partial_\psi\end{pmatrix}.$$

Each solution of the homogeneous equation $t\,\frac{du}{dt} = \lambda u$ can be represented in the form

$$\text{(39)}\qquad u = t^\lambda h(\psi) \qquad \text{(h is a } 2\pi\text{-periodic function on } \mathbb{R})$$

and it is easily seen that this solution is in $L^p(\Omega)$ if and only if

$$h \in L^p(\mathbb{R}\ mod\ 2\pi) \quad \text{and} \quad Re\lambda > -(1+\mu)/p \qquad (1\le p\le\infty).$$

A particular solution of the inhomogeneous equation is given by

$$(40) \qquad u_o(x,y) = -\int_1^{1/t(x,y)} f(sx,s^{\mu}y)s^{-1-\lambda}ds$$

provided f is locally integrable.

LEMMA 4.7. *The resolvent sets of* T_o *in* $L^p(\Omega)$ *and* $C^o(\Omega)$ *are the sets*

$$(41) \qquad \rho(T_o) = \begin{cases} \{\lambda \in \mathbb{C} \mid Re\lambda > -(1+\mu)/p\}, & \textit{if } T_o \textit{ acts in } L^p(\Omega), \\ \{\lambda \in \mathbb{C} \mid Re\lambda > 0\}, & \textit{if } T_o \textit{ acts in } C^o(\Omega); \end{cases}$$

moreover, each $\lambda \in \rho(T_o)$ *is contained in* $\rho(T_\varepsilon)$, *provided* $\varepsilon \in \mathbb{R}^+$ *is sufficiently small.*

PROOF. The dual of the operator T_o (acting in L^p or C^o) is the operator $T_o^* = -x\partial_x - \mu y\partial_y - \mu - 1$ (acting in the dual space), whose domain is not restricted by any boundary conditions. From (39) we infer that the solutions of $T_o^* u = \lambda u$ cannot be continuous functionals on L^p and C^o if $Re\lambda > -(\mu+1)/p$ and $Re\lambda > 0$ respectively (cf. [29] ch. 4 §9) and hence that $N(T_o^*-\lambda) = \{0\}$. In conjunction with lemma 4.6 this proves (41).

If $\varepsilon > 0$, L^2-invertibility of $T_\varepsilon - \lambda$ with $\lambda \in \mathbb{C}\setminus\Lambda$ and ε sufficiently small is proved in theorem 4.5. Since the inclusions $L^p(\Omega) \subset L^q(\Omega) \subset C^o(\Omega)$ are dense for all p, $q \in [1,\infty]$ with $p < q$, the invertibility in $L^2(\Omega)$ and the lower estimate (34) imply invertibility of $T_\varepsilon - \lambda$ in $L^p(\Omega)$ for all $p \in [1,\infty]$ provided $Re\lambda > -(1+\mu)/p + K\varepsilon$ and in $C^o(\Omega)$ provided $Re\lambda > K\varepsilon$. □

By analogy to theorem 3.7 we now find strong convergence of the resolvent operator $(T_\varepsilon-\lambda)^{-1}$ to $(T_o-\lambda)^{-1}$ for $\varepsilon \to +0$ and for all $\lambda \in \rho(T_o)$:

THEOREM 4.8. *The resolvent operator* $(T_\varepsilon-\lambda)^{-1}$ *converges for* $\varepsilon \to +0$ *to* $(T_o-\lambda)^{-1}$ *strongly in all* $L^p(\Omega)$*-norms with* $1 \le p \le \infty$ *and in the uniform norm, provided* $\lambda \in \rho(T_o)$. *Furthermore, if* $\lambda - 2 \in \rho(T_o)$ *we have the stronger estimate*

(42) $$|(T_\varepsilon-\lambda)^{-1}f - (T_o-\lambda)^{-1}f|_{o,p} = \mathcal{O}(\varepsilon\|f\|_{2,p}), \qquad (\varepsilon\to+0)$$

provided $|f|_{2,p} < \infty$.

REMARK. It is clear that this theorem implies also L^p - or C^o-convergence of the solution of (1+) with inhomogeneous boundary conditions.

PROOF. Formula (40) implies

(40') $$(T_o-\lambda)^{-1}f = -\int_1^{1/t(x,y)} f(sx,s^\mu y)s^{-1-\lambda}ds.$$

Differentiating once with respect to x we obtain with use of formula (38b):

(43a) $$\partial_x(T_o-\lambda)^{-1}f = (T_o-\lambda+1)^{-1}(\partial_x f) + \frac{t^{\lambda-1}\cos\psi f(\cos\psi,\sin\psi)}{\cos^2\psi+\mu\sin^2\psi}$$

and for the other first and second order derivatives we obtain similar expressions. Since by the trace theorem (cf. lemma 1.9 and [4] §7.58) the $L^p(\partial\Omega)$-norms of the restrictions to the boundary $f_{|\partial\Omega}$ and $\partial_\psi(f_{|\partial\Omega})$ are bounded by $\|f\|_{2,p}$, we find from lemma 4.6 the estimate

(43b) $$|L(T_o-\lambda)^{-1}f|_{o,p} = \mathcal{O}(\|f\|_{2,p})$$

for all $p \in (1,\infty]$ and $\lambda \in \rho(T_o)$.
The remainder of the proof is equal to the proof of theorem 3.7. □

This theorem generalizes the results of [13] §5 and [14] §5 as far as convergence of the solution of (1+) to the solution of the reduced equation (without internal boundary layer terms) is concerned.

4.3. CONVERGENCE OF THE SOLUTION ON AN ANNULAR SUBDOMAIN OF Ω

Theorem 4.8 shows that the norm, with respect to which we proved convergence, deteriorates as $Re\lambda$ decreases. The reason is that the singularity of the solutions of the reduced equation at the origin deteriorates as $Re\lambda$ decreases. In this section we shall restrict the problem (1+) to a subdomain not containing the origin and we shall show that we can achieve convergence of the solution of (1+) on that subdomain for all $\lambda \in \mathbb{C}\setminus\dot{\Lambda}$ with the aid of the cut-off method of §3.6. This method is based on the fact that an estimate (independent of ε) for the norm of the resolvent of $\tilde{T}_\varepsilon$ is available for all $\lambda \in \mathbb{C}\backslash\Lambda$, cf. (3) and (29), while such an estimate is not known for T_ε.

Define E_γ and its Ω-complement F_γ as the domains

(44) $$E_\gamma := \left\{(x,y) \mid x^2 + \mu y^2 \le \gamma^2\right\} \quad \text{and} \quad F_\gamma := \Omega\backslash E_\gamma .$$

We begin with a study of the restriction of problem (1+) to the subdomain F_γ ($\gamma<1$). In order to make this restriction "well-posed" for $\varepsilon \neq 0$, we add a boundary condition at ∂E_γ; we define the operators M_ε and M_o in $L^p(F_\gamma)$ and $C^o(F_\gamma)$ as the restrictions of T_ε and T_o, cf. (33),

(45a) $$M_\varepsilon u := T_\varepsilon u \quad \text{for all } u \in \mathcal{D}(M_\varepsilon) := \left\{v \in \mathcal{D}(T_\varepsilon) \cap L^1(F_\gamma) \;\middle|\; v_{|\partial E_\gamma} = 0\right\}$$

(45b) $$M_o u := T_o u \quad \text{for all } u \in \mathcal{D}(M_o) := \mathcal{D}(T_o) \cap L^1(F_\gamma).$$

By removing the singular point (0,0) from the domain, we obtain a problem of the same type as problem (2.1) is, in the more general setting of L^p-spaces. Using the same technique as in the proof of lemma 4.6 we can show, as in lemma 2.1, that the spectrum of M_ε recedes to $-\infty$ for $\varepsilon \to +0$ and we can prove the inverse stability of $M_\varepsilon - \lambda$ for all $\lambda \in \mathbb{C}$ in $C^o(F_\gamma)$ and in all $L^p(F_\gamma)$-spaces with $1 \le p \le \infty$. In the proof we use the weighted L^p-norm $u \mapsto |t^s u|_{o,p,F_\gamma}$ with $s \in \mathbb{R}^+$ (which is equivalent to the ordinary $L^p(F_\gamma)$-norm).

<u>LEMMA 4.9</u>. *Constants* K_1 *and* $K_2 \in \mathbb{R}^+$, *depending only on the coefficients of* L, *exist such that* $M_\varepsilon - \lambda$ *satisfies for all* $p \in [1,\infty]$ *the estimate*

(46a) $$|t^s(M_\varepsilon u-\lambda u)|_{o,p,F_\gamma} \ge B_\varepsilon(\lambda,s,\gamma,p)\,|t^s u|_{o,p,F_\gamma}$$

and in particular for $p = 2$

(46b) $$\| t^s u\|_{F_\gamma} \, \| t^s(M_\varepsilon u-\lambda u)\|_{F_\gamma} \ge \varepsilon K_2 \| t^s \nabla u \|^2_{F_\gamma} + B_\varepsilon(\lambda,s,\gamma,p) \| t^s u\|^2_{F_\gamma} ,$$

with

(46c) $$B_\varepsilon(\lambda,s,\gamma,p) := Re\lambda + s + (1+\mu)/p - \varepsilon K_1 (1+s/\gamma)^2 ,$$

for all $u \in \mathcal{D}(M_\varepsilon)$, $\varepsilon \in [0,1]$, $\gamma \in (0,1]$, $s \in \mathbb{R}$ *and* $\lambda \in \mathbb{C}$. *Moreover, if*

$B_\varepsilon(\lambda,s,\gamma,p) > 0$, *then* $M_\varepsilon - \lambda$ *has a bounded inverse in* $L^p(F_\gamma)$.

PROOF. Define $\tilde{L}u := t^s L t^{-s} u$, then

$$\tilde{L}u = Lu - 2st^{-1}A(\nabla u,\nabla t) + s(s+1)t^{-2}A(\nabla t,\nabla t) - st^{-1}u(L-d_3)t, \tag{47}$$

where $t = t(x,y)$ is defined in (38a), and we find

$$t^s(M_\varepsilon-\lambda)u = (\varepsilon\tilde{L}+x\partial_x+\mu y\partial_y-s-\lambda)(t^s u).$$

Let p and q be finite, i.e. $p \in (1,\infty)$. If $u \in \mathcal{D}(T_\varepsilon)$ with $\varepsilon \neq 0$, then $u_{|\partial F_\gamma} = 0$ and we can use the analogues of the formulae (37a-b-c), in which the integration is taken over F_γ instead of Ω. By substituting $\tilde{L}$ for L and $t^s u$ for u in (34) we find that (46a) is true for $\varepsilon \neq 0$, provided K_1 satisfies

$$K_1(1+s/\gamma)^2 \geq \Big[\partial_x^2 a+2\partial_x\partial_y b+\partial_y^2 c-\partial_x d_1-\partial_y d_2+(s+1)d_3-st^{-1}(Lt+2L_p t) + $$
$$+ s(s-1)t^{-2}A(\nabla t,\nabla t)\Big]_{F_\gamma}.$$

From (38) it follows that such a constant exists.

If $\varepsilon = 0$ we cannot use (37b) since $u_{|\partial E_\gamma}$ is not zero for all $u \in \mathcal{D}(T_0)$. We have instead, if $|t^s u|_{0,p} = 1$,

$$- Re\left\langle t^s(x\partial_x+\mu y\partial_y-\lambda u),\ t^{ps-s}u|u|^{p-2}\right\rangle_{F_\gamma} = \tag{48}$$
$$= (Re\lambda+s+(\mu+1)/p)\,|t^s u|^p_{o,p,F_\gamma} + \frac{1}{p}\int_{\partial E_\gamma}(x^2t^{\mu-1}+\mu y^2 t^{1-\mu})|t^s u|^p dE_\gamma$$

and this proves (46a) for $\varepsilon = 0$. Since the constant K_1 in (46a) does not depend on p, the formula remains true when we take the limits $p \to 1+0$ or $p \to \infty$ in it.

In case $p = 2$ and $\varepsilon \neq 0$ we find by integration by parts for each $u \in \mathcal{D}(T_\varepsilon)$ the identity

$$Re\left\langle t^s Lu, t^s u\right\rangle_{F_\gamma} = -\iint_{F_\gamma} A(\nabla u,\nabla u)t^{2s}dxdy + \tag{49}$$
$$+\iint_{F_\gamma} \tfrac{1}{2}\Big\{\partial_x^2(at^{2s}) + 2\partial_x\partial_y(bt^{2s}) + \partial_y^2(ct^{2s}) - \partial_x(d_1t^{2s}) -$$
$$- \partial_y(d_2t^{2s}) + 2d_3t^{2s}\Big\}\, u\bar{u}dxdy$$

and this implies (46b).

The invertibility of M_o is a direct consequence of the invertibility of T_o; by analytic continuation (cf. the proof of theorem 3.7) this property is transferred to all $\lambda \in \mathbf{C}$. The invertibility of M_ε in L^2 is proved by the continuity method from the fact that Δ is a one-to-one mapping from $H^2(F_\gamma) \cap H_o^1(F_\gamma)$ onto $L^2(F_\gamma)$; by the density argument, used in lemma 4.7, we extend this result to all L^p-spaces and to C^o; by analytic continuation we extend it to all $\lambda \in \mathbf{C}$ for which the right-hand side of (46a) is positive. □

REMARK. This lemma is important because it provides *a priori estimates* in the supremum norm and the L^2-norm.

Let u_o be as defined in (40), i.e. $u_o = (M_o-\lambda)^{-1}f$ on F_γ and let v_ε be the solution of the boundary value problem on F_γ

(50) $$\varepsilon Lv + x\partial_x v + \mu y\partial_y v - \lambda v = f, \qquad v\Big|_{\partial\Omega} = 0 \text{ and } v\Big|_{\partial E_\gamma} = u_o\Big|_{\partial E_\gamma}$$

which has a unique solution by the previous lemma, provided ε is small enough. By definition we now have, if f is smooth enough,

$$v_\varepsilon - u_o \in \mathcal{D}(M_\varepsilon) \quad \text{and} \quad (M_\varepsilon-\lambda)(v_\varepsilon-u_o) = \varepsilon Lu_o.$$

Since lemma 4.9 provides estimates of the norms of u_o and its derivatives by the norms of f and its derivatives, we find from (38) and (43a) positive constants C_i such that

(51a) $$\| t^s(M_\varepsilon-\lambda)(v_\varepsilon-u_o)\|_{F_\gamma} \le C_1\varepsilon(1+|\lambda|)B_o^{-\frac{1}{2}}\|f\|_{1,\partial\Omega} + C_2\varepsilon B_o^{-1}\left[[t^sf]\right]$$

where $\left[[t^sf]\right]$ denotes

(51b) $$\left[[t^sf]\right] := \sum_{k,j\ge 0,k+j\le 2} \| t^s\partial_x^k\partial_y^j f\|_{F_\gamma} .$$

Applying again lemma 4.9 and the trace-theorem (lemma 1.9) we find

(51c) $$\| t^s(v_\varepsilon-u_o)\|_{F_\gamma} \le C_3\varepsilon\left[[t^sf]\right]\left\{1+|Im\lambda|+(B_\varepsilon(\lambda-2,s,\gamma,2))^{-2}\right\},$$

(51d) $$\| t^s\nabla(v_\varepsilon-u_o)\|_{F_\gamma} \le C_4\varepsilon^{\frac{1}{2}}\left[[t^sf]\right]\left\{1+|Im\lambda|+(B_\varepsilon(\lambda-2,s,\gamma,2))^{-3/2}\right\},$$

provided $Re\lambda > -s - \frac{1}{2}\mu + 3/2 + \varepsilon K_1(1+s/\gamma)^2$. In the same way we find the estimate with respect to the supremum norm on F_γ

$$\text{(51e)} \qquad \left[t^s(v_\varepsilon - u_o)\right]_{F_\gamma} \le C_5\varepsilon\left[[t^s f]\right]\left\{1+|Im\lambda|+(B_\varepsilon(\lambda-2,s,\gamma,2))^{-2}\right\},$$

provided $Re\lambda > 2 - s + \varepsilon K_1(1+s/\gamma)^2$. This proves that u_o approximates v_ε if ε is small enough.

In order to show that v_ε in its turn approximates $u_\varepsilon := (T_\varepsilon-\lambda)^{-1}f$, we choose cut-off functions $z \in C^\infty(\mathbb{R})$ and $z_\gamma \in C^\infty(\Omega)$ which satisfy

$$\text{(52a)} \qquad z(\xi) = \begin{cases} 0 & \text{if } \xi < 1, \\ 1 & \text{if } \xi > 2, \end{cases} \qquad 0 \le z'(\xi) \le 2 \text{ and } [z'']_{\mathbb{R}} \le 4$$

$$\text{(52b)} \qquad z_\gamma(x,y) := z((x^2+\mu y^2)^{\frac{1}{2}}/\gamma) .$$

We continue the function $z_\gamma v_\varepsilon$ into E_γ by zero and we consider the difference $w_\varepsilon := u_\varepsilon - z_\gamma v_\varepsilon$. Applying $T_\varepsilon - \lambda$ to it we find that the result f_ε satisfies

$$\text{(53)} \qquad f_\varepsilon := (T_\varepsilon-\lambda)(u_\varepsilon - z_\gamma v_\varepsilon) = (1-z_\gamma)f - v_\varepsilon(T_\varepsilon-\varepsilon d_3)z_\gamma - 2\varepsilon A(\nabla v_\varepsilon,\nabla z_\gamma) ,$$

and has a support which is contained in $E_{2\gamma}$; moreover, since $w_\varepsilon \in \mathcal{D}(T_\varepsilon)$ we have $w_\varepsilon = (T_\varepsilon-\lambda)^{-1}f_\varepsilon$. We now transform w_ε and f_ε into $\tilde{w}_\varepsilon$ and $\tilde{f}_\varepsilon$ as follows

$$\tilde{w}_\varepsilon(x,y) := w_\varepsilon(x,y)\exp\{(x^2+\mu y^2-9\gamma^2)/4\varepsilon\}$$

$$\tilde{f}_\varepsilon(x,y) := f_\varepsilon(x,y)\exp\{(x^2+\mu y^2-9\gamma^2)/4\varepsilon\} ,$$

then we find by (3) the relation

$$\tilde{w}_\varepsilon = (\tilde{T}_\varepsilon-\lambda)^{-1}f_\varepsilon$$

and by (29) the estimate

$$\text{(54)} \qquad \|\tilde{w}_\varepsilon\| = \mathcal{O}(\|\tilde{f}_\varepsilon\|) , \qquad (\varepsilon\to+0),$$

provided $\lambda \notin \Lambda$ (and λ fixed). Since $\mathrm{supp}(f_\varepsilon) \subset E_{2\gamma}$ and the exponent of the transforming factor is negative in $E_{3\gamma}$, the order estimate $\mathcal{O}(\|\tilde{f}_\varepsilon\|)$ in (54) is exponentially small. Moreover, since positive constants C_i exist such that

(55) $\|\nabla u\| \le \nu\|\Delta u\| + C_1\|u\|/\nu$ and $\|\Delta u\| \le C_2\|Lu\| + C_3\|u\|$

for all $u \in H^2(\Omega)$ and $\nu \in (0,1]$ we find from the equation, cf. (3),

$$\varepsilon L\tilde{w}_\varepsilon = (-\omega_1\partial_x - \omega_2\partial_y + \omega_3/\varepsilon - \tfrac{1}{2} - \tfrac{1}{2}\mu - \omega_4)\tilde{w}_\varepsilon + \tilde{f}_\varepsilon$$

the estimate

$$\|\Delta\tilde{w}_\varepsilon\| = \mathcal{O}(\varepsilon^{-2}\|\tilde{w}_\varepsilon\| + \varepsilon^{-1}\|\tilde{f}_\varepsilon\|) = \mathcal{O}(\varepsilon^{-2}\|\tilde{f}_\varepsilon\|).$$

By Sobolev's inequality (in two dimensions), cf. (2.19) and [9] ch. 9,

(56) $[u]^2 \le C_4\|u\|^2 + C_5\|u\|\|\Delta u\|$,

valid for all $u \in H^2(\Omega)$ and certain positive constants C_i, we obtain the estimate

$$[\tilde{w}_\varepsilon] = \mathcal{O}(\varepsilon^{-1}\|\tilde{f}_\varepsilon\|) .$$

Hence a constant C exists, depending only on μ,L and the distance between λ and Λ such that

(57) $|w_\varepsilon(x,y)| \le C\varepsilon^{-1}\|\tilde{f}_\varepsilon\| \exp\{(9\gamma^2 - x^2 - \mu y^2)/4\varepsilon\}$

for all $(x,y) \in \Omega$, $\gamma \in (0,1/3)$, $\varepsilon \in (0,1]$ and $f \in L^2(\Omega)$.

In order to estimate $\|\tilde{f}_\varepsilon\|$ we use formula (53) and the estimates of $v_\varepsilon - u_o$ and u_o, derived in (51) and (46); we find a constant C_1 such that

(58) $$\|\tilde{f}_\varepsilon\| \le \gamma C_1 \exp(-5\gamma/4\varepsilon)\Big\{[f]_{E_{2\gamma}} + \\ + \gamma^{-s}\big[[t^s f]\big](1+\varepsilon\gamma^{-2})\{1+|Im\lambda| + (B_\varepsilon(\lambda-2,s,\gamma,\infty))^{-2}\}\Big\},$$

provided $Re\lambda > 2 - s + \varepsilon K_1(1+s/\gamma)^2$; C_1 depends on μ,L and s, but not on $\varepsilon,\gamma,\lambda$ and f. In conjunction with (57) this implies

(59) $|w_\varepsilon(x,y)| = \mathcal{O}(\varepsilon^{-1}\gamma^{-s+1}([f]+[\Delta f])\exp\{(4\gamma^2 - x^2 - \mu y^2)/4\varepsilon\})$,

provided $\lambda \notin \Lambda$ and $Re\lambda > 2 - s + \varepsilon K_1(1+s/\gamma)^2$. Since γ can be chosen arbitrarily within (0,1/3), we insert $8\gamma^2 = x^2 + \mu y^2$ in (59) and we find from this formula and from (51d) that the difference between u_ε and u_o satisfies the estimate

$$(60)\qquad |u_\varepsilon(x,y) - u_o(x,y)| = \mathcal{O}(\varepsilon[f]+\varepsilon[\Delta f]) \qquad (\varepsilon\to+0),$$

uniformly for all (x,y) in the annular subdomain Ω/E_γ, provided $\gamma > 0$, $\lambda \notin \Lambda$ and γ and λ are fixed. More precisely stated we have:

THEOREM 4.10. *Positive constants* C_1 *and* C_2 *exist such that the difference between* $u_\varepsilon := (T_\varepsilon-\lambda)^{-1}f$ *and* $u_o := (T_o-\lambda)^{-1}f$ *satisfies the inequality*

$$(61)\qquad (x^2+\mu y^2)^{\frac{1}{2}s}|u_\varepsilon(x,y) - u_o(x,y)| \le$$

$$\le C_1\{\varepsilon + \varepsilon^{-\frac{1}{2}}\exp(-(x^2+\mu y^2)/8\varepsilon)\}([f]+[\Delta f])$$

uniformly for all $(x,y) \in \Omega$ *satisfying*

$$x^2 + \mu y^2 \ge \gamma^2(\varepsilon) \ge C_2\varepsilon^{\frac{1}{2}},$$

provided $Re\lambda > -s+2+\varepsilon K_1(1+s/\gamma)^2$. C_2 *depends only on* μ, s *and* L; C_1 *depends on* μ,s,L *and* λ, *its* λ*-dependence being*

$$C_1(\lambda) = \mathcal{O}(\{1+(Re\lambda+s-2-\varepsilon K_1(1+s/\gamma)^2)^{-2}\}\{1+1/\mathrm{dist}(\lambda,\Lambda)\}) .$$

REMARKS 1. Approximations of higher order on an annular subdomain are obtained by iteration of the above procedure; e.g. we find by analogy to (60):

$$(62)\qquad |u_\varepsilon(x,y) - u_o(x,y) + \varepsilon(M_o-\lambda)^{-1}Lu_o(x,y)| = \mathcal{O}(\varepsilon^2([f]+[\Delta^2 f])) .$$

2. The assertion of theorem 4.10 can easily be extended to the solution of the inhomogeneous problem (1+): we merely have to add the term $t^\lambda(x,y)g(\psi(x,y))$ to the approximation u_o and the term $[g]_{\partial\Omega} + [g'']_{\partial\Omega}$ to the factor $[f] + [\Delta f]$ in the order estimate.

4.4. A REPELLING NODE; CONVERGENCE FOR $Re\lambda > 0$

We now consider problem (1-) and begin by studying the asymptotic behaviour of its solution in the case $Re\lambda > 0$. As we observed earlier in §3.6, the change of sign in problem (1) radically alters the asymptotic behaviour of the solution: the region of non-uniformity is transferred from a neighbourhood of the origin in the plus-sign case to a neighbourhood of the boundary in the minus-sign case.

In connection with problem (1-) we define the operators U_ε and U_o in the spaces $L^p(\Omega)$ and $C^o(\Omega)$ by

$$\text{(63a)} \qquad U_\varepsilon u := \varepsilon L u - x\partial_x u - \mu y \partial_y u \qquad \text{for all } u \in \mathcal{D}(U_\varepsilon) := \mathcal{D}(T_\varepsilon) \ ,$$

$$\text{(63b)} \qquad U_o u := -x\partial_x u - \mu y \partial_y u \qquad \text{for all } u \in \mathcal{D}(U_o),$$

$$\mathcal{D}(U_o) := \begin{cases} \{u \in L^p(\Omega) \mid x\partial_x u + \mu y \partial_y u \in L^p(\Omega)\}, \text{ or} \\ \{u \in C^o(\Omega) \mid x\partial_x u + \mu y \partial_y u \in C^o(\Omega)\}. \end{cases}$$

These operators satisfy:

<u>LEMMA 4.11</u>. *A constant* K *exists such that* U_ε *satisfies the inequality*

$$\text{(64)} \qquad |U_\varepsilon u - \lambda u|_{o,p} \geq (\mathit{Re}\lambda - (1+\mu)/p - \varepsilon K)\,|u|_{o,p}$$

for all $p \in [1,\infty]$, $u \in \mathcal{D}(U_\varepsilon)$, $\varepsilon \geq 0$ *and* $\lambda \in \mathbb{C}$. *Moreover,* $U_\varepsilon - \lambda$ *is invertible if the right-hand side of* (64) *is positive.*

<u>PROOF</u>. The proof of the estimate (64) is similar to the proof of (34) and the proof of the invertibility is the same as the one of lemma 4.7. □

In a manner analogous to §2.2 we now construct an approximation to $(U_\varepsilon-\lambda)^{-1}f$. The solution of the reduced equation $U_o u - \lambda u = f$ of (1-) is, cf. (38-39-40),

$$\text{(65)} \qquad (U_o-\lambda)^{-1}f = -\int_0^1 f(xs, ys^\mu)\, s^{\lambda-1} ds.$$

Differentiation under the integral sign shows the identities

$$\partial_x (U_o-\lambda)^{-1}f = (U_o-\lambda-1)^{-1}(\partial_x f),\ \partial_y (U_o-\lambda)^{-1}f = (U_o-\lambda-\mu)^{-1}(\partial_y f) \ ,$$

hence we find a constant C such that

$$\text{(66)} \qquad |L(U_o-\lambda)^{-1}f|_{o,p} \leq C\|f\|_{2,p} / (\mathit{Re}\lambda - (\mu+1)/p),$$

provided $Re\lambda > (\mu+1)/p$.

The solution of the reduced equation $(U_o-\lambda)^{-1}f$ will approximate $(U_\varepsilon-\lambda)^{-1}f$ in the major part of Ω, but since it does not satisfy the boundary condition at $\partial\Omega$, we have to construct a boundary layer there. We introduce the local coordinate $\xi := (1-t)/\varepsilon$ and define the substitution operator s_ε by

(67) $$(s_\varepsilon u)(\xi,\psi) := u((1-\varepsilon\xi)\cos\psi,\ (1-\varepsilon\xi)^\mu \sin\psi)$$

and the formal expansion of order m

(68a) $$s_\varepsilon(\varepsilon L - x\partial_x - \mu y\partial_y)s_\varepsilon^{-1} = \sum_{j=0}^{m} \varepsilon^{j-1}\rho_j + \varepsilon^m\rho_m^{\#};$$

in particular we find from (38b)

(68b) $$\rho_o = \hat{a}(\psi)\partial_\xi^2 - \partial_\xi$$

$$\text{where } \hat{a}(\psi) := (x^2+\mu y^2)(x^2a+2xyb+y^2c)\big|_{(x,y) = (\cos\psi,\sin\psi)}\ .$$

As in §2.2 we define the kernel k by

(69a) $$k(\xi,\eta,\psi) := \begin{cases} \exp(-\xi/\hat{a}(\psi)) - \exp((\eta-\xi)/\hat{a}(\psi)), & \text{if } \xi > \eta \\ \exp(-\xi/\hat{a}(\psi)) - 1\ , & \text{if } \xi < \eta \end{cases}$$

and the functions w_j and v_j by

(69b) $$w_o := (U_o-\lambda)^{-1}f, \quad w_j := -(U_o-\lambda)^{-1}Lw_{j-1} \quad \text{for } j \geq 1$$

$$\tilde{v}_o := 0,$$

(69c) $$\tilde{v}_j(\xi,\psi) := \int_0^\infty k(\xi,\eta,\psi)\Big(\lambda v_{j-1}(\eta,\psi) - \sum_{\ell=0}^{j-1} \rho_{j-\ell}v_\ell(\eta,\psi)\Big)d\eta,$$

(69d) $$v_j(\xi,\psi) := \tilde{v}_j(\xi,\psi) - w_j(\cos\psi,\sin\psi)\exp(-\xi/\hat{a}(\psi)).$$

By analogy to theorem 2.7 we find from lemma 4.11 and the formulae (66) and (69):

<u>THEOREM 4.12</u>. *Positive constants* C *and* ε_o *exist, such that*

(70) $$\Big|(U_\varepsilon-\lambda)^{-1}f - \sum_{j=0}^{n-1} \varepsilon^j(w_j + z_{1/3}s_\varepsilon^{-1}v_j)\Big|_{o,p} \leq C\varepsilon^n \|f\|_{2n+4,p}$$

for all $p \in [1,\infty]$, $\lambda \in \mathbb{C}$ *with* $Re\lambda > (\mu+1)/p$ *and* $\varepsilon \in (0,\varepsilon_o]$. C *and* ε_o *depend on* λ,μ,p,n *and the coefficients of* L, *but not on* f *and* ε.

PROOF. By definition we have

$$\sum_{j=0}^{n-1} \varepsilon^j (w_j + z_{1/3} s_\varepsilon^{-1} v_j) + \varepsilon^n z_{1/3} s_\varepsilon^{-1} \tilde{v}_n \in \mathcal{D}(U_\varepsilon)$$

and when we apply $U_\varepsilon - \lambda$ to it we find as result f plus a remainder of the same order as (70) is; since $|\varepsilon^n \tilde{v}_n|_{o,p}$ is also of this order, the validity of (70) follows from lemma 4.11. □

REMARKS. 1. If $f \in C^{2n+4}(\Omega)$ we obtain in (70) an estimate in the maximum norm, provided $Re\lambda > 0$.

2. An asymptotic expansion of the solution of problem (1-) with inhomogeneous boundary conditions is easily obtained from (70) by adding $g(\psi)\exp(-\xi/\hat{a}(\psi))$ to v_o in (69d) and adding $O(\varepsilon^n \| g \|_{2n+4,p,\partial\Omega})$ to the order estimate.

3. The L^p-norm of the boundary layer part in the expansion of $(U_\varepsilon-\lambda)^{-1}f$ tends to zero iff $p < \infty$; hence we conclude that $(U_\varepsilon-\lambda)^{-1}$ converges strongly to $(U_o-\lambda)^{-1}$ in L^p-norm with $p < \infty$ but not in the L^∞-norm and the maximum norm.

4. The constants C and ε_o in theorem 4.12 can be chosen independently of λ for all λ within a fixed compact subset of $\rho(U_o)$; this follows from the fact that the estimate (64) depends continuously on λ.

4.5. A PROOF OF CONVERGENCE FOR ALL $\lambda \in \mathbb{C}\backslash\Lambda^*$ BY A CUT-OFF METHOD

In order to enlarge the part of the λ-plane in which convergence of $(U_\varepsilon-\lambda)^{-1}f$ can be proved at least for a restricted class of functions from which f can be chosen, we re-employ the cut-off method, used in §3.6 and §4.3, and formula (31), which gives a bound for $\| (\tilde{U}_\varepsilon-\lambda)^{-1} \|$ independent of ε. The result obtained is dual to the result of §4.3: we shall prove convergence of $(U_\varepsilon-\lambda)^{-1}f$ on all of Ω, provided the support of f does not contain a neighbourhood of the origin and $\lambda \notin \Lambda^*$.

In $L^p(F_\gamma)$ and $C^o(F_\gamma)$ we define the restriction N_ε of U_ε for $\varepsilon \geq 0$ by

(71) $$N_\varepsilon u := U_\varepsilon u \quad \text{for all } u \in \mathcal{D}(N_\varepsilon),$$

$$\mathcal{D}(N_\varepsilon) := \{ v \in \mathcal{D}(U_\varepsilon) \cap L^1(F_\gamma) \mid v_{|\partial E_\gamma} = 0\} ;$$

it satisfies:

LEMMA 4.13. *A constant* $K_1 \in \mathbb{R}^+$, *depending only on the coefficients of* L, *exists such that*

$$(72) \qquad |t^{-s}(N_\varepsilon u-\lambda u)|_{o,p,F_\gamma} \geq \left(Re\lambda+s-(\mu+1)/p-\varepsilon K_1(1+s/\gamma)^2\right)|t^{-s}u|_{o,p,F_\gamma}$$

for all $u \in \mathcal{D}(N_\varepsilon)$, $\varepsilon \in [0,1]$, $\gamma \in (0,1]$, $s \geq 0$, $\lambda \in \mathbb{C}$ *and* $p \in [1,\infty]$. *Moreover, if the right-hand side of* (72) *is positive,* $N_\varepsilon - \lambda$ *has a bounded inverse in* $L^p(F_\gamma)$.

The proof is identical to the proof of lemma 4.9. □

If $f \in C^o(\Omega)$ (or $f \in L^p(\Omega)$) and if the support of f is contained in F_γ, then by lemma 4.13

$$(U_o-\lambda)^{-1}f = (N_o-\lambda)^{-1}f = -\int_0^1 f(xs,ys^\mu)s^{\lambda-1}ds$$

is well-defined and is an element of $C^o(\Omega)$ (or $L^p(\Omega)$) for all $\lambda \in \mathbb{C}$; moreover, its support is contained in F_γ too. This implies that the asymptotic approximation of $(U_\varepsilon-\lambda)^{-1}f$, given in (70) and defined for $Re\lambda > 0$, can be continued analytically to the entire complex plane in this case; by lemma 4.13 it is an asymptotic approximation of $(N_\varepsilon-\lambda)^{-1}f$ of the same order as (70) is, i.e.

$$(73) \qquad \left|(N_\varepsilon-\lambda)^{-1}f - \sum_{j=0}^{n-1} \varepsilon^j(w_j+z_{1/3}s_\varepsilon^{-1}v_j)_{o,p,F_\gamma}\right| = \mathcal{O}(\varepsilon^n\|f\|_{2n+4,p}),$$

for all $\lambda \in \mathbb{C}$, $\gamma \in (0,1/3)$ and f with $supp(f) \cap E_\gamma = \emptyset$.

In order to show that $(N_\varepsilon-\lambda)^{-1}f$ approximates $(U_\varepsilon-\lambda)^{-1}f$ for all $\lambda \in \mathbb{C}\backslash\Lambda^*$, we assume until further notice that $supp(f) \cap E_\beta = \emptyset$ with $\beta > \gamma$ and we define

$$u_\varepsilon := (U_\varepsilon-\lambda)^{-1}f ,$$
$$\tilde{u}_\varepsilon := u_\varepsilon \exp((\gamma^2-x^2-\mu y^2)/4\varepsilon),$$
$$\tilde{f}_\varepsilon := f \exp((\gamma^2-x^2-\mu y^2)/4\varepsilon) ,$$

then

$$\tilde{u}_\varepsilon = (\tilde{U}-\lambda)^{-1}\tilde{f}_\varepsilon$$

and by (31) we infer

$$\| \tilde{u}_\varepsilon \| = O(\| \tilde{f}_\varepsilon \|) \qquad (\varepsilon \to +0)$$

uniformly with respect to f, provided $\lambda \notin \Lambda^*$. By an argument, similar to that of (54-57), we find

$$[\tilde{u}_\varepsilon] = O(\varepsilon^{-1} \| \tilde{f}_\varepsilon \|) = O(\varepsilon^{-1}[f] \exp((\gamma^2-\beta^2)/4\varepsilon))$$

and hence

(74a) $$|u_\varepsilon(x,y)| \le C\varepsilon^{-1}[f] \exp((x^2+\mu y^2-\beta^2)/4\varepsilon) \ ,$$

where C is a constant, depending on L,μ and λ, but not on β,γ,ε and f; explicitly the λ-dependence of C is

(74b) $$C = O(1/\mathrm{dist}(\lambda,\sigma(U_\varepsilon)))$$

uniformly for all $\lambda \in \mathbb{C}$. In particular we find from (74a)

(74c) $$[u_\varepsilon]_{\partial E_\gamma} \le \varepsilon^{-1}C[f] \exp((\gamma^2-\beta^2)/4\varepsilon).$$

We continue the restriction of u_ε to ∂E_γ into F_γ by defining

$$\hat{u}_\varepsilon := (1-z_\gamma)u_\varepsilon(\gamma\cos\psi,\gamma^\mu\sin\psi);$$

this function is bounded by (74c) and its first and second derivatives are bounded by the first and second tangential derivatives of u_ε along ∂E_γ, which in its turn are bounded by $[\nabla u_\varepsilon]_{E_\gamma}$ and $[\Delta u_\varepsilon]_{E_\gamma}$. Since as a consequence of the mean value theorem we have the inequality

$$[\nabla u]_{E_\gamma} \le \nu[\Delta u]_{E_\gamma} + 4\nu^{-1}[u]_{E_\gamma} \qquad \text{for all } u \in C^2(E_\gamma)$$

we find from the differential equation $U_\varepsilon u_\varepsilon = \lambda u_\varepsilon$ on E_γ a constant C_1 such that

$$[\Delta u_\varepsilon]_{E_\gamma} \le C_1\varepsilon^{-2}[u_\varepsilon]_{E_\gamma} \ .$$

Since $u_\varepsilon - \hat{u}_\varepsilon \in \mathcal{D}(N_\varepsilon)$ this implies the estimate

$$(75)\qquad \left[(N_\varepsilon-\lambda)(u_\varepsilon-\hat{u}_\varepsilon) - f\right]_{F_\gamma} = \mathcal{O}(\varepsilon^{-2}[f]\exp((\gamma^2-\beta^2)/4\varepsilon)) .$$

From lemma 4.13, the formulae (73-75) and the equivalence of the norms $u \mapsto [u]_{F_\gamma}$ and $u \mapsto [t^{-s}u]_{F_\gamma}$ we conclude:

<u>THEOREM 4.14</u>. *Positive constants* C *and* ε_o *exist such that*

$$(76)\qquad \left[(U_\varepsilon-\lambda)^{-1}f - \sum_{j=0}^{n-1} \varepsilon^j(w_j+z_{1/3}s_\varepsilon^{-1}v_j)\right] \le C\varepsilon^n([f]+[\Delta^{n+2}f])$$

for all $f \in C^{2n+4}(\Omega)$ *with* $\mathrm{supp}(f) \cap E_\gamma = \emptyset$, $\gamma \in (0,1]$, $\lambda \in \mathbb{C}\setminus\Lambda^*$, $n \in \mathbb{N}$ *and* $\varepsilon \in (0,\varepsilon_o]$. C *and* ε_o *depend on* γ,λ,μ,n *and the coefficients of* L, *but not on* f *and* ε.

<u>REMARK</u>. 1. The constants C and ε can be chosen independently of λ for all λ within a fixed compact subset K of $\mathbb{C}\setminus\Lambda^*$; this applies even if K depends on ε in such a way that $K(\varepsilon)$ is contained in a circle with fixed radius and if the distance between $K(\varepsilon)$ and $\sigma(U_\varepsilon)$ is larger than some positive power of ε. This follows from the fact that the distance between λ and $\sigma(U_\varepsilon)$ enters the estimate (76) only through formula (74c) and that the order terms in (73) and (75) depend continuously on λ by lemma 4.13; since the right-hand side of (74c) decreases faster than any power of ε, multiplication by a negative power of ε does not destroy convergence.

2. An asymptotic expansion of the solution of problem (1-) is obtained in the same manner as in remark 2 of the previous section.

4.6. CONVERGENCE IN $\ddot{H}^{2n}(\Omega)$

The restriction on the support of the right-hand side f of the differential equation (1-) can be removed, when we strengthen the smoothness conditions on f, as we did in §3.7. Therefore we define in $\ddot{H}^{2n}(\Omega)$ the auxiliary operator $U_{\varepsilon,n}$, which is a restriction of $\varepsilon L - x\partial_x - \mu y\partial_y$ by a boundary condition on the highest possible derivative.

Let M be a uniformly elliptic differential operator on Ω of second order, which is such that the coefficients of the principal part of

$$M(x\partial_x+\mu y\partial_y) - (x\partial_x+\mu y\partial_y+2\mu)M$$

are non-negative C^∞-functions which are zero in a neighbourhood of the boundary. The following construction yields such an operator. Choose a function $\beta \in C_o^\infty(\Omega)$ satisfying

$$0 \le \beta(x,y) \le 2 - 2\mu, \qquad \text{if } (x,y) \in \Omega$$

$$\beta(x,y) = 2 - 2\mu, \qquad \text{if } x^2 + y^2 \le \tfrac{1}{2}$$

and define α by, cf. (65),

$$\alpha(x,y) := 1 + \int_0^1 (2-2\mu-\beta(xs,ys^\mu))s^{2\mu-3}ds;$$

since the integrand is non-negative and zero in a neighbourhood of $s = 0$, α is C^∞ and $\alpha \ge 1$. This implies that the operator

(77a) $$M := \partial_y^2 + \partial_x \alpha \partial_x$$

is uniformly elliptic on Ω and satisfies the relation

(77b) $$M(x\partial_x+\mu y\partial_y) - (x\partial_x+\mu y\partial_y+2\mu)M = (2-2\mu)\partial_x\beta\partial_x.$$

By analogy to (3.69) we define in $H^{2n}(\Omega)$ the operators $U_{\varepsilon,n}$ and $U_{o,n}$ for all $n \in \mathbb{N}$ by

(78a) $$U_{\varepsilon,n}u := \varepsilon Lu - x\partial_x u - \mu y\partial_y u$$

$$\text{for all } u \in \mathcal{D}(U_{\varepsilon,n}) := \{v \in H^{2n+2}(\Omega) \mid (x\partial_x+\mu y\partial_y)M^n v|_{\partial\Omega} = 0\},$$

(78b) $$U_{o,n}u := -x\partial_x - \mu y\partial_y u \quad (= U_o u)$$

$$\text{for all } u \in \mathcal{D}(U_{o,n}) := \{v \in H^{2n}(\Omega) \mid U_o v \in H^{2n}(\Omega)\}.$$

LEMMA 4.15. *The spectrum of* $U_{o,n}$ *is the set*

(79) $$\sigma(U_{o,n}) := \{\lambda \in \mathbb{C} \mid Re\lambda \le \tfrac{1}{2} + \tfrac{1}{2}\mu - 2n\mu\} \cup \Lambda^*$$

and a constant $C_{2n} > 0$ *exists such that* $U_{o,n}$ *satisfies the estimate*

(80) $$\| U_{o,n}u-\lambda u\|_{2n} \geq C_{2n}\nu\| u \|_{2n}\,\mathrm{dist}(\lambda,\Lambda^{*}\cup\{\lambda\in\mathbb{C}\,|\,Re\lambda>-2n\mu+\mu\nu+\tfrac{1}{2}\mu+\tfrac{1}{2}\})$$

for all $n \in \mathbb{N}$, $u \in \mathcal{D}(U_{o,n})$, $\lambda \in \mathbb{C}$ *and* $\nu \in (0,2n]$.

PROOF. Instead of the usual inner product, we use in $H^{2n}(\Omega)$ the equivalent inner product $\left\langle\cdot,\cdot\right\rangle_{2n}^{(\nu)}$, cf. lemma 1.12. It admits the orthogonal decomposition (1.30) of $H^{2n}(\Omega)$, which is invariant under the action of U_o.

If $u \in \mathcal{D}(U_{o,n})$ and $v := \partial_x^{2n-j}\partial_y^j u$, we find integrating by parts

(81a) $$\| \partial_x^{2n-j}\partial_y^j(U_{o,n}u-\lambda u)\| \geq \left|Re\left\langle(U_o-\lambda-\mu j-2n+j)v,v\right\rangle\right|/\|v\| =$$

$$= (Re\lambda+2n+\mu j-j-\tfrac{1}{2}\mu-\tfrac{1}{2})\| \partial_x^{2n-j}\partial_y^j u\| +$$

$$+ \int_{\partial\Omega} (x^2+\mu y^2)|\partial_x^{2n-j}\partial_y^j u|^2 d\phi/\| \partial_x^{2n-j}\partial_y^j u\| .$$

If $u = Z_{2n}u$, cf. (1.30), we find

(81b) $$\| r^{\nu-2n}(U_{o,n}u-\lambda u)\|\,\| r^{\nu-2n}u\| =$$

$$= \| (U_o-\lambda-2\mu n+\mu\nu)r^{\nu-2n}u + (1-\mu)(\nu-2n)x^2r^{\nu-2n-2}u\|\,\| r^{\nu-2n}u\| \geq$$

$$\geq \left|Re\left\langle(U_o-\lambda-2\mu n+\mu\nu)r^{\nu-2n}u + (1-\mu)(\nu-2n)x^2r^{\nu-2n-2}u,r^{\nu-2n}u\right\rangle\right| =$$

$$= (Re\lambda+2n\mu-\mu\nu-\tfrac{1}{2}\mu-\tfrac{1}{2})\| r^{\nu-2n}u\|^2 + (1-\mu)(2n-\nu)\| xr^{\nu-2n-1}u\|^2 +$$

$$+ \int_{\partial\Omega} (x^2+\mu y^2)u\bar{u}d\phi.$$

If $u = x^ky^m$ is a monomial of degree less than $2n - 1$, we find

(81c) $$\left|(U_{o,n}-\lambda)x^ky^m\right|_{2n}^{(\nu)} = \left|(\lambda+k+\mu m)x^ky^m\right|_{2n}^{(\nu)} .$$

The orthogonal decomposition (1.30) of $H^{2n}(\Omega)$ and the formulae (81a-b-c) imply the estimate

(81d) $$\left|U_{o,n}u-\lambda u\right|_{2n}^{(\nu)} \geq \left|u\right|_{2n}^{(\nu)}\mathrm{dist}(\lambda,\Lambda^{*}\cup\{\lambda\in\mathbb{C}\,|\,Re\lambda>-2n\mu+\mu\nu+\tfrac{1}{2}+\tfrac{1}{2}\mu\}) +$$

$$+ \left\{\sum_{j=0}^{2n} (Re\lambda+2n+\mu j-j-\tfrac{1}{2}\mu-\tfrac{1}{2})\| \partial_x^{2n-j}\partial_y^j\|_{\partial\Omega}^2\right\}^{\frac{1}{2}} ,$$

provided $0 < \nu \leq 2n$. Lemma 1.12, concerning the equivalence of the norms $|\cdot|_{2n}^{(\nu)}$ and $\|\cdot\|_{2n}$, and inequality (81d) imply (80).

Since $U_{o,n}$ is a restriction of U_o, lemma 4.11 implies that a solution of the equation $U_{o,n}u - u = f$ exists for each $f \in H^{2n}(\Omega)$; formula (80) implies that this solution is unique and hence that $U_{o,n} - 1$ has a bounded inverse. By analytic continuation it follows from (80) that $U_{o,n} - \lambda$ is invertible for all λ for which the right-hand side of (80) is non-zero for some $\nu > 0$, hence the complement of the set given in (79) is contained in the resolvent set of $U_{o,n}$. For other values of λ the operator $U_{o,n} - \lambda$ is not invertible: the equation $U_o u = \lambda u$ has in $H^{2n}(\Omega)$ the non-trivial solutions

$$u = t^{\alpha}y^{\alpha+2n}, \qquad \text{if } \lambda = -\alpha - \alpha\mu - 2n\mu \qquad \text{with } Re\alpha > -\tfrac{1}{2}$$

$$u = x^j y^k, \qquad \text{if } \lambda = -j - \mu k \qquad \text{with } j,k \in \mathbb{N};$$

this proves formula (79). □

LEMMA 4.16. *Positive constants* $\eta_1,\ldots,\eta_4$ *exist, such that* $U_{\varepsilon,n}$ *satisfies the estimate*

$$\text{(82)} \qquad \|U_{\varepsilon,n}u-\lambda u\|_n \geq \|u\|_n \{\eta_1 \nu \text{dist}(\lambda,\Lambda^* \cup \{\alpha \mid Re\alpha > -2n\mu+\mu\nu+\tfrac{1}{2}\mu+\tfrac{1}{2}\}) - \varepsilon^{\frac{1}{2}} n^{\frac{1}{2}} \eta_2\}$$

for all $u \in \mathcal{D}(U_{\varepsilon,n})$, $n \in \mathbb{N}$, $\nu \in (0,n]$ *and* $\lambda \in \mathbb{C}$, *provided* $Re\lambda > -2n\mu + \eta_3$ *and* $Im\lambda < \varepsilon^{-\frac{1}{2}}\eta_4$. *If, moreover, the right-hand side of* (82) *is positive, then* $U_{\varepsilon,n} - \lambda$ *is invertible.*

PROOF. We consider in $H^{2n}(\Omega)$ the (equivalent) inner product

$$u,v \longmapsto \langle M^n u, M^n v\rangle + \langle u,v\rangle ,$$

cf. (1.41). With respect to this inner product we have for any $u \in \mathcal{D}(U_{\varepsilon,n})$

$$\text{(83)} \qquad 2\|M^n(U_{\varepsilon,n}-\lambda)u\|^2 + 2\|U_{\varepsilon,n}u-\lambda u\|^2 \geq \|U_{o,n}u-\lambda u\|^2 - 2\|\varepsilon Lu\|^2 +$$

$$+ \|M^n(U_{o,n}-\lambda)u\|^2 + \|\varepsilon L_p M^n u\|^2 - 2\|\varepsilon(L_p M^n - M^n L)u\|^2 +$$

$$- 2\varepsilon Re \langle M^n(x\partial_x+\mu y\partial_y+\lambda)u,\ L_p M^n u\rangle ;$$

for this formula we find an estimate from below as follows. From (81d) and the equivalence of the norms $u \mapsto |u|_{2n}^{(\nu)}$ and $u \mapsto \| M^n u\| + \|u\|$ we find a constant $C_1 > 0$ such that

$$\text{(84)} \qquad \| M^n(U_{o,n}u-\lambda u)\|^2 + \| (U_{o,n}u-\lambda u)\|^2 \geq$$

$$\geq C_1\nu^2\Big\{(\| M^n u\|^2 + \|u\|^2)\mathrm{dist}(\lambda,\Lambda^* \cup\{\alpha\in\mathbb{C}|Re\alpha>-2n\mu+\mu\nu+\tfrac12+\tfrac12\mu\})^2 +$$

$$+ \sum_{j=0}^{n} (Re\lambda+2n+\mu j-j-\tfrac12\mu-\tfrac12)\| \partial_x^{2n-j}\partial_y^j u\|^2_{\partial\Omega}\Big\} .$$

Since the operator $L_pM^n - M^nL$ is at most of order $2n + 1$, we can find a constant C_2 such that

$$\text{(85)} \qquad 2\| Lu\|^2 + 2\| (L_pM^n-M^nL)u\|^2 \leq \| L_pM^n u\|^2 + C_2(\| M^n u\|^2 + \|u\|^2).$$

In order to estimate the inner product in (83) we introduce in $H^2(\Omega)$ the sesquilinear forms $\mathcal{A}$, cf. (1.33), and $\mathcal{B}$,

$$\text{(86)} \qquad \mathcal{A}(u,v) := \iint_\Omega A(\nabla u,\nabla v)dxdy, \quad \mathcal{B}(u,v) := \iint_\Omega B(\nabla u,\nabla v)dxdy,$$

where A and B are sesquilinear forms in $\mathbb{C}^2$, defined by (36) and by

$$B(\alpha,\beta) := (\mu a-a+x\partial_x a+\mu y\partial_y a)\alpha_1\overline{\beta}_1 + (x\partial_x b+\mu y\partial_y b)(\alpha_1\overline{\beta}_2+\alpha_2\overline{\beta}_1) +$$

$$+ (c-\mu c+x\partial_x c+\mu y\partial_y c)\alpha_2\overline{\beta}_2 .$$

Since L_p is a uniformly elliptic operator, positive constants ξ_j exist such that

$$\text{(87)} \qquad \mathcal{A}(v,v) \geq \xi_1|v|_1^2 \quad\text{and}\quad |\mathcal{B}(v,v)| \leq \xi_2\mathcal{A}(v,v) + \xi_3\|v\|^2$$

for all $v \in H^1(\Omega)$. If $w \in H^2(\Omega)$ and satisfies the boundary condition

$$\text{(88a)} \qquad (x\partial_x w+\mu y\partial_y w)\big|_{\partial\Omega} = 0,$$

we find from (1.35a)

$$\text{(88b)} \qquad \left\langle L_p w,v\right\rangle + \mathcal{A}(w,v) = \int_0^{2\pi} h(\phi)\overline{v}(\cos\phi,\sin\phi)\partial_\phi w(\cos\phi,\sin\phi)d\phi .$$

Integrating by parts we find in the same way

(89a) $$2Re\left\langle x\partial_x v+\mu y\partial_y v, L_p v\right\rangle - \mathcal{B}(v,v) =$$

$$= \int_0^{2\pi} \{(a+c/\mu)|x\partial_x v+\mu y\partial_y v|^2-(x^2c-2\mu xyb+\mu^2y^2a)(|\partial_y v|^2+|\partial_x v|^2/\mu)\}|_{r=1}\, d\phi$$

for all $v \in H^2(\Omega)$; if in particular v satisfies the boundary condition (88a), the right-hand side of (89a) is non-positive due to the uniform ellipticity of L and we find a positive constant ξ_4 such that

(89b) $$- 2Re\left\langle x\partial_x v+\mu y\partial_y v, L_p v\right\rangle + \mathcal{B}(v,v) =$$

$$= \mu^{-1}\int_0^{2\pi} \{(x^2+\mu y^2)^{-1}(a\mu^2y^2-2b\mu xy+cx^2)|\partial_\phi v|^2\}|_{r=1}\, d\phi \geq \xi_4|v|^2_{1,\partial\Omega}.$$

Using formula (77b) we reduce the inner product term in the right-hand side of (83) to

(90) $$- 2\varepsilon Re\left\langle M^n(x\partial_x+\mu y\partial_y+\lambda)u, L_p M^n u\right\rangle =$$

$$= - 2\varepsilon Re\left\langle (x\partial_x+\mu y\partial_y+2n\mu+\lambda)M^n u, L_p M^n u\right\rangle - 2\varepsilon Re\left\langle Ru, L_p M^n u\right\rangle ,$$

where R is the operator of order 2n, cf. (77b),

$$R := (2-2\mu)\sum_{j=0}^{n-1} M^j\partial_x\beta\partial_x M^{n-j-1} =$$

$$= 2n(1-\mu)\beta\partial_x^2 M^{n-1} + \text{derivatives of order less than } 2n.$$

Since the coefficients of all terms of R are zero in a neighbourhood of the boundary, we find integrating by parts repeatedly

(91a) $$- Re\left\langle Ru, L_p M^n u\right\rangle = 2n(1-\mu)\iint_\Omega \alpha\beta A(\nabla\partial_x^2 M^{n-1}u, \nabla\partial_x^2 M^{n-1}u)dxdy +$$

$$+ 2n(1-\mu)\iint_\Omega \beta A(\nabla\partial_x\partial_y M^{n-1}u, \nabla\partial_x\partial_y M^{n-1}u)dxdy +$$

$$+ 2n(1-\mu)\iint_\Omega \sum_{i,j=1}^{2n} \gamma_{ij}|\partial_x^i\partial_y^j u|^2\, dxdy ,$$

where the coefficients γ_{ij} are derivatives of products of α and $\alpha\beta$ with a, b and c. The positivity of α and β implies the existence of a positive constant ξ_5 such that

$$\text{(91b)} \qquad - Re \left\langle Ru, L_p M^n u \right\rangle \geq - 2n(1-\mu)\xi_5 (\| M^n u\|^2 + \|u\|^2) .$$

Using the formulae (1.35a), (87), (88b), (89b) and (91b) we can estimate the right-hand side of (90) as follows:

$$\text{(92)} \qquad - 2\varepsilon Re \left\langle M^n(x\partial_x+\mu y\partial_y+\lambda)u, L_p M^n u \right\rangle =$$

$$= \varepsilon\mathcal{B}(M^n u, M^n u) + \varepsilon \int_0^{2\pi} \{(x^2+\mu y^2)^{-1}(a\mu y^2-2bxy+cx^2/\mu)|\partial_\phi M^n u|^2\}_{|r=1} d\phi +$$

$$+ \varepsilon(\lambda+\bar{\lambda}+4n\mu)\mathcal{A}(M^n u, M^n u) + 2\varepsilon Re \int_0^{2\pi} h(\phi)\{(\lambda+2n\mu)(M^n u)(\partial_\phi \overline{M^n u})\}_{|r=1} d\phi +$$

$$- 2\varepsilon Re \left\langle Ru, L_p M^n u \right\rangle \geq$$

$$\geq \varepsilon(\lambda+\bar{\lambda}+4n\mu-\xi_2)\mathcal{A}(M^n u, M^n u) - \varepsilon(\xi_5(n-n\mu)+\xi_3)(\| M^n u\|^2 + \|u\|^2) +$$

$$+ \varepsilon\xi_4 |M^n u|^2_{1,\partial\Omega} - \varepsilon Im\lambda[h] |M^n u|_{1,\partial\Omega} \| M^n u\|_{\partial\Omega} +$$

$$- \varepsilon(Re\lambda+2n\mu)[h'] \| M^n u\|^2_{\partial\Omega} .$$

If $Re\lambda + 2n\mu - \tfrac{1}{2}\mu - \tfrac{1}{2} - \varepsilon[h'](Re\lambda+2n\mu) - \tfrac{1}{4}\varepsilon\xi_4^{-1}([h]Im\lambda)^2 \geq 0$, the boundary terms of (84) and (92) add up to a non-negative quantity and we find from the formulae (83), (84), (85) and (92) the estimate

$$\| M^n(U_{\varepsilon,n}u-\lambda u)\|^2 + \| U_{\varepsilon,n}u-\lambda u\|^2 \geq$$

$$\geq (\| M^n u\|^2 + \|u\|^2)\Big\{C_1\nu^2 \text{dist}(\lambda, \Lambda^* \cup \{\alpha\in\mathbb{C} | Re\alpha > -2n\mu+\mu\nu+\tfrac{1}{2}+\tfrac{1}{2}\mu\})^2 +$$

$$- \varepsilon^2 C_2 - \varepsilon(\xi_5(n-n\mu)+\xi_3)\Big\},$$

provided $Re\lambda > - 2n\mu + \xi_4$. This proves (82).

The invertibility of $U_{\varepsilon,n} - \lambda$ is now a simple consequence of estimate (82) and corollary (1.14). □

Using this lemma we can prove convergence of formal approximations of the solution of the auxiliary equation $U_{\varepsilon,n}u - \lambda u = f$ and show that we can derive from it convergence of the analytic continuation (in the λ-plane) of the approximation of $(U_\varepsilon-\lambda)^{-1}$, which is given in (70), provided f is smooth enough and $\lambda \notin \Lambda^*$. If $f \in H^n(\Omega)$ and $Re\lambda + n\mu > \frac{1}{2}\mu + \frac{1}{2}$, we find from lemma 4.15 the analytic continuation

$$(U_o-\lambda)^{-1}f = - \sum_{0\le i+\mu j<n\mu-\mu} \frac{x^i y^j}{i!\,j!} \frac{\partial_x^i \partial_y^j f(0,0)}{\lambda+i+\mu j} - \int_0^1 \tilde{f}(xs,ys^\mu)s^{\lambda-1}ds$$

with

$$\tilde{f}(x,y) := f(x,y) - \sum_{0\le i+\mu j<n\mu-\mu} \frac{x^i y^j}{i!\,j!} \partial_x^i \partial_y^j f(0,0).$$

Let z_γ be as defined in (52b) and $f \in H^{2n+2}(\Omega)$; we split f up in two parts,

$$f = f_\lambda + \tilde{f}_\lambda \quad \text{with} \quad f_\lambda := (U_o-\lambda)(1-z_{\frac{1}{4}})(U_o-\lambda)^{-1}f\ , \tag{93}$$

such that $\tilde{f}_\lambda$ is zero in a neighbourhood of (0,0) and $(U_o-\lambda)^{-1}f_\lambda$ is zero in a neighbourhood of the boundary and is contained in the domain of $U_{\varepsilon,n}$. Lemma 1.16 now implies

$$\| (U_{\varepsilon,n}-\lambda)^{-1}f_\lambda - (U_o-\lambda)^{-1}f_\lambda \|_{2n} = O(\varepsilon \| Lf_\lambda \|_{2n}) = O(\varepsilon \| f \|_{2n+2}) \tag{94a}$$

provided $\lambda \notin \Lambda^*$ and $Re\lambda + 2n\mu > \frac{1}{2} + \frac{1}{2}\mu + \eta_4$. The trace theorem (lemma 1.12) implies

$$\| (U_{\varepsilon,n}-\lambda)^{-1}f_\lambda \|_{2n-1,\partial\Omega} = O(\varepsilon \| f \|_{2n+2}).$$

Since $(U_{\varepsilon,n}-\lambda)^{-1}f_\lambda$ and $(U_{\varepsilon,o}-\lambda)^{-1}f_\lambda$ differ by a solution of the homogeneous equation $U_{\varepsilon,o}u = \lambda u$, we can estimate the difference between $(U_{\varepsilon,n}-\lambda)^{-1}f_\lambda$ and $(U_{\varepsilon,o}-\lambda)^{-1}f_\lambda$ with the aid of theorem 4.14 and we find

$$\left[(U_{\varepsilon,n}-\lambda)^{-1}f_\lambda - (U_{\varepsilon,o}-\lambda)^{-1}f_\lambda\right] = O(\varepsilon \| f \|_{2n+2}). \tag{94b}$$

Applying theorem 4.14 directly to the remainder $\tilde{f}_\lambda$ we find from the estimates (94):

<u>THEOREM 4.17</u>. *Positive constants* C *and* ε_0 *exist, such that*

$$\left[(U_\varepsilon-\lambda)^{-1}f - w_0 - z_{1/3}s_\varepsilon^{-1}v_0\right] \le C\varepsilon\| f \|_{2n+2} \tag{95}$$

for all $f \in H^{2n+2}(\Omega)$, $n \in \mathbb{N}$, $\varepsilon \in (0,\varepsilon_0]$ *and* $\lambda \in \mathbb{C}\backslash\Lambda^*$ *satisfying* $Re\lambda + 2n\mu > \frac{1}{2} + \frac{1}{2}\mu + \eta_4$. C *and* ε_0 *depend on* n,λ,μ *and the coefficients of* L *but not on* f *and* ε. *The functions* v_0 *and* w_0 *are (the analytic continuations of the functions) defined in* (69b *and* d).

<u>REMARK</u>. In the same way we can prove convergence of the analytic continuation of the higher order approximations given in theorem 4.12.

4.7. DISCUSSION OF THE RESULTS

In this chapter we have constructed (formal) approximations to the solutions of the Dirichlet-problems (1+) and (1-) for all $\lambda \in \mathbb{C}\backslash\Lambda$ and $\lambda \in \mathbb{C}\backslash\Lambda^*$ respectively, provided the right-hand side f is smooth enough, and we have proved convergence of these approximations for $\varepsilon \to +0$. This convergence is uniform in all of Ω for the formal approximation to the solution of (1-).

For a first order approximation of the solution of (1+) we obtain uniform convergence of order $\mathcal{O}(\varepsilon)$ if and only if $Re\lambda > 2$ (and by regularisation, cf. [12], we obtain uniform convergence of order $\mathcal{O}(\varepsilon^\nu)$ iff $Re\lambda > 2\nu$ and $\nu \in (0,1]$). If $-(1+\mu)/p < Re\lambda \le 0$ with $p \ge 1$, the difference $(T_\varepsilon-\lambda)^{-1}f$ + - $(T_0-\lambda)^{-1}f$ cannot converge to zero uniformly, since $(T_0-\lambda)^{-1}f$ is (in general) not continuous at the origin, however it converges still in L^p-sense; moreover, we can construct a uniformly convergent approximation, which contains an internal boundary layer in a neighbourhood of the origin, cf. [13] and [14]. If $Re\lambda$ is smaller than or equal to the first eigenvalue, i.e. if $Re\lambda \le -\mu - 1$, we can prove (uniform) convergence for approximations of (1+) only in an annular subdomain of Ω not containing a neighbourhood of the origin and we do not know how convergence of any formal approximation in a neighbourhood of (0,0) can be proved.

In the one-dimensional analogue we find that any formal approximation, which satisfies the differential equation (3.1+) and the boundary conditions up to the order $\mathcal{O}(\varepsilon)$, is a (valid) asymptotic approximation of the solution up to $\mathcal{O}(\varepsilon)$ with respect to the weighted norm

$$u \mapsto [|x|^{k+\frac{1}{2}}u]_{(-1,1)} ,$$

provided $Re\lambda > -k + 3/2$ and provided λ is not the limit of an eigenvalue. The analogous statement for problem (1+) in two dimensions would be that any formal approximation converges in the weighted norm

$$u \mapsto [r^s u], \quad s \in \mathbb{R}^+ ,$$

provided $Re\lambda > s\mu - \frac{1}{2}\mu + 3/2$ and $\lambda \notin \Lambda$. However, when we try to generalize the proof of theorem 3.15 and the lemma's, on which it depends, we encounter the fact that lemma 3.13 is essentially one-dimensional. The inequalities (3.43a and b) depend on the fact that every differential operator D in one dimension is "elliptic", such that all derivatives of lower order are D-bounded with arbitrarily small D-bound (cf. §1.1). In several dimensions this is not true: for $\mu = 1$ and $k = 2$ the analogue of (3.43b) would be

$$\text{(96)} \qquad \| r^2\Delta w\| \le t\| r^2(x\partial_x+y\partial_y)\Delta w\| + Ct^{-2}\|w\|$$

for all $t \in (0,1]$ and $w \in H^3(\Omega)$; with the choice $w = \chi(r)e^{im\phi}$, with $\chi \in C_o^\infty(0,1)$, χ nonnegative and $m \in \mathbb{N}$ we have for $m \to \infty$

$$\| r^2\Delta w\| = m^2\| r^2\chi\|_{(0,1)} + O(m) ,$$

$$\| r^3\partial_r\Delta w\| = m^2\| r^3\partial_r\chi\|_{(0,1)} + O(m) ,$$

$$\| w\| = O(1) ;$$

this contradicts (96).

The results of this chapter can easily be extended to the more general Dirichlet-problem on the bounded domain $\Omega \subset \mathbb{R}^n$

$$\varepsilon Lu + \sum_{j=1}^{n} p_j\partial_j u - \lambda u = f, \quad u_{|\partial\Omega} = g \qquad (\partial_j := \partial/\partial x_j) ,$$

where L is a second order uniformly elliptic operator on Ω, where $\sum p_j\partial_j$ is a first order operator with C^∞-coefficients and with exactly one critical point of nondegenerate nodal type, cf. §1.3, inside Ω and where Ω is an open bounded set in $\mathbb{R}^n$ whose boundary is a connected C^∞-manifold of dimension n-1 which is nowhere tangent to the characteristics of $\sum p_j\partial_j$. According to STERNBERG [28] we can linearize the equations for the characteristics of $\sum p_j \partial_j$, cf. §1.3, and then we can apply the entire machinery developed in this chapter.

CHAPTER V

PERTURBATION OF A FIRST ORDER OPERATOR OF VORTEX TYPE

In this chapter we study degeneration of an elliptic operator on the unit disk $\Omega \subset \mathbb{R}^2$ to a first order operator, which has a critical point of vortex type at $(x,y) = (0,0)$. In the domain Ω we consider the singularly perturbed boundary value problems

$$(1\pm) \qquad \varepsilon Lu \pm \big((x-\kappa y)\partial_x u + (y+\kappa x)\partial_y u\big) - \lambda u = f, \qquad u\big|_{\partial\Omega} = g,$$

where Ω, L, ε, λ, f and g are as in (4.1±) and $\kappa \in \mathbb{R}$; without loss of generality we can assume $\kappa > 0$. We shall use polar coördinates (r,ϕ) and rectangular coordinates $(x,y) = (r\cos\phi, r\sin\phi)$ collateral for the same point of Ω; e.g. we have

$$(2) \qquad (x-\kappa y)\partial_x + (y+\kappa x)\partial_y = r\partial_r + \kappa\partial_\phi .$$

The asymptotic behaviour of the solutions of the problems (1±) is the same as that of the problems (4.1±) of the previous chapter and their proofs can easily be adapted to this case. We shall therefore merely state the results and for a proof refer to the corresponding results in the nodal case. Only the proof of the convergence of the eigenvalues will be reconsidered in detail, since a part of it differs considerably from the proof theorem 4.5.

Let the operators T_ε, $\tilde{T}_\varepsilon$, R_ε, A and B and the functions ω_j be as defined in chapter 4 formulae (4.2-3-6) and (4.4) respectively with $\mu = 1$ and define in connection with (1+) the operator $T_{\varepsilon,\kappa}$ by

$$(3) \qquad T_{\varepsilon,\kappa} := T_\varepsilon + \kappa\partial_\phi, \qquad \mathcal{D}(T_{\varepsilon,\kappa}) := \mathcal{D}(T_\varepsilon).$$

Applying the transformation (4.3) to $T_{\varepsilon,\kappa}$ we find

$$(4) \qquad \tilde{T}_{\varepsilon,\kappa}u := \exp(r^2/4\varepsilon)T_{\varepsilon,\kappa}(u\exp(-r^2/4\varepsilon)) =$$

$$= \tilde{T}_\varepsilon u + \kappa\partial_\phi u = R_\varepsilon u + \kappa\partial_\phi u + Au + Bu.$$

We shall show that the spectrum of $T_{\varepsilon,\kappa}$ converges for $\varepsilon \to +0$ to the set Λ_κ,

(5) $$\Lambda_\kappa := \{- 2n - |m| + i\kappa m \mid n \in \mathbb{N},\ m \in \mathbb{Z}\}.$$

By separation of variables it is easy to show that the spectrum of the special operator $S_{\varepsilon,\kappa} := \varepsilon\Delta + \kappa\partial_\phi - \frac{1}{4}r^2/\varepsilon$ converges to Λ_κ. However, it is not possible to transfer this property directly to $R_\varepsilon + \kappa\partial_\phi$ by the continuity method of lemma 4.4. Since $R_\varepsilon + \kappa\partial_\phi$ is not normal (it cannot be made selfadjoint by a transformation of type (4.3) since its spectrum is non-real), we do not know how to estimate the norm of its resolvent by a function of the distance to the spectrum; consequently no criterion is available for the smallness of additional perturbations. Therefore we shall use a slightly different method.

We construct an alternative set of approximate eigenfunctions for R_ε, which is simultaneously a set of eigenfunctions for ∂_ϕ and we show that the commutant of R_ε and ∂_ϕ is R_ε-bounded and is small on the span of a finite number of such approximate eigenfunctions; this implies that the eigenvalues of R_ε and ∂_ϕ add up approximately, provided ε is small enough.

The approximate eigenfunctions $\chi_{n,m}$, defined in (4.11), are (for $\mu=1$) the eigenfunctions of the selfadjoint operator $\varepsilon\Delta - r^2/4\varepsilon$ on the domain $H^2(\mathbb{R}^2)$. Since the operator ∂_ϕ (with domain $H^1(\mathbb{R}^2)$) is normal and since it commutes with $\varepsilon\Delta - r^2/4\varepsilon$, a complete set of simultaneous eigenfunctions exists. Separation of variables in the equation $\varepsilon\Delta u - r^2u/4\varepsilon = \lambda u$ with respect to polar coordinates yields the normalized eigenfunctions

(6) $$\psi_{n,m}(r,\phi;\varepsilon) := h_{n,m} r^{|m|} e^{im\phi} \exp(r^2/4\varepsilon) F(n+|m|;1+|m|;-r^2/2\varepsilon)$$

of the operators $\varepsilon\Delta - r^2/4\varepsilon$ and ∂_ϕ at the eigenvalues $- 2n - |m|$ and im respectively, with $n \in \mathbb{N}$ and $m \in \mathbb{Z}$; $\psi_{n,m}$ is a (finite) linear combination of the functions $\chi_{k,j}$ with $k + j + 2 = 2n + |m|$. Clearly these functions are approximate eigenfunctions of $\tilde{T}_{\varepsilon,\kappa}$ at the approximate eigenvalues $- 2n - |m|$; they satisfy lemma 4.3 and the set

(7) $$\{P_{\varepsilon,j}\psi_{n,m} \mid 2n + |m| \le j,\ n \in \mathbb{N} \text{ and } m \in \mathbb{Z}\}$$

is a nearly orthogonal basis in $R(P_{\varepsilon,j})$ in the sense of (4.26), where $P_{\varepsilon,j}$ is the orthogonal projection on the joint eigenspace of R_ε, belonging to all eigenvalues of R_ε, contained in $D(0,j+\frac{1}{2})$, cf. (4.16).

In addition to lemmas 4.2 and 4.3 we show that ∂_ϕ is R_ε-bounded and that the commutant of R_ε and ∂_ϕ has an arbitrarily small R_ε-bound.

LEMMA 5.1. *Positive constants* ξ_j *exist such that all* $u \in \mathcal{D}(T_\varepsilon)$ *satisfy the estimates*

(8a) $$\| \partial_\phi u\| \le \xi_1 \| R_\varepsilon u\| + \xi_2 \| u \|$$

(8b) $$|\langle R_\varepsilon \partial_\phi u - \partial_\phi R_\varepsilon u, u\rangle| \le \xi_3 \| R_\varepsilon u\| \, \| u \| + \xi_4 \| u \|^2$$

and such that the approximate eigenfunctions satisfy

(8c) $$\| (R_\varepsilon \partial_\phi - \partial_\phi R_\varepsilon)\psi_{n,m}\| \le \xi_5 \varepsilon^{\frac{1}{2}}(n+|m|)^{3/2}$$

for all $n \in \mathbb{N}$, $m \in \mathbb{Z}$ *and* $\varepsilon \in (0,1]$.

PROOF. Integrating by parts once we find for any $u \in \mathcal{D}(T_\varepsilon)$

$$\| \partial_\phi u\|^2 \le 2\| x\partial_y u\|^2 + 2\| y\partial_x u\|^2 \le$$

$$\le 2|\langle x\partial_y^2 u, xu\rangle| + 2|\langle y\partial_x^2 u, yu\rangle|$$

$$\le 2\| r^2 u\| \, (\| \partial_x^2 u\| + \| \partial_y^2 u\|);$$

hence a constant C exists such that

$$\| \partial_\phi u\|^2 \le C(\| \varepsilon L_p u\|^2 + \| \omega_3 u/\varepsilon\|^2).$$

In conjunction with the two-dimensional analogue of inequality (3.11) this proves (8a). The commutant of R_ε and ∂_ϕ is the formally selfadjoint second order operator

(9a) $$R_\varepsilon \partial_\phi - \partial_\phi R_\varepsilon = {}^t\nabla M \nabla - \omega_5/\varepsilon, \qquad {}^t\nabla = (\partial_x, \partial_y),$$

where $\omega_5 := (x\partial_y - y\partial_x)\omega_3$ and where M is the matrix

(9b) $$M := \begin{pmatrix} y\partial_x a - x\partial_y a - 2b & a - c + y\partial_x b - x\partial_y b \\ a - c + y\partial_x b - x\partial_y b & y\partial_x c - x\partial_y c - 2b \end{pmatrix}.$$

Since $a(0,0) = c(0,0) = 1$ and $b(0,0) = 0$ we have

(9c) $$M = (0) + \mathcal{O}(r), \qquad r^2 = x^2 + y^2 \to 0$$

and from (4.4c) we infer

(9d) $$\omega_3 = \mathcal{O}(r^3), \qquad r \to 0.$$

Since $\psi_{n,m}$ is a finite linear combination of the functions $\chi_{k,j}$, cf. (4.11), estimate (8b) is a consequence of formula (3.16). The proof of (8a) is similar to the proofs of formulae (3.10a) and (4.10a). □

THEOREM 5.2. *The eigenvalues of the operator* $T_{\varepsilon,\kappa}$ *can be numbered in such a way that*

(10a) $$\sigma(T_{\varepsilon,\kappa}) = \{\pi_{n,m}(\varepsilon,\kappa) \mid n \in \mathbb{N},\ m \in \mathbb{Z}\}$$

and a constant $K > 0$, *not depending on* ε,κ,n *and* m, *exists such that*

(10b) $$|\pi_{n,m}(\varepsilon,\kappa) - 2n - |m| - i\kappa m| \le K\varepsilon^{\frac{1}{2}}(n+|m|)^{3/2}.$$

PROOF. First we shall deduce a lower bound for $\|(R_\varepsilon+\kappa\partial_\phi+A-\lambda)u\|$ from the known lower bound of $\|(R_\varepsilon-\lambda)u\|$ derived in lemma 4.4. Any $u \in \mathcal{D}(\tilde{T}_\varepsilon)$ satisfies

$$\langle R_\varepsilon u,\partial_\phi u\rangle + \langle \partial_\phi u,R_\varepsilon u\rangle = \langle \partial_\phi^* R_\varepsilon u + R_\varepsilon^* \partial_\phi u,u\rangle =$$
$$= \langle (R_\varepsilon\partial_\phi-\partial_\phi R_\varepsilon)u,u\rangle;$$

if $\lambda = \alpha + i\beta$ with $\alpha,\beta \in \mathbb{R}$, this implies

$$2\|(R_\varepsilon+A+\kappa\partial_\phi-\lambda)u\|^2 \ge \|(R_\varepsilon+\kappa\partial_\phi-\lambda)u\|^2 - 2\|Au\|^2 =$$
$$= \|R_\varepsilon u-\alpha u\|^2 + \|\kappa\partial_\phi u-i\beta u\|^2 + \langle \kappa(R_\varepsilon\partial_\phi-\partial_\phi R_\varepsilon)u,u\rangle - 2\|Au\|^2.$$

Using the method by which we derived (4.28b) from (4.25), we obtain from this inequality and from the lemmas 5.1 and 4.2-3-4 the estimate

$$(11)\qquad \|\tilde{T}_{\varepsilon,\kappa}u - \lambda u\|^2 = \|(R_\varepsilon + A + \kappa\partial_\phi + B - \lambda)u\|^2 \geq$$

$$\geq \tfrac{1}{4}\|R_\varepsilon u - \alpha u\|^2 + \tfrac{1}{2}\|\kappa\partial_\phi u - i\beta u\|^2 - \varepsilon^{\frac{1}{2}}C(1+\kappa^2)|\alpha|^3\|u\|^2$$

where C is a constant not depending on λ,κ and ε. We remark that the negative term in the right-hand side of (11) is of order $\mathcal{O}(\varepsilon^{\frac{1}{2}})$ only (and not of order $\mathcal{O}(\varepsilon)$ as it is in (28b)); this is due to the fact that (8c) is of order $\mathcal{O}(\varepsilon^{\frac{1}{2}})$. Estimate (11) considerably restricts the freedom of movement of the eigenvalues of $\tilde{T}_{\varepsilon,\kappa}$: since all eigenvalues of $\tilde{T}_{\varepsilon,\kappa}$ depend analytically on κ and since the eigenvalues of R_ε are contained in small disks around the points $-k-1$ with $k \in \mathbb{N}$, no eigenvalue of $\tilde{T}_{\varepsilon,\kappa}$ can cross a line $Re\lambda = -k-\frac{1}{2}$ if ε and $\varepsilon^{\frac{1}{4}}\kappa$ are small enough. Also the imaginary part of an eigenvalue cannot grow too fast: the spectrum is contained in the (semi-) cone

$$(12)\qquad K := \{\lambda \mid |Im\lambda| \leq -2\kappa\xi_1 Re\lambda + 2\kappa\xi_2\}.$$

In order to prove this we use the inequality

$$\|\kappa\partial_\phi u - i\beta u\|^2 \geq s(2-s)\|\beta u\|^2 - 2\kappa s\|\beta u\|\;\|\partial_\phi u\|,$$

valid for all $s \in (0,1]$; estimating its right-hand side from below, using (8a) and Young's inequality and inserting the result in (11) we obtain the inequality

$$(13)\qquad \|\tilde{T}_{\varepsilon,\kappa}u-\lambda u\|^2 \geq \{s(\beta^2-2s\beta^2\xi_1^2\kappa^2-2\kappa|\beta|(\xi_1|\alpha|+\xi_2))-\varepsilon^{\frac{1}{2}}C(1+\kappa^2|\alpha|^3)\}\|u\|^2;$$

the coefficient of $\|u\|^2$ in its right-hand side is bounded away from zero if λ is outside the cone K and s and ε are small enough. We conclude that the eigenvalues of $\tilde{T}_{\varepsilon,\kappa}$, contained in the strip $|Re\lambda+k+1| < \frac{1}{2}$ cannot escape a fixed bounded set in the limit for $\varepsilon \to +0$; their total multiplicity is constant and it is equal to k, since this is true for $\tilde{T}_{\varepsilon,0}$.

Let $Q_{\varepsilon,k}$ be the orthogonal projection on the joint eigenspace of R_ε belonging to all eigenvalues contained in the intersection

$$\{\lambda \mid -\tfrac{1}{2} < Re\lambda + k + 1 < \tfrac{1}{2}\} \cap K,$$

cf. (4.22a), and let $N_{\varepsilon,k}$ be the orthogonal projection onto the span of the (orthonormal) set

(14) $$\{\psi_{j,m} \mid 2j + |m| = k + 1,\ j \in \mathbb{N} \text{ and } m \in \mathbb{Z}\}.$$

From (4.19) we infer

$$\| Q_{\varepsilon,k}\psi_{j,m} - \psi_{j,m}\| = O(\varepsilon^{\frac{1}{2}}k^{3/2}),$$

where $2j + |m| = k + 1$, and hence, since the ranks of $Q_{\varepsilon,k}$ and $N_{\varepsilon,k}$ are equal, we have

$$\| (Q_{\varepsilon,k}-1)N_{\varepsilon,k}\| = O(\varepsilon^{\frac{1}{2}}k^{3/2});$$

this implies (by [19] ch. I theorem 6.34) the identities

(15) $$\| Q_{\varepsilon,k} - N_{\varepsilon,k}\| = \| (1-N_{\varepsilon,k})Q_{\varepsilon,k}\| = \| (1-Q_{\varepsilon,k})N_{\varepsilon,k}\| = O(\varepsilon^{\frac{1}{2}}k^{3/2}).$$

Since $\kappa\partial_\phi$ commutes with $N_{\varepsilon,k}$ and is normal and since the spectrum of its restriction to $R(N_{\varepsilon,k})$ is the set

$$s_k := \sigma\left(\kappa\partial_\phi\big|_{R(N_{\varepsilon,k})}\right) = \{i\kappa(k-2j+1) \mid j \in \mathbb{N},\ j \le k\},$$

we find from (15) a constant η_k such that

(16) $$\begin{aligned} \| \kappa\partial_\phi u - i\beta u\| &\ge \| N_{\varepsilon,k}(\kappa\partial_\phi u - i\beta u)\| \ge \\ &\ge \operatorname{dist}(i\beta,s_k)\| N_{\varepsilon,k}u\|^2 \ge \\ &\ge \operatorname{dist}(i\beta,s_k)(\| Q_{\varepsilon,k}u\| - \| Q_{\varepsilon,k}u - N_{\varepsilon,k}u\|) \ge \\ &\ge \operatorname{dist}(i\beta,s_k)(\|Q_{\varepsilon,k}u\| - \eta_k\varepsilon^{\frac{1}{2}}|\beta|\|u\|). \end{aligned}$$

If λ is in the strip $|Re\lambda + k + 1| < \frac{1}{2}$, lemma 4.4 yields the inequalities

$$\| (1-Q_{\varepsilon,k})(R_\varepsilon u-\alpha u)\| \ge \tfrac{1}{2}\| (1-Q_{\varepsilon,k})u\| , \qquad (\alpha := Re\lambda),$$

$$\| Q_{\varepsilon,k}(R_\varepsilon u-\alpha u)\| \ge (\alpha+k+1-\varepsilon^{\frac{1}{2}}k^{3/2}\hat{\eta}_k)\| Q_{\varepsilon,k}u\| ;$$

hence from formulae (11) and (16) we find a constant $\tilde{\eta}_k$ such that

$$\| \tilde{T}_{\varepsilon,\kappa}u-\lambda u\| \geq \left(\tfrac{1}{2}\,\mathrm{dist}(\lambda,\{k+1+i\kappa(k-2j+1)\,|\,j\in\mathbb{N},j\leq k\}-\tilde{\eta}_k\varepsilon^{\frac{1}{4}}k^{3/2}\right)\|u\|. \tag{17}$$

Moreover, if u is orthogonal to $\psi_{n,m}$ with $2n + |m| = k + 1$ and if λ is contained in the disk $D(k+1+im\kappa,\min(\frac{1}{2},\kappa))$, then the formulae (16) and (17) imply

$$\| \tilde{T}_{\varepsilon,\kappa}u-\lambda u\| \geq \tfrac{1}{2}\|u\|\left(\min(\tfrac{1}{2},|\kappa|) - C\varepsilon^{\frac{1}{4}}\right), \qquad C > 0; \tag{18}$$

hence $\tilde{T}_{\varepsilon,\kappa} - \lambda$ is invertible modulo $\psi_{n,m}$ for all λ in the disk. Formula (17) implies that the eigenvalues of $\tilde{T}_{\varepsilon,\kappa}$, which are contained in the strip $|Re\lambda + k + 1\,| < \frac{1}{2}$, are already contained in the union of disks of radius $\mathcal{O}(\varepsilon^{\frac{1}{4}})$ around the points $k + 1 + i\kappa(k-2j+1)$ with $j \in \mathbb{N}$ and $j \leq k$ and formula (18) implies that the rank of the eigenprojection

$$M_{\varepsilon,n,m} := \int_{\partial D(2n+|m|+i\kappa m,\rho)} (\tilde{T}_{\varepsilon,\kappa}-\lambda)^{-1}d\lambda$$

with $2n + |m| = k + 1$ and $0 < \rho < \min(\frac{1}{2},\kappa)$ is at most one. Since the total eigenprojection of the strip $|Re\lambda + k + 1| < \frac{1}{2}$ is of rank k, the rank of $M_{\varepsilon,n,m}$ is one and $D(2n+|m|+i\kappa m,C\varepsilon^{\frac{1}{4}})$ contains precisely one eigenvalue. From (17) we find $\| M_{\varepsilon,n,m}\| \leq 3$ and choosing $\rho = \mathcal{O}(\varepsilon^{\frac{1}{4}})$ we find from (18) a constant $K > 0$ such that

$$\| M_{\varepsilon,n,m}u\| \leq \varepsilon^{\frac{1}{4}}K\|u\|$$

for all u in the orthogonal complement of $\psi_{n,m}$; since $M_{\varepsilon,n,m}$ is a non-trivial projection of rank one this implies

$$\| M_{\varepsilon,n,m}\psi_{n,m}\| \geq \tfrac{1}{2}$$

for all sufficiently small ε. Since by lemma 4.3 a constant $C > 0$ exists, independent of κ and ε, such that

$$\| (\tilde{T}_{\varepsilon,\kappa}-2n-|m|-i\kappa m)\psi_{n,m}\| \leq \varepsilon^{\frac{1}{2}}C(n+|m|)^{3/2}$$

we find

$$(19)\qquad 3\varepsilon^{\frac{1}{2}}C(n+m)^{3/2} \ge \| M_{\varepsilon,n,m}(\tilde{T}_{\varepsilon,\kappa}-2n-|m|-i\kappa m)\psi_{n,m}\| \ge$$

$$\ge |\pi_{n,m}(\varepsilon,\kappa) - 2n - |m| - i\kappa m|\ \| M_{\varepsilon,n,m}\psi_{n,m}\| .$$

This proves the theorem. □

REMARK. The formulae (17) - (18) - (19) imply the analogue of formula (4.29):

$$(20)\qquad \| \tilde{T}_{\varepsilon,\kappa}u - \lambda u\| \ge \tfrac{1}{2}\|u\|\{\mathrm{dist}(\lambda,\Lambda_\kappa) - \varepsilon^{\frac{1}{2}}C|Re\lambda|^{3/2}\}$$

and an analogous one for the operator associated with problem (1-).

In the spaces $L^p(\Omega)$ and $C^o(\Omega)$ we define the family of operators $T_{\varepsilon,\kappa} := T_\varepsilon + \kappa\partial_\phi$ with $\varepsilon \in [0,1]$, $\kappa \in \mathbb{R}$ and T_ε as defined in (4.33). The characteristics of $T_{o,\kappa}$ are parametrized by

$$(x(t),y(t)) = (e^t\cos(\kappa t+\phi_o),\ e^t\sin(\kappa t+\phi_o)),\qquad t \in \mathbb{R},$$

and the solution of the reduced equation of (1+),

$$(x\partial_x+y\partial_y u+\kappa x\partial_y-\kappa y\partial_x)u = \lambda u + f,\qquad u|_{\partial\Omega} = 0,$$

is the function

$$(21)\qquad u(r\cos\phi,r\sin\phi;\lambda,\kappa) := -\int_r^1 f\left(t\cos(\phi+\kappa\log\tfrac{t}{r}),t\sin(\phi+\kappa\log\tfrac{t}{r})\right)\left(\tfrac{r}{t}\right)^\lambda \frac{dt}{t}.$$

By analogy to the theorems 4.8 and 4.10 we find

THEOREM 5.3. *The resolvent set of* $T_{o,\kappa}$ *is the set*

$$(22a)\qquad \rho(T_{o,\kappa}) := \begin{cases} \{\lambda \mid Re\lambda > -2/p\} & \text{if } \mathcal{D}(T_{o,\kappa}) \subset L^p(\Omega), \\ \{\lambda \mid Re\lambda > 0\} & \text{if } \mathcal{D}(T_{o,\kappa}) \subset C^o(\Omega). \end{cases}$$

The resolvent $(T_{\varepsilon,\kappa}-\lambda)^{-1}$ *converges strongly to* $(T_{o,\kappa}-\lambda)^{-1}$ *in* $L^p(\Omega)$ *or* $C^o(\Omega)$ *if* $\lambda \in \rho(T_{o,\kappa})$ *and it satisfies for* $\varepsilon \to +0$ *the asymptotic formulae*

$$(22b)\qquad \left|(T_{\varepsilon,\kappa}-\lambda)^{-1}f - (T_{o,\kappa}-\lambda)^{-1}f\right|_{o,p} = O(\varepsilon\|f\|_{2,p}).$$

provided $Re\lambda > 2 - 2/p$ *and*

$$\text{(22c)} \qquad \left[(T_{\varepsilon,\kappa}-\lambda)^{-1}f - u(\cdot,\cdot;\lambda,\kappa)\right]_{F_\gamma} = \mathcal{O}(\varepsilon[f]+\varepsilon[\Delta f])$$

provided $\lambda \notin \Lambda_\kappa$ *and* $\gamma > 0$.

In connection with problem (1-) we define the family of operators $U_{\varepsilon,\kappa} := U_\varepsilon + \kappa\partial_\phi$, where U_ε as defined in (4.63). If $\lambda \in \rho(U_{o,\kappa}) = \rho(T^*_{o,\kappa}+2/p)$, we find

$$\text{(23)} \qquad ((U_{o,\kappa}-\lambda)^{-1}f)(r\cos\phi,r\sin\phi) = - \int_0^1 f(rt\cos(\phi-\kappa\log t),rt\sin(\phi-\kappa\log t))t^{\lambda-1}dt;$$

if $f \in H^n(\Omega)$, we can continue $(U_{o,\kappa}-\lambda)^{-1}$ analytically up to the line $Re\lambda = - n - 1$. In order to construct the boundary layer terms at $\partial\Omega$ we introduce the substitution operator

$$(s_{\varepsilon,\kappa}u)(\xi,\psi) := u(\zeta\cos(\psi-\kappa\log\zeta),\zeta\sin(\psi-\kappa\log\zeta)) \text{ with } \zeta := 1 - \varepsilon\xi$$

and the formal expansion of order m

$$s_{\varepsilon,\kappa}(\varepsilon L-r\partial_r+\kappa\partial_\phi)s^{-1}_{\varepsilon,\kappa} = \sum_{j=0}^{m} \varepsilon^{j-1}\rho_j + \varepsilon^m\rho^\#_m;$$

in particular we find

$$\rho_o = \hat{a}(\psi)\partial^2_\xi - \partial_\xi,$$

where

$$\hat{a}(\psi) := \left((x+\kappa y)^2 a + 2\kappa(y^2-x^2)b + (y-\kappa x)^2 c\right)\Big|_{(x,y)=(\cos\psi,\sin\psi)}$$

By analogy to (69) we define

$$k(\xi,\eta,\psi) := \begin{cases} \exp(-\xi/\hat{a}(\psi)) - \exp((\eta-\xi)/\hat{a}(\psi)), & \text{if } \xi > \eta, \\ \exp(-\xi/\hat{a}(\psi)) - 1, & \text{if } \xi < \eta, \end{cases}$$

$$w_o := (U_{o,\kappa}-\lambda)^{-1}f ,$$

$$w_j := -(U_{o,\kappa}-\lambda)^{-1}\, Lw_{j-1} \qquad \text{for } j \geq 1,$$

$$\tilde{v}_o := 0,$$

$$\tilde{v}_j(\xi,\psi) := \int_0^\infty k(\xi,\eta,\psi)\Big(\lambda v_{j-1}(\eta,\psi) - \sum_{\ell=o}^{j-1} \rho_{j-\ell}v_\ell(\eta,\psi)\Big)d\eta,$$

$$v_j(\xi,\psi) := \tilde{v}_j(\xi,\psi) - w_j(\cos\psi,\sin\psi)\exp\big(-\xi/\hat{a}(\psi)\big).$$

Continuing these expressions analytically into the negative half-plane as far as possible we find by analogy to the theorems 4.12 and 4.17:

THEOREM 5.4. *Positive constants* C, ε_o *and* η *exist such that*

$$(24) \qquad \Big[(U_{\varepsilon,\kappa}-\lambda)^{-1}f - \sum_{j=0}^{k-1} \varepsilon^j(w_j+z_{1/3}s_{\varepsilon,\kappa}^{-1}v_j)\Big] \leq C\varepsilon^k\|f\|_{2k+2\ell+2},$$

for all $k,\ell \in \mathbb{N}$, $f \in H^{2k+2\ell+2}(\Omega)$ *and* $\varepsilon \in (0,\varepsilon_o]$, *provided*

$$\lambda \notin \{-2n-|m|+i\kappa m \mid n \in \mathbb{N}_o,\ m \in \mathbb{Z}\} \quad \text{and} \quad Re\lambda + 2\ell > 1 + \eta.$$

The constants C, ε_o *and* η *do not depend on* ε *and* f; η *does not depend on* ℓ *and* n.

CHAPTER VI

PERTURBATION OF A FIRST ORDER OPERATOR OF SADDLE-POINT TYPE

On the unit square $\Omega := \{(x,y) \mid |x| < 1, |y| < 1\}$ in $\mathbb{R}^2$ we consider the singular perturbation problem

$$(1) \qquad \varepsilon Lu + x\partial_x u - \mu y\partial_y u - \lambda u = f, \quad u_{|\partial\Omega} = g,$$

where L, ε, λ, f and g are as in (4.1±) and $\mu \in \mathbb{R}^+$. We shall investigate the behaviour of the solution of (1) for $\varepsilon \to +0$ and we shall show that the spectrum of the differential operator in $L^2(\Omega)$, connected with (1) converges to the set

$$(2) \qquad \Lambda := \{-k - \mu j - 1 \mid k, j \in \mathbb{N}_0\}.$$

We have chosen a domain Ω with a non-smooth boundary, such that the characteristics of the formal limit operator $x\partial_x - \mu y\partial_y$, the curves $|x|^\mu y$ = constant, are nowhere tangent to the boundary. By doing this we avoid in the construction of a first order formal approximation complications caused by tangency problems, cf. [11], [17] and [18].

We have already studied problem (1) in [13] and [14]; on that occasion we constructed a first order approximation to its solution and we proved its validity by the maximum principle, provided $Re\lambda$ is larger than the largest eigenvalue. Here we shall mainly state some results on local convergence of the solution of the general problem (1) for all $\lambda \in \mathbb{C}/\Lambda$; moreover, in the particular case $L = \Delta$ we shall obtain global results, by considering a related problem in a non-isotropic space.

1. CONVERGENCE OF THE SPECTRUM

In connection with the boundary value problem (1) we define the differential operator T_ε on $L^2(\Omega)$ by

$$(3) \qquad T_\varepsilon u := \varepsilon Lu + x\partial_x u - \mu y\partial_y u \qquad (\varepsilon>0)$$

$$\text{for all } u \in \mathcal{D}(T_\varepsilon) := \{v \in H^2(\Omega) \mid v_{|\partial\Omega} = 0\}.$$

The spectrum of T_ε satisfies:

THEOREM 6.1. *The eigenvalues of* T_ε *can be numbered in such a way that*

$$\sigma(T_\varepsilon) = \left\{\lambda_{n,m}(\varepsilon) \mid (n,m) \in \mathbb{N}_o^2\right\} \tag{4}$$

and such that they satisfy for $\varepsilon \to +0$

$$\lambda_{n,m}(\varepsilon) = -n - \mu m - 1 + \mathcal{O}(\varepsilon^{\frac{1}{2}}(n+m+1)^{3/2}) \tag{5}$$

uniformly with respect to $(n,m) \in \mathbb{N}_o^2$.

PROOF. Let $w \in C^\infty(\mathbb{R}^2)$ satisfy

$$\left.\begin{aligned} &w(x,y) = \tfrac{1}{4}x^2 - \tfrac{1}{4}\mu y^2 + \mathcal{O}(r^3) \\ &\partial_x^2 w(x,y) = \tfrac{1}{2} + \mathcal{O}(r) \\ &\partial_y^2 w(x,y) = -\tfrac{1}{2}\mu + \mathcal{O}(r) \\ &\partial_x\partial_y w(x,y) = \mathcal{O}(r) \end{aligned}\right\} \quad r^2 = x^2 + y^2 \to 0 \tag{6}$$

and define the transformed operator $\tilde{T}_\varepsilon$ by

$$\begin{aligned} \tilde{T}_\varepsilon u &:= \exp(w/\varepsilon)T_\varepsilon\{u\exp(-w/\varepsilon)\} = \\ &= \varepsilon L u + \tilde{\omega}_1\partial_x u + \tilde{\omega}_2\partial_y u - \tilde{\omega}_3 u/\varepsilon - (\tfrac{1}{2}-\tfrac{1}{2}\mu+\tilde{\omega}_4)u. \end{aligned} \tag{7}$$

Since the functions $\tilde{\omega}_i$ satisfy the relations (4.5) we can apply theorem 4.5 to $\tilde{T}_\varepsilon$. □

REMARKS: 1. By analogy to (4.29-31) the proof yields a constant $K \in \mathbb{R}^+$, depending on the function w, such that $\tilde{T}_\varepsilon - \lambda$ satisfies the estimate

$$\|\tilde{T}_\varepsilon u - \lambda u\| \geq \tfrac{1}{2}\|u\|\left\{|\lambda - \ell(\lambda)| - \varepsilon^{\frac{1}{2}}K|\ell(\lambda)|^{3/2}\right\} \tag{8}$$

for all $u \in \mathcal{D}(\tilde{T}_\varepsilon)$, $\lambda \in \mathbb{C}$ and $\varepsilon \in \mathbb{R}^+$ and small enough; $\ell(\lambda)$ denotes the point of Λ that is nearest to λ.

2. The limiting set of the spectrum does not depend on the form of the domain Ω considered, provided (0,0) is contained in the interior of Ω.

2. STRONG CONVERGENCE

We begin by proving convergence of the solution of (6.1) for λ in the right half of the complex plane, using the analogue of the method of §4.2. We extend T_ε to an operator in $L^p(\Omega)$ with $1 \le p \le \infty$ and in $C^o(\Omega)$ by defining its domain in $L^p(\Omega)$ by

$$\text{(9a)}\qquad \mathcal{D}(T_\varepsilon) := \left\{u \in L^p(\Omega) \mid \Delta u \in L^p(\Omega) \ \&\ u_{|\partial\Omega} = 0\right\}$$

and in $C^o(\Omega)$ by $\mathcal{D}(T_\varepsilon) := C^2(\Omega) \cap C^o_o(\Omega)$. The presumed limit operator T_o is the restriction of $x\partial_x - \mu y\partial_y$ to the sets

$$\text{(9b)}\qquad \mathcal{D}(T_o) := \begin{cases} \{u \in L^p(\Omega) \mid x\partial_x u - \mu y\partial_y u \in L^p(\Omega) \ \&\ u(\pm 1,y) = 0\} \\ \{u \in C^o(\Omega) \mid x\partial_x u - \mu y\partial_y u \in C^o(\Omega) \ \&\ u(\pm 1,y) = 0\} \end{cases}$$

in $L^p(\Omega)$ and $C^o(\Omega)$ respectively. We emphasize the fact that the boundary condition of T_o applies only to that part of the boundary, from which the characteristics emanate: the value of a solution of a first order (partial) differential equation cannot be prescribed at more than one point on each characteristic.

LEMMA 6.2. *A constant* $K \in \mathbb{R}$ *exists such that*

$$\text{(10)}\qquad |T_\varepsilon u - \lambda u|_{o,p} \ge (Re\lambda + (1-\mu)/p - K\varepsilon)\,|u|_{o,p}$$

for all $\varepsilon \in [0,1]$, $u \in \mathcal{D}(T_\varepsilon)$, $p \in [1,\infty]$ *and* $\lambda \in \mathbb{C}$. *Moreover,* $T_\varepsilon - \lambda$ *has a bounded inverse on* $L^p(\Omega)$ *if* $Re\lambda + (1-\mu)/p > K\varepsilon$ *and* $T_o - \lambda$ *has a bounded inverse on* $L^p(\Omega)$ *if and only if* $Re\lambda > (\mu-1)/p$. *The same is true in* $C^o(\Omega)$ *if* $1/p$ *is replaced by zero.*

PROOF. Consider for $p \in (1,\infty)$ and $u \in \mathcal{D}(T_\varepsilon)$ with $|u|_{o,p} = 1$ the inner product

$$Re\left\langle T_\varepsilon u - \lambda u,\ u|u|^{p-2}\right\rangle$$

and proceed as in the proofs of the lemmas 4.6 and 4.7. □

This lemma implies convergence of a formal approximation to the solution of problem (1), provided $Re\lambda > (\mu-1)/p$. Similarly to remark 3 of §4.4

(pag.112) we find as a first result:

THEOREM 6.3. *If* $1 \le p < \infty$ *and if* $Re\lambda > (\mu-1)/p$, *then* $(T_\varepsilon-\lambda)^{-1}$ *converges strongly in* $L^p(\Omega)$ *to* $(T_o-\lambda)^{-1}$ *for* $\varepsilon \to +0$.

PROOF. If $Re\lambda > 2$ and if $f \in C^2(\Omega)$, the function u, defined by

(11) $$u_o(x,y) := (T_o-\lambda)^{-1}f(x,y) = -\int_{|x|}^{1} f(xt^{-1},yt^{\mu})t^{\lambda-1}dt,$$

is an element of $C^2(\Omega)$. It satisfies the differential equation of (1) and the boundary value at $x = \pm 1$ up to $\mathcal{O}(\varepsilon)$. By the usual matching technique, cf. (4.67-69) and [8], we match it to the boundary value at $y = \pm 1$. Using the local coordinates $\eta_\pm := (1\mp y)/\varepsilon$ and the substitution operators $s_\varepsilon^\pm$,

(12a) $$(s_\varepsilon^\pm u)(x,\eta_\pm) := u(x,\pm 1\mp\varepsilon\eta_\pm)$$

we find the formal expansions of the operator

(12b) $$s_\varepsilon^\pm(\varepsilon L+x\partial_x-\mu y\partial_y)(s_\varepsilon^\pm)^{-1} = \sum_{j=0}^{m} \varepsilon^{j-1}\rho_j^\pm + \varepsilon^m\rho_m^{\pm\#}$$

in the upper and lower boundary layers along the lines $y = \pm 1$ respectively; in particular the lowest order parts of the operators are

(12c) $$\rho_o^\pm := c(x,\pm 1)\partial_\eta^2 + \mu\partial_\eta,$$

and the lowest order parts of the boundary layer expansions are

(12d) $$v_o^\pm(x,\eta) := -u_o(x,\pm 1)\exp(-\mu\eta/a(x,\pm 1)),$$

cf. (2.22) and (4.69). The composition

(13) $$P_\lambda := u_o + z(4y)(s_\varepsilon^+)^{-1}v_o^+ + z(-4y)(s_\varepsilon^-)^{-1}v_o^-,$$

with z as in (4.52), satisfies by definition $P_\lambda \in \mathcal{D}(T_\varepsilon)$ and

$$|(T_\varepsilon-\lambda)P_\lambda - f|_{o,p} = \mathcal{O}(\varepsilon^{1/p}|f|_{2,p}), \qquad \varepsilon \to +0,$$

hence by lemma (6.2) we find

$$(14)\qquad |(T_\varepsilon-\lambda)^{-1}f-(T_o-\lambda)^{-1}f|_{o,p} = |P_\lambda-(T_\varepsilon-\lambda)^{-1}f|_{o,p}+\mathcal{O}(\varepsilon^{1/p}|f|_{2,p}) =$$

$$= \mathcal{O}(\varepsilon^{1/p}|f|_{2,p}),\qquad \varepsilon\to+0,$$

provided $Re\lambda > (\mu-1)/p$. Since $C^2(\Omega)$ is dense in $L^p(\Omega)$, this implies strong L^p-convergence of $(T_\varepsilon-\lambda)^{-1}$ for all $\lambda\in\mathbb{C}$ with $Re\lambda > (\mu-1)/p$ and for all finite values of p. □

If $Re\lambda > 2$ and if $f\in C^2(\Omega)$, then the function P_λ, cf. (12b), is in fact an approximation of $(T_\varepsilon-\lambda)^{-1}f$ of order $\mathcal{O}(\varepsilon)$ in the maximum norm. In order to obtain an approximation of order $\mathcal{O}(\varepsilon)$ in the max-norm for $Re\lambda\le 2$ we have to add to P_λ an expansion in the interior boundary layer along the line $x = 0$ with the local variable $\zeta = x/\sqrt{\varepsilon}$; the complexity of the formal approximation increases as $Re\lambda$ decreases. In [13] and [14] we constructed such a formal approximation and proved its validity for $\lambda\in\mathbb{R}$ and $\lambda > -1$ by a maximum principle. Using lemma 6.2 we can extend the validity of that approximation to non-real λ satisfying $Re\lambda > -1$.

3. CONVERGENCE ON SUBDOMAINS OF Ω

The restriction $Re\lambda > -1$, necessary in the previous section for a proof of convergence, can be removed either by assuming that the support of the right-hand side of (1) does not contain the line $y = 0$ or by restricting the domain of convergence to a closed subset of Ω that does not contain the line $x = 0$. This is achieved by a cut-off method analogous to the method used in §§3.6, 4.3 and 4.5.

Let w be as defined in (6) and let it, moreover, be such that the level curves $w(x,y) = \gamma$ are nowhere tangent to the characteristics $|x|^\mu y =$ constant of $x\partial_x - \mu y\partial_y$ for any $\gamma\in\mathbb{R}$. We define the subdomain E_γ and its complement F_γ by

$$(15)\qquad E_\gamma := \{(x,y)\in\Omega \mid w(x,y)\le\gamma\} \quad\text{and}\quad F_\gamma := \Omega\backslash E_\gamma;$$

clearly the line $y = 0$ is contained in F_γ if $\gamma < 0$ and the line $x = 0$ is contained in E_γ if $\gamma\ge 0$. We stipulate that we can choose the function w in such a way, that F_γ with $\gamma < 0$ is only a small strip along the line $y = 0$ and (by another choice) that E_γ with $\gamma > 0$ is only a small strip along the line $x = 0$. On these subsets of Ω we define the auxiliary operators M_ε and

N_ε as the restrictions of T_ε to the domains

$$\text{(16a)} \qquad \mathcal{D}(M_\varepsilon) := \left\{ u \in \mathcal{D}(T_\varepsilon) \cap L^1(F_\gamma) \;\middle|\; u_{|\partial F_\gamma \backslash \partial\Omega} = 0 \quad \text{if } \varepsilon \neq 0 \right\},$$

$$\text{(16b)} \qquad \mathcal{D}(N_\varepsilon) := \left\{ u \in \mathcal{D}(T_\varepsilon \cap L^1(E_\gamma) \;\middle|\; u_{|\partial E_\gamma \backslash \partial\Omega} = 0 \right\}.$$

By analogy to the lemmas 4.9 and 4.13 we find:

<u>LEMMA 6.4</u>. $M_\varepsilon - \lambda$ *has a bounded inverse in* $L^p(F_\gamma)$ *and* $C^o(F_\gamma)$ *for every* $\lambda \in \mathbb{C}$ *and* $\gamma > 0$ *and* $N_\varepsilon - \lambda$ *has a bounded inverse in* $L^p(E_\gamma)$ *and* $C^o(E_\gamma)$ *for every* $\lambda \in \mathbb{C}$ *and* $\gamma < 0$, *if* $\varepsilon \in [0,\varepsilon_o]$ *and if* ε_o, *depending on* λ, *is small enough. Moreover, constants* $\tilde{K}$ *and* K *exist such that* M_ε *and* N_ε *satisfy the estimates*

$$\text{(17a)} \qquad |x^k(M_\varepsilon u - \lambda u)|_{o,p,F_\gamma} \geq B_\varepsilon(\lambda,k,\gamma,p)\,|x^k u|_{o,p,F_\gamma} ,$$

$$\text{(17b)} \qquad \| x^k u\|_{F_\gamma} \, \| x^k (M_\varepsilon - \lambda) u\|_{F_\gamma} \geq \varepsilon\tilde{K}\| x^k \nabla u\|^2_{F_\gamma} + B_\varepsilon(\lambda,k,\gamma,2)\,\| x^k u\|^2_{F_\gamma} ,$$

for all $u \in \mathcal{D}(M_\varepsilon)$, *provided* $\gamma > 0$, *and*

$$\text{(17c)} \qquad |y^{-k}(N_\varepsilon u - \lambda u)|_{o,p,E_\gamma} \geq B_\varepsilon(\lambda,\mu k,\gamma,p)\,|y^{-k} u|_{o,p,E_\gamma}$$

for all $u \in \mathcal{D}(N_\varepsilon)$, *provided* $\gamma < 0$. B_ε *is defined by* (4.46),

$$B_\varepsilon(\lambda,k,\gamma,p) := \mathit{Re}\lambda + k + (1-\mu)/p - \varepsilon K(1+k/\gamma)^2 .$$

The constants K *and* $\tilde{K}$ *depend only on the function* w *and on the coefficients of* L.

The proof of this lemma is similar to that of 4.9 and 4.13.

With the aid of this lemma we shall show that (the analytic continuation of) P_λ approximates $(T_\varepsilon - \lambda)^{-1} f$ up to $\mathcal{O}(\varepsilon)$ for $\varepsilon \to +0$ on F_γ with $\gamma > 0$ or on Ω if $\mathrm{supp}(f) \subset E_\gamma$ with $\gamma < 0$, provided $\lambda \in \rho(T_\varepsilon)$; in order to do so we first construct a better formal approximation than P_λ is.

For all $\lambda \in \sigma(T_o)$ we define u_o as the analytic continuation of the integral in formula (11); lemma 6.4 implies that the restriction of u_o to F_γ with $\gamma > 0$ is as smooth as f is and that this is even true in Ω if $\mathrm{supp}(f) \subset E_\gamma$ with $\gamma < 0$. In order to construct in the boundary layers at

$y = \pm 1$ terms of higher order than $v_o^{\pm}$, cf. (12d), we define the kernels

$$\text{(18a)} \qquad k^{\pm}(\xi,\eta,x) := \begin{cases} \exp(-\mu\xi/a(x,\pm 1)) - \exp(\mu(\eta-\xi)/a(x,\pm 1)), & \text{if } \xi > \eta, \\ \exp(-\mu\xi/a(x,\pm 1)) - 1, & \text{if } \xi < \eta \end{cases}$$

and the functions

$$\text{(18b)} \qquad v_1^{\pm}(x,\eta) := \int_0^{\infty} k^{\pm}(\eta,\xi,x)(\lambda-\rho_1^{\pm})v_o^{\pm}(x,\xi)\,d\xi/\mu$$

with the restriction $x \neq 0$ if necessary.

Since the second terms $v_1^{\pm}$ of the boundary layer expansions are non-zero at the lines $x = \pm 1$, we take a closer look at the corner points: we stretch also the x-variable there. In a neighbourhood of (1,1) we introduce the local coordinate $\zeta := (1-x)/\varepsilon$ and the substitution operator σ_ε,

$$(\sigma_\varepsilon u)(\zeta,y) := u(1-\varepsilon\zeta,y)$$

and we make the formal expansion of the transformed operator

$$\text{(19)} \qquad \sigma_\varepsilon s_\varepsilon^{+}(\varepsilon L + x\partial_x - \mu y\partial_y)(\sigma_\varepsilon s_\varepsilon^{+})^{-1} = \varepsilon^{-1}R_o + R^{\#}.$$

We find that R_o is the operator

$$R_o := a(1,1)\partial_\zeta^2 + 2b(1,1)\partial_\zeta\partial_\eta + c(1,1)\partial_\eta^2 + \partial_\zeta - \mu\partial_\eta$$

and that the coefficients of the remainder $R^{\#}$ are bounded by a polynomial of degree (at most) one in ζ and η, independently of ε. Let V be the solution of the equation $R_oV = 0$ in the quadrant $\zeta > 0$ and $\eta > 0$ satisfying the boundary conditions

$$V(0,\eta) = -v_1^{+}(1,\eta) \quad \text{and} \quad V(\zeta,0) = 0, \quad (\text{N.B.}: v_1^{+}(1,0) = 0).$$

Since v_1^{+} satisfies

$$v_1^{+}(1,\eta) = \mathcal{O}(\eta \exp\{-\eta/a(1,1)\}(\partial_x u_o)(1,1)),$$

the Phragmèn-Lindelöf theorem, cf. [24], implies that V and all derivatives of it are of the order

$$(20)\qquad \mathcal{O}(\exp\{-\kappa(\eta^2+\zeta^2)^{\frac{1}{2}}\}),\quad \eta^2+\zeta^2\to\infty,$$

for some $\kappa \in \mathbb{R}^+$; this implies that $R^{\#}V$ is uniformly bounded (independently of ε) and also exponentially decreasing. We cut the function V off outside a neighbourhood of the corner by defining

$$\tilde{V}_1(x,y) := z(4y)z(4x)\big((\sigma_\varepsilon s_\varepsilon^+)^{-1}V\big)(x,y).$$

In the other corners of Ω we construct in the same manner functions $\tilde{V}_2$, $\tilde{V}_3$ and $\tilde{V}_4$ and we define the formal approximation

$$(21)\qquad \tilde{P}_\lambda := u_0 + z(4y)(s_\varepsilon^+)^{-1}(v_0^+ + \varepsilon v_1^+) + z(-4y)(s_\varepsilon^-)(v_0^- + \varepsilon v_1^-) + \sum_{j=1}^{4} \varepsilon\tilde{V}_j.$$

(with the restriction $x \neq 0$ if necessary). If $f \in C^3(\Omega)$, the construction implies

$$(22a)\qquad \Big[(\varepsilon L + x\partial_x - \mu y\partial_y - \lambda)\tilde{P}_\lambda - f\Big]_{F_\gamma} = \mathcal{O}(\varepsilon[f]+\varepsilon[\nabla\Delta f]),\qquad \varepsilon\to+0,$$

$$(22b)\qquad P_{\lambda\,|\,\partial\Omega\cap\partial F_\gamma} = 0,$$

for each $\gamma > 0$; if, in addition, $\mathrm{supp}(f) \subset E_\gamma$ with $\gamma < 0$, then $\tilde{P}_\lambda$ is an element of $\mathcal{D}(T_\varepsilon)$ and it satisfies

$$(23a)\qquad \Big[(T_\varepsilon-\lambda)\tilde{P}_\lambda - f\Big]_\Omega = \mathcal{O}(\varepsilon[f]+\varepsilon[\nabla\Delta f]),\qquad \varepsilon\to+0,$$

$$(23b)\qquad \mathrm{supp}(\tilde{P}_\lambda) \subset E_\gamma \cup \{(x,y)\mid |y| > \tfrac{1}{4}\}.$$

<u>REMARK</u>. Formula (21) implies $\Big[\tilde{P}_\lambda - P_\lambda\Big]_{F_\gamma} = \mathcal{O}(\varepsilon)$ for $\varepsilon\to+0$.

<u>THEOREM 6.5</u>. *If* $f \in C^3(\Omega)$ *and* $\lambda \in \mathbb{C}\backslash\Lambda$, *the formal approximation* P_λ *satisfies for every* $\alpha \in \mathbb{R}^+$ *the estimate*

$$(24a)\qquad \Big[(T_\varepsilon-\lambda)^{-1}f - P_\lambda\Big]_{F_\alpha} = \mathcal{O}(\varepsilon[f]+\varepsilon[\nabla\Delta f]),\qquad \varepsilon\to+0;$$

if, in addition, $\mathrm{supp}(f) \subset E_\gamma$ *with* $\gamma < 0$, *then*

(24b) $$\left[(T_\varepsilon-\lambda)^{-1}f - P_\lambda\right]_\Omega = \mathcal{O}(\varepsilon[f]+\varepsilon[\nabla\Delta f]), \qquad \varepsilon \to +0.$$

The order terms in (23) *are uniform with respect to* $f \in C^3(\Omega)$ *and depend on* λ,α,μ,w *and the coefficients of* L.

PROOF. We define $u_\varepsilon := (T_\varepsilon-\lambda)^{-1}f$. If the support of f is contained in E_γ we find from (8) the estimate

$$\| u_\varepsilon \exp((w-\gamma)/\varepsilon)\| = \| (\tilde{T}_\varepsilon-\lambda)^{-1} \exp((w-\gamma)/\varepsilon)\| \le$$

$$\le C_\lambda \| f \exp((w-\gamma)/\varepsilon)\| \le C_\lambda \| f \|$$

with $C_\lambda := 2\left\{|\lambda-\ell(\lambda)| - \varepsilon^{\frac{1}{2}}K|\ell(\lambda)|^{3/2}\right\}^{-1}$, provided $\lambda \in \Lambda$ and ε is small enough. By analogy to (4.74a) and (4.75a-b) this implies

(25a) $$|u_\varepsilon(x,y)| \le \tilde{C}_\lambda \varepsilon^{-1} \exp((\gamma-w(x,y))/\varepsilon)\| f \|$$

(25b) $$|\nabla u_\varepsilon(x,y)| \le \hat{C}_\lambda \varepsilon^{-2} \exp((\gamma-w(x,y))/\varepsilon)\| f \|$$

where $\hat{C}_\lambda$ and $\tilde{C}_\lambda$ are (constant) multiples of C_λ; we see that u_ε and its derivatives are exponentially small in F_γ.

Let $z_{\alpha\beta}$ with $\alpha < \beta$ be a C^∞-function satisfying

(26) $$z_{\alpha\beta}(x,y) = \begin{cases} 1 & \text{if } (x,y) \in E_\alpha \\ 0 & \text{if } (x,y) \in F_\beta \end{cases}$$

$$[\nabla z_{\alpha\beta}] \le C(\beta-\alpha) \qquad \text{for all } \alpha,\beta \in \mathbb{R} \text{ and some } C \in \mathbb{R}^+ .$$

If $\alpha,\beta,\gamma \in \mathbb{R}$ and $\alpha < \beta < \gamma$ and if $\mathrm{supp}(f) \subset E_\alpha$ we find

$$\mathrm{supp}(f-(N_\varepsilon-\lambda)(u_\varepsilon z_{\beta\gamma})) \subset F_\beta \backslash E_\gamma,$$

hence formula (25) implies

$$\left[f-(N_\varepsilon-\lambda)(u_\varepsilon z_{\beta\gamma})\right] = \mathcal{O}(\varepsilon^{-1}\exp((\alpha-\beta)/\varepsilon))$$

and, since $u_\varepsilon z_{\beta\gamma} \in \mathcal{D}(N_\varepsilon)$, (19c) implies

$$(27)\qquad \left[(N_\varepsilon-\lambda)^{-1}f - (T_\varepsilon-\lambda)^{-1}f\right] = \mathcal{O}(\varepsilon^{-1}\exp((\alpha-\beta)/\varepsilon)).$$

provided $\alpha < \beta < \gamma < 0$. In conjunction with the formulae (17c) and (23) formula (27) implies estimate (24b).

If the support of f is not restricted and if $\gamma > 0$, we define $\tilde{u}_\varepsilon$ as the solution of

$$(28)\qquad (\varepsilon L+x\partial_x-\mu y\partial_y-\lambda)u = f \quad \text{in } F_\gamma$$

$$u\Big|_{\partial F_\gamma} = \tilde{P}_\lambda\Big|_{\partial F_\gamma}, \quad \text{i.e.} \quad \tilde{u}_\varepsilon - \tilde{P}_\lambda \in \mathcal{D}(M_\varepsilon).$$

Assuming $0 < \gamma < \beta < \alpha$ and continuing $\tilde{u}_\varepsilon z_{\gamma\beta}$ into E_γ by zero we find, cf. (4.53),

$$(29)\qquad (T_\varepsilon-\lambda)(u_\varepsilon-z_{\gamma\beta}\tilde{u}_\varepsilon) = (1-z_{\gamma\beta})f + \tilde{u}_\varepsilon(\varepsilon L+x\partial_x-\mu y\partial_y-\varepsilon\omega_3)z_{\gamma\beta} + 2\varepsilon A(\nabla v_\varepsilon,\nabla z_{\gamma\beta}).$$

Since the support of the right-hand side of (29) is contained in E_β, formula (25a) implies

$$(30)\qquad |(u_\varepsilon-z_{\gamma\beta}\tilde{u}_\varepsilon)(x,y)| \le \tilde{C}_\lambda\varepsilon^{-1}\exp((\beta-w(x,y))/\varepsilon)\|(T_\varepsilon-\lambda)(u_\varepsilon-z_{\gamma\beta}\tilde{u}_\varepsilon)\| =$$

$$= \mathcal{O}(\varepsilon^{-1}\exp\{(\beta-w(x,y))/\varepsilon\}(\|f\| + \|\tilde{u}_\varepsilon\|_{E_\beta\cap F_\gamma} + \varepsilon\|\nabla\tilde{u}_\varepsilon\|_{E_\beta\cap F_\gamma})),$$

for $\varepsilon \to +0$. In conjunction with the formulae (17a-b) and (28) this implies estimate (24a). □

<u>REMARK</u>. In order to prove convergence of $\tilde{P}_\lambda$ in the maximum norm we can use the maximum principle for elliptic differential operators as an alternative to lemma 6.4. It has the advantage that we need not construct the local expansions εV_j at the corners of Ω for an approximation of order $\mathcal{O}(\varepsilon)$, since it yields this order of approximation already if the difference between the formal approximation and the solution at the boundary is of order $\mathcal{O}(\varepsilon)$, cf. [8] theorem 3. However, the maximum principle has the drawback that it is less suitable for complex-valued problems. In such cases we have to consider the equations for the real and imaginary parts as a system of two coupled real equations and we have to apply the usual maximum principle

to both equations separately in a suitable way. We obtain an a priori estimate in the norm $u \mapsto [x^k u]_{F_\gamma}$, $\gamma > 0$, only if λ is in the sector $Re\lambda > -k + \frac{1}{2}|Im\lambda|$; for details we refer to the proof of lemma 5.10 in [15].

4. CONVERGENCE IN NON-ISOTROPIC SPACES

The solution u_o of the reduced equation of (1), cf.(11), shows the remarkable effect that, if f is smooth enough, it becomes smoother (at the line x = 0 only) by differentiation with respect to y: if $f \in C^\infty(\Omega)$, then

(31) $$\partial_y^j u_o \in C^k(\Omega) \quad \text{if } Re\lambda > k - \mu j \quad \text{and} \quad k,j \in \mathbb{N}_o .$$

This suggests that it would be advantageous to consider problem (1) in a space of functions which are differentiable with respect y a number of times (and not with respect to x). We shall restrict the analysis to the case $L = \Delta$; it is not known whether it can be generalized to all elliptic perturbations.

We define in $H^{(o,n)}(\Omega)$ the auxiliary operator

(32a) $$T_{\varepsilon,n}u := \varepsilon\Delta u + x\partial_x u - \mu y\partial_y u, \quad \text{for all } u \in \mathcal{D}(T_{\varepsilon,n}) ,$$

(32b) $$\mathcal{D}(T_{\varepsilon,n}) := \left\{u \in H^{(o,n)}(\Omega) \,|\, \Delta u \in H^{(o,n)}(\Omega), u\big|_{x=\pm 1} = 0 \ \&\ \partial_y^{n+1}u\big|_{y=\pm 1} = 0\right\},$$

(note that $T_{\varepsilon,o} \neq T_\varepsilon$). By theorem 1.17 this operator is semibounded from above and has a compact inverse. For any $u \in \mathcal{D}(T_{\varepsilon,n})$ and $\varepsilon \geq 0$ we have the estimate

(33) $$\| \partial_y^n(T_{\varepsilon,n}-\lambda)u\| \, \| \partial_y^n u\| \geq \left|\left\langle(\varepsilon\Delta + x\partial_x - \mu y\partial_y - (\lambda+n\mu))\partial_y^n u, \partial_y^n u\right\rangle\right| \geq$$
$$\geq \varepsilon\| \nabla\partial_y^n u\|^2 + (Re\lambda + n\mu + \tfrac{1}{2} - \tfrac{1}{2}\mu)\| \partial_y^n u\|^2 ,$$

provided $Re\lambda > -n\mu - \frac{1}{2} + \frac{1}{2}\mu$. This inequality cannot be used in $H^{(o,n)}(\Omega)$ directly since $u \mapsto \| \partial_y^n u\|$ is not a norm in that space. Therefore we shall split up this space into two invariant subspaces in such a way that equation (32a) disintegrates in n ordinary differential equations in one of them and such that the other is isomorphic (and approximately isometric) to $H_1^{(o,n)}(\Omega)$, cf.(1.45), and is equipped with the norm $u \mapsto \| \partial_y^n u\|$.

We define the polynomials $h_{\varepsilon,j}$ by

$$h_{\varepsilon,j}(y) := (\varepsilon/2\mu)^{\frac{1}{2}j} H_j(y\sqrt{\mu/2\varepsilon}), \quad j \in \mathbb{N}_o, \tag{34a}$$

where H_j is the j-th Hermite polynomial; they satisfy

$$h_{\varepsilon,j}(y) = y^j + \mathcal{O}(\varepsilon|y|^{j-2} + \varepsilon^2|y|^{j-4} + \ldots.) \qquad \varepsilon \to +0 \tag{34b}$$

uniformly with respect to $y \in [-1,1]$. In $L^2(\mathbb{R};\ \exp(-\mu y^2/2\varepsilon))$ these polynomials form a complete orthogonal system of eigenfunctions of the Hermite operator $\varepsilon d^2/dy^2 - \mu y d/dy$. We continue any $f \in H^{(o,n)}(\Omega)$ by zero outside Ω and we expand it in a Hermite series with respect to y,

$$f = \sum_{j=0}^{\infty} f_{\varepsilon,j} h_{\varepsilon,j} \tag{35a}$$

$$f_{\varepsilon,j}(x) := (2\pi)^{-\frac{1}{2}}(\mu/\varepsilon)^{j+\frac{1}{2}} \frac{1}{j!} \int_{-\infty}^{\infty} h_{\varepsilon,j}(y) f(x,y) \exp(-\mu y^2/2\varepsilon)\,dy, \tag{35b}$$

the integral existing almost everywhere in (-1,1) and $f_{\varepsilon,j} \in L^2(-1,1)$. Inserting Rodrigues' relation for H_j, integrating by parts j times and using the identity (1.27b) we find

$$f_{\varepsilon,j}(x) = (\mu/2\pi\varepsilon)^{\frac{1}{2}} \frac{1}{j!} \int_{-\infty}^{\infty} (-1)^j f(x,y)\,\partial_y^j \exp(-\mu y^2/2\varepsilon)\,dy =$$

$$= \frac{1}{j!}(\partial_y^j f)(x,0) + (\mu/2\pi\varepsilon)^{\frac{1}{2}} \frac{1}{j!} \sum_{k=0}^{j-1} (-1)^{k+j} (\partial_y^k f)(\partial_y^{j-k-1} \exp(-\mu y/2\varepsilon))\Big|_{y=-1}^{y=1} +$$

$$+ (\mu/2\pi\varepsilon)^{\frac{1}{2}} \frac{1}{j!} \int_{-\infty}^{\infty} \exp(-\mu y^2/2\varepsilon) y^2 \int_0^1 (1-t)(\partial_y^{j+2} f)(x,yt)\,dt\,dy.$$

Denoting by $U_{o,o}$ the operator defined in (3.69b) we find

$$\int_0^1 (1-t)(\partial_y^{j+2} f)(\cdot,yt)\,dt = \left\{(U_{o,o}-2)^{-1} - (U_{o,o}-1)^{-1}\right\}(\partial_y^{j+2} f)(\cdot,y)$$

and by (3.72) we find the estimate

$$\Big\| \int_0^1 (1-t)(\partial_y^{j+2} f)(x,yt)\,dt \Big\|_{(-1,1)} \le \frac{8}{3} \,\|\, (\partial_y^{j+2} f)(x,y) \,\|_{(-1,1)}$$

for almost every $x \in (-1,1)$. By Schwarz' inequality and lemma 1.15 we find a constant C_j such that

$$\text{(36)}\qquad \| f_{\varepsilon,j} - \frac{1}{j!}\,\partial_y^j f|_{y=0} \|_{(-1,1)} \le C_j \varepsilon^{-j+\frac12} \exp(-\mu/2\varepsilon)(\| \partial_y^j f\| + \| f \|) + $$

$$+ \frac{8}{3j!}\,(\mu/2\pi\varepsilon)^{\frac12} \| \partial_y^{j+2} f\| \left\{ \int_{-\infty}^{\infty} y^4 \exp(-\mu y^2/\varepsilon)\,dy \right\}^{\frac12} =$$

$$= \mathcal{O}(\varepsilon(\| \partial_y^{j+2} f\| + \| f \|)), \qquad \varepsilon \to +0.$$

Analogously we find

$$\| f_{\varepsilon,j} - \frac{1}{j!}\,\partial_y^j f|_{y=0} \|_{(-1,1)} = \mathcal{O}(\varepsilon^{\frac12}(\| \partial_y^{j+1} f\| + \| f \|)), \qquad \varepsilon \to +0,$$

and approximations of higher order can be derived similarly.

In $H^{(o,n)}(\Omega)$ we define for $\varepsilon \ge 0$ the projection operator $Z_{\varepsilon,n}$ by

$$\text{(37a)}\qquad Z_{\varepsilon,n} f := f - \sum_{j=0}^{n-1} f_{\varepsilon,j} h_{\varepsilon,j}\,,$$

where $f_{o,j} := \lim_{\varepsilon\to+0} f_{\varepsilon,j}$ and $h_{o,j} := y^j$. Since $h_{\varepsilon,j}$ is a polynomial, it satisfies $\partial_y^n Z_{\varepsilon,n} f = \partial_y^n f$. From (36) we infer that the range of $Z_{o,n}$ is the subspace $H_1^{(o,n)}(\Omega)$, cf. (1.45), and that $Z_{\varepsilon,n}$ satisfies the estimates

$$\text{(37b)}\qquad \| Z_{\varepsilon,n} f - Z_{o,n} f \| = \begin{cases} \mathcal{O}(\varepsilon^{\frac12}(\| f \| + \| \partial_y^n f\|)), \\ \\ \mathcal{O}(\varepsilon(\| f \| + \| \partial_y^{n+1} f\|)), \end{cases} \qquad \varepsilon \to +0,$$

uniformly with respect to f. Moreover, since the norms

$$\text{(38a)}\qquad f \mapsto \left\{ \| f \|^2 + \| \partial_y^n f \|^2 \right\}^{\frac12} \quad\text{and}\quad f \mapsto \left\{ \| \partial_y^n f \|^2 + \sum_{j=0}^{n-1} \| f_{o,j} \|_{(-1,1)}^2 \right\}^{\frac12}$$

are equivalent in $H^{(o,n)}(\Omega)$, cf. (1.43b) and (1.47), the norm

$$\text{(38b)}\qquad f \mapsto \left\{ \| \partial_y^n f \|^2 + \sum_{j=0}^{n-1} \| f_{\varepsilon,j} \|_{(-1,1)}^2 \right\}^{\frac12}$$

is equivalent to these two norms. Hence, in $\mathcal{R}(Z_{\varepsilon,n})$ the norms

(38c) $$f \mapsto \left\{\| f \|^2 + \| \partial_y^n f \|^2\right\}^{\frac{1}{2}} \quad \text{and} \quad f \mapsto \| \partial_y^n f \|$$

are equivalent and we see that we can use estimate (33) in that subspace.

If $u \in \mathcal{D}(T_{\varepsilon,n})$ is written as

(39) $$u = \sum_{j=0}^{n-1} u_{\varepsilon,j} h_{\varepsilon,j} + Z_{\varepsilon,n} u,$$

then it is easily seen that $Z_{\varepsilon,n}u$ is an element of $\mathcal{D}(T_{\varepsilon,n})$ and that $u_{\varepsilon,j}$ is in $H^2(-1,1) \cap C_0^o(-1,1)$; if u is a solution of the equation $T_{\varepsilon,n}u - \lambda u = f$, then $u_{\varepsilon,j}$ is a solution of the equation

(40a) $$\varepsilon u''_{\varepsilon,j} + xu'_{\varepsilon,j} - (\lambda+\mu j)u_{\varepsilon,j} = f_{\varepsilon,j}, \qquad u(\pm 1) = 0, \qquad (\; ' = d/dx)$$

and the remainder of (39) satisfies

(40b) $$(T_{\varepsilon,n}-\lambda)Z_{\varepsilon,n}u = Z_{\varepsilon,n}f, \qquad Z_{\varepsilon,n}u \in \mathcal{D}(T_\varepsilon),$$

by virtue of the Hermite expansion (35). Hence

$$u_{\varepsilon,j} = (\Pi_\varepsilon - \lambda - \mu j)^{-1} f_{\varepsilon,j}, \qquad \text{provided } \lambda \notin \sigma(\Pi_\varepsilon - \mu j),$$

where Π_ε is the operator defined in 3.5. From theorem 3.15 we find the estimate

(41) $$\left\| x^k\left\{u_{\varepsilon,j}(x) - \int_{|x|}^1 f_{\varepsilon,j}(x/t)t^{\lambda+\mu j-1}dt\right\}\right\|_{(-1,1)} =$$

$$= \mathcal{O}\big(\varepsilon \| f_{\varepsilon,j}\|_{1,(-1,1)} \Gamma(\lambda+\mu j+1)/(Re\lambda+k+\mu j-3/2)\big),$$

provided $k \in \mathbb{N}$ and $Re\lambda + k + \mu j > 3/2$. Defining $u_{o,j}$ by

$$u_{o,j}(x) := \int_{|x|}^1 f_{o,j}(x/t)t^{\lambda+\mu j-1}dt \quad \big(=(E_k-\lambda-\mu j)^{-1} f_{o,j}, \text{ cf. } (3.35a)\big),$$

we find from lemma 3.12 and formula (36) the estimate

$$\left\| x^k\left\{u_{o,j}(x) - \int_{|x|}^1 f_{\varepsilon,j}(x/t)t^{\lambda+\mu j-1}dt\right\}\right\|_{(-1,1)} =$$

$$= \mathcal{O}\big(\varepsilon(\| f \| + \| \partial_y^{j+2} f\|)/(Re\lambda+k+\mu j+\tfrac{1}{2})\big), \qquad \varepsilon \to +0.$$

In conjunction with (41) this implies the estimate

$$\text{(42a)} \qquad \| x^k(u_{\varepsilon,j}-u_{o,j})\|_{(-1,1)} = \mathcal{O}(\varepsilon(\|f\|+\|\partial_y^{j+2}f\|)\Gamma(\lambda+\mu j+1)/(Re\lambda+k+\mu j-3/2))$$

for $\varepsilon \to +0$ and likewise we obtain from theorem 3.15 the estimate

$$\text{(42b)} \qquad \left[x^{k+\frac{1}{2}}(u_{\varepsilon,j}-u_{o,j})\right]_{(-1,1)} = \mathcal{O}(\varepsilon(\|f\|+\|\partial_y^{j+2}f\|)\Gamma(\lambda+\mu j+1)/(Re\lambda+k+\mu j-3/2))$$

for $\varepsilon \to +0$, provided $Re\lambda > -k-\mu j+3/2$.

Now we shall approximate the solution of (40b). We restrict the operator T_o to $\mathcal{R}(Z_{o,m}) \cap \mathcal{D}(T_o)$. Inequality (33) with $\varepsilon = 0$ and the equivalence of the norms (38c) in $\mathcal{R}(Z_{o,m})$ imply the invertibility of the restriction of $T_o - \lambda$ and the existence of a constant C_m such that

$$\text{(44)} \qquad \|(T_o-\lambda)u\|+\|\partial_y^m(T_o-\lambda)u\| \geq C_m(\|u\|+\|\partial_y^m u\|)/(Re\lambda+m\mu+\tfrac{1}{2}-\tfrac{1}{2}\mu)$$

for all $u \in \mathcal{R}(Z_{o,m}) \cap \mathcal{D}(T_o)$, provided $Re\lambda + m\mu + \frac{1}{2} > \frac{1}{2}\mu$. By analogy to (11), (12) and (13) we define

$$\text{(45a)} \qquad \hat{u}_{o,n} := (T_o-\lambda)^{-1}Z_{o,n}Z_{\varepsilon,n}f \quad \text{and} \quad u_{o,n} := (T_o-\lambda)^{-1}Z_{o,n}f$$

$$\text{(45b)} \qquad \hat{v}^{\pm}_{o,n}(x,\eta) := -(-\mu)^{-n-1}\left(\partial_y^{n+1}\hat{u}_{o,n}\Big|_{y=\pm1}\right)\exp(-\mu\eta)$$

$$\text{(45c)} \qquad \hat{P}_{\lambda,n} := \hat{u}_{o,n} + \varepsilon^{n+1}\left\{z(4y)(s_\varepsilon^+)^{-1}\hat{v}^+_{o,n} + z(-4y)(s_\varepsilon^-)^{-1}\hat{v}^-_{o,n}\right\}$$

and we define $P_{\lambda,n}$ by skipping the hats in (45b and c). We remark that we have to define $\hat{u}_{o,n}$ in the manner as it is done in (45a) and that we cannot take $(T_o-\lambda)^{-1}Z_{\varepsilon,n}f$: since this last expression and its y-derivatives of order less than n need not be zero at the line $y = 0$, it cannot be continued to all λ in the negative half-plane with $Re\lambda + n\mu + \frac{1}{2} > \frac{1}{2}\mu$. Moreover, in order to be able to use the equivalence of the norms (38c) we have to project the formal approximation $\hat{P}_{\lambda,n}$ back into $\mathcal{R}(Z_{\varepsilon,n})$. From (44) and (36) we find the estimate

$$\text{(46a)} \qquad \|\hat{P}_{\lambda,n}-P_{\lambda,n}\| + \|\partial_y^n(\hat{P}_{\lambda,n}-P_{\lambda,n})\| =$$

$$= \mathcal{O}(\varepsilon(\|f\|+\|\partial_y^{n+2}f\|)/(Re\lambda+n\mu+\tfrac{1}{2}-\tfrac{1}{2}\mu))$$

and analogously

(46b) $$\| Z_{\varepsilon,n}\hat{P}_{\lambda,n}-P_{\lambda,n}\| + \| \partial_y^n(Z_{\varepsilon,n}\hat{P}_{\lambda,n}-P_{\lambda,n})\| =$$

$$= O(\varepsilon(\| f\| + \| \partial_y^{n+2}f\|)/(Re\lambda+n\mu+\tfrac{1}{2}-\tfrac{1}{2}\mu))$$

for all $f \in H^{(o,n+2)}(\Omega)$, provided $Re\lambda > - n\mu - \tfrac{1}{2} + \tfrac{1}{2}\mu$. By definition we now have

$$Z_{\varepsilon,n}\hat{P}_{\lambda,n} \in \mathcal{D}(T_{\varepsilon,n}) \cap R(Z_{\varepsilon,n}).$$

Since $\partial_y^n Z_{\varepsilon,n} f = \partial_y^n f$ for all $f \in H^{(o,n)}(\Omega)$ we find

(47) $$\| \partial_y^n\{(T_{\varepsilon,n}-\lambda)Z_{\varepsilon,n}\hat{P}_{\lambda,n} - Z_{\varepsilon,n}f\}\| =$$

$$= \| (\varepsilon\Delta+x\partial_x-\mu y\partial_y-\lambda-n\mu)\partial_y^n\hat{P}_{\lambda,n} - \partial_y^n f\| =$$

$$= \| \varepsilon\Delta\partial_y^n\hat{P}_{\lambda,n}\| = O(\varepsilon(\| f \| + \| \partial_y^n\Delta f\|)/(Re\lambda+r_n)),$$

provided $Re\lambda > - r_n$ with

$$r_n := \tfrac{1}{2} \min \{2n\mu - \mu -3,\ 2n\mu - 5\mu + 1\}.$$

In conjunction with formula (33) this implies for $\varepsilon \to +0$

(48) $$\| \partial_y^n\{(T_{\varepsilon,n}-\lambda)^{-1}Z_{\varepsilon,n}f - Z_{\varepsilon,n}\hat{P}_{\lambda,n}\}\| =$$

$$= O(\varepsilon(\| f \| + \| \partial_y^n\Delta f\|)(Re\lambda+r_n)^{-1}(Re\lambda+n\mu+\tfrac{1}{2}-\tfrac{1}{2}\mu)^{-1})$$

for $\varepsilon \to +0$ and $Re\lambda > - r_n$; the equivalence of the norms (38c) in $R(Z_{\varepsilon,n})$ implies that this estimate is also true with respect to the norm of $H^{(o,n)}(\Omega)$ and in conjunction with estimate (46b) we find

(49a) $$\| (T_{\varepsilon,n}-\lambda)^{-1}Z_{\varepsilon,n}f - P_{\lambda,n}\| + \| \partial_y^n\{(T_\varepsilon-\lambda)^{-1}Z_{\varepsilon,n}f - P_{\lambda,n}\}\| =$$

$$= O(\varepsilon(\| f \| + \| \partial_y^n\Delta f\|)(Re\lambda+n\mu+\tfrac{1}{2}-\tfrac{1}{2}\mu)^{-1}(Re\lambda+r_n)^{-1})$$

for $\varepsilon \to +0$, provided $Re\lambda > - r_n$.

With the aid of lemma 1.16 and the estimate of $\varepsilon\|\nabla\partial_y^n u\|^2$ in formula (33) we obtain instead of (49a) an estimate of order $O(\varepsilon^{\frac{3}{4}})$ with respect to the maximum norm. Straightforward computations yield the estimate

(49b) $$\left[(T_{\varepsilon,n}-\lambda)^{-1}Z_{\varepsilon,n}f - u_{o,n}\right] + \left[\partial_y^n\left\{(T_{\varepsilon,n}-\lambda)^{-1}Z_{\varepsilon,n}f - u_{o,n}\right\}\right] =$$
$$= O(\varepsilon^{\frac{3}{4}}(\|f\| + \|\partial_y^n\Delta f\|)(Re\lambda+n\mu+\tfrac{1}{2}-\tfrac{1}{2}\mu)^{-1}(Re\lambda+r_n)^{-1})$$

for $\varepsilon \to +0$, provided $Re\lambda > -r_n$. Formulae (42) and (49) yield an approximation of the composition

(50) $$(T_{\varepsilon,n}-\lambda)^{-1}f = (T_{\varepsilon,n}-\lambda)^{-1}Z_{\varepsilon,n}f + \sum_{j=0}^{n-1} h_{\varepsilon,j}(\Pi_\varepsilon-\lambda-\mu j)^{-1}f_{\varepsilon,j}.$$

Defining integers $k(j)$ such that

$$r_n \le k(j) + \mu j - 3/2 < r_n + 1$$

and defining the norms $|||\cdot|||_n$ and $\ast\cdot\ast_n$ by

(51a) $$|||u|||_n := \|\partial_y^n u\|_\Omega + \sum_{j=0}^{n-1}\|x^{k(j)}\partial_y^j u|_{y=0}\|_{(-1,1)}$$

(51b) $$\ast u \ast_n := \left[\partial_y^n u\right]_\Omega + \sum_{j=0}^{n-1}\left[x^{k(j)+\frac{1}{2}}\partial_y^j u|_{y=0}\right]_{(-1,1)}$$

we find from formulae (42) and (49):

<u>LEMMA 6.6</u>. *For any* $f \in L^2(\Omega)$ *with* $\Delta f \in H^{(o,n)}(\Omega)$ *the resolvent operator* $(T_{\varepsilon,n}-\lambda)^{-1}$ *satisfies for* $\varepsilon \to +0$ *the estimates*

(52a) $$|||(T_{\varepsilon,n}-\lambda)^{-1}f - \int_{|x|}^{1} f(xt^{-1},yt^\mu)t^{\lambda-1}dt|||_n = O(\varepsilon K_{n,\lambda}(f)),$$

(52b) $$\ast(T_{\varepsilon,n}-\lambda)^{-1}f - \int_{|x|}^{1} f(xt^{-1},yt^\mu)t^{\lambda-1}dt\ast_n = O(\varepsilon^{\frac{3}{4}}K_{n,\lambda}(f)),$$

where

$$K_{n,\lambda}(f) := (\|f\|+\|\partial_y^n\Delta f\|)\sum_{j=0}^{n-1}\Gamma(\lambda+\mu j+1)(Re\lambda+r_n)^{-1}(Re\lambda+n\mu+\tfrac{1}{2}-\tfrac{1}{2}\mu)^{-1},$$

provided $Re\lambda > - r_n$ *and* $\lambda \notin \Lambda$.

<u>REMARK</u>. The norm $u \mapsto |||u|||_n$, with respect to which we have proved convergence, is strictly weaker than the norm of $H^{(o,n)}(\Omega)$.

The max-norm estimate (52b) does not give a bound for the value of $(T_{\varepsilon,n}-\lambda)^{-1}f$ at $x = 0$. We shall show that it is bounded by some negative power of ε by reconsidering the terms $h_{\varepsilon,j}(\Pi_\varepsilon-\lambda-\mu j)^{-1}f_{\varepsilon,j}$ of formula (50), which are possibly unbounded. If $k \in \mathbb{N}$, $g \in H^1(-1,1)$ and $Re\alpha > - k + 3/2$, we find by theorem 3.15

$$\left[x^{k+\frac{1}{2}}\left\{(\Pi_\varepsilon-\alpha)^{-1}g - \int_{|x|}^{1} g(x/t)t^{\alpha-1}dt\right\}\right]_{(-1,1)} =$$

$$= \mathcal{O}\big(\varepsilon\|g\|_{1,(-1,1)}\,\Gamma(\alpha+1)/(Re\alpha+k-3/2)\big), \qquad \varepsilon \to +0.$$

Hence at the points $x = \pm\tau\sqrt{\varepsilon}$ with $\tau \in [1,2]$ we have

$$(53) \qquad A_{\varepsilon,\tau} \pm B_{\varepsilon,\tau} := (\Pi_\varepsilon-\alpha)^{-1}g\Big|_{x=\pm\tau\sqrt{\varepsilon}} = \int_{\tau\sqrt{\varepsilon}}^{1} g(\pm\tau\sqrt{\varepsilon}/t)t^{\alpha-1}dt + \mathcal{O}(\varepsilon^{-k+\frac{1}{2}}) =$$

$$= \mathcal{O}(\varepsilon^{-k+\frac{1}{2}}), \qquad \varepsilon \to +0.$$

Defining the substitution operator θ_ε by $(\theta_\varepsilon u)(\xi) := u(\xi/\sqrt{\varepsilon})$ and the function p_ε by

$$p_\varepsilon(\xi) = \exp(\tfrac{1}{4}\xi^2)\big(\theta_\varepsilon(\Pi_\varepsilon-\lambda)^{-1}g\big)(\xi)$$

we find by (3.7) that p_ε is the solution of the boundary value problem on the interval $(-\tau,+\tau)$:

$$(54) \qquad \partial_\xi^2 p_\varepsilon - \tfrac{1}{4}\xi^2 p_\varepsilon - \alpha p_\varepsilon = \theta_\varepsilon g, \qquad p_\varepsilon(\pm\tau) = A_{\varepsilon,\tau} \pm B_{\varepsilon,\tau},$$

provided τ is chosen such that α is not an eigenvalue of the problem. Since problem (54) is selfadjoint and since α is not an eigenvalue, a constant C exists, cf. thm.1.2, such that

$$\|p_\varepsilon\|_{(-\tau,\tau)} \le C(\|\theta_\varepsilon g\|_{(-\tau,\tau)} + |A_{\varepsilon,\tau}| + |B_{\varepsilon,\tau}|).$$

By Sobolev's inequality and the differential equation of (54) we find a constant C' such that

$$\text{(55)}\qquad \left[p_\varepsilon\right]_{(-\tau,\tau)} + \left[\partial_\xi^2 p_\varepsilon\right]_{(-\tau,\tau)} \le C'([g] + |A_{\varepsilon,\tau}| + |B_{\varepsilon,\tau}|).$$

Transforming back we find that $(\Pi_\varepsilon-\alpha)^{-1}g$ satisfies

$$\text{(56)}\qquad \left[(\Pi_\varepsilon-\alpha)^{-1}g\right] + \left[\varepsilon\partial_x^2(\Pi_\varepsilon-\alpha)^{-1}g\right] =$$

$$= (\varepsilon^{-k+\frac{1}{2}}\|g\|_{1,(-1,1)}\,\Gamma(\alpha+1)/(\mathit{Re}\alpha+k-3/2)),\qquad \varepsilon\to+0,$$

provided $k\in\mathbb{N}$ and $\mathit{Re}\alpha > -k+3/2$. In conjunction with (49b) this yields the bound for $(T_{\varepsilon,n}-\lambda)^{-1}f$:

$$\text{(57)}\qquad \left[(T_{\varepsilon,n}-\lambda)^{-1}f\right] = \mathcal{O}(\varepsilon^{-k(n-1)+\frac{1}{2}}K_{n,\lambda}(f)),\qquad \varepsilon\to+0,$$

provided $\mathit{Re}\lambda > -r_n$ and $\lambda\notin\Lambda$.

Finally we can compare $(T_{\varepsilon,n}-\lambda)^{-1}f$ and $(T_\varepsilon-\lambda)^{-1}f$; we shall show that their difference is exponentially small (with respect to ε) outside neighbourhoods of the lines $y=\pm1$. We consider the difference

$$\text{(58a)}\qquad d_\varepsilon := (T_\varepsilon-\lambda)^{-1}f - (1-\exp(\mu(y^2-1)/2\varepsilon))(T_{\varepsilon,n}-\lambda)^{-1}f;$$

it is an element of $\mathcal{D}(T_\varepsilon)$ and it satisfies the equation

$$\text{(58b)}\qquad (T_\varepsilon-\lambda)d_\varepsilon = \left\{f+\mu(T_{\varepsilon,n}-\lambda)^{-1}f+2\mu y(T_{\varepsilon,n-1}-\lambda-\mu)^{-1}\partial_y f\right\}\exp(\mu(y^2-1)/2\varepsilon).$$

For the function w in transformation (7) we make the specific choice

$$w(x,y) := \tfrac{1}{4}\mu x^2(1+\mu x^2)(1-y^2)/(\mu+x^2) - \tfrac{1}{4}\mu y^2;$$

it satisfies (6), its level curves are nowhere in $\overline{\Omega}$ tangent to the characteristics $|x|^\mu y$ = constant and it is constant at the lines $y=\pm1$. Defining $\tilde{d}_\varepsilon$ by

$$\tilde{d}_\varepsilon := d_\varepsilon\exp((w+\tfrac{1}{4}\mu)/\varepsilon)$$

and using (7) we find

(58c) $$(\tilde{T}_\varepsilon-\lambda)\tilde{d}_\varepsilon = \left\{f+\mu(T_{\varepsilon,n}-\lambda)^{-1}f+2\mu y(T_{\varepsilon,n}-\lambda-\mu)^{-1}\partial_y f\right\}\exp\left(\frac{\mu^2(1-y^2)(x^4-1)}{4\varepsilon(\mu+x^2)}\right).$$

Since the exponential is smaller than one in Ω, we find from (57) the estimate

$$\|(\tilde{T}_\varepsilon-\lambda)^{-1}\tilde{d}_\varepsilon\| = O(\varepsilon^{-k(n-1)+\frac{1}{2}}\tilde{K}_{n,\lambda}(f)), \qquad \varepsilon \to +0,$$

where $\tilde{K}_{n,\lambda}(f) := K_{n,\lambda}(f) + K_{n,\lambda+\mu}(\partial_y f)$; by (8) this implies

$$\|d_\varepsilon\| = O(\varepsilon^{-k(n-1)+\frac{1}{2}}\tilde{K}_{n,\lambda}(f)), \qquad \varepsilon \to +0,$$

provided $Re\lambda > -r_n$ and $\lambda \notin \Lambda$. As in (4.74) and (4.75a-b) we find from the differential equation (58c) and from Sobolev's inequality the estimate

$$\left[\tilde{d}_\varepsilon\right] = O(\varepsilon^{-k(n-1)-\frac{1}{2}}\tilde{K}_{n,\lambda}(f)), \qquad \varepsilon \to +0;$$

hence a constant C exists, such that

(59) $$|(T_\varepsilon-\lambda)^{-1} - (T_{\varepsilon,n}-\lambda)^{-1}f| \le C\varepsilon^{-k(n-1)-\frac{1}{2}}\exp(-(w+\tfrac{1}{4}\mu)/\varepsilon)\tilde{K}_{n,\lambda}(f),$$

for all $(x,y) \in \Omega$, provided $Re\lambda > -r_n$ and $\lambda \notin \Lambda$. Since $w + \frac{1}{4}\mu$ is positive in the interior of Ω, we find from lemma 6.6, theorem 6.5 and estimate (59) the final result:

<u>THEOREM 6.7</u>. *If Ω^* is a subset of Ω which is equal to Ω minus small neighbourhoods of the points $(0,\pm1)$, then $(T_\varepsilon-\lambda)^{-1}f$ satisfies on Ω^* the estimates*

(60a) $$\|x^k((T_\varepsilon-\lambda)^{-1}f-P_\lambda)\|_{\Omega^*} = O(\varepsilon\hat{K}_{n,\lambda}(f)), \qquad \varepsilon \to +0,$$

(60b) $$\left[x^{k+\frac{1}{2}}(T_\varepsilon-\lambda)^{-1}f-P_\lambda)\right]_{\Omega^*} = O(\varepsilon^{\frac{3}{4}}\hat{K}_{n,\lambda}(f)), \qquad \varepsilon \to +0,$$

where $k := k(n-1)$ is the integer satisfying $r_n \le k + \mu n - \mu - 3/2 < r_n + 1$, where r_n is defined by $r_n := \frac{1}{2}\min\{2n\mu - \mu - 3,\ 2n\mu - 5\mu + 1\}$ and where $\hat{K}$ is defined by

$$\hat{K}_{n,\lambda}(f) := ([f]+[\nabla\Delta f]+\|\partial_y^n\Delta f\|)\sum_{j=0}^{n-1}\Gamma(\lambda+\mu j+1)(Re\lambda+r_n)^{-1}(Re\lambda+n\mu+\tfrac{1}{2}-\tfrac{1}{2}\mu)^{-1};$$

the estimates are uniform with respect to $f \in H^{(0,n)}(\Omega)$ satisfying

$$[f] + [\nabla\Delta f] + \| \partial_y^n \Delta f \| < \infty$$

and $\lambda \in \mathbb{C}\backslash\Lambda$ *satisfying* $Re\lambda > - r_n$.

REMARK. If we enlarge the power of the weight-factor in (60b), we obtain an estimate which is valid on the entire domain:

$$\text{(60c)} \qquad \left[x^{k+2}((T_\varepsilon-\lambda)^{-1}f-P_\lambda)\right]_\Omega = O(\varepsilon^{\frac{3}{4}}\hat{K}_{n,\lambda}(f)), \qquad \varepsilon \to +0,$$

provided $Re\lambda > - r_n$ and $\lambda \notin \Lambda$. From (59) we infer that this estimate is true in a strip of width $O(\sqrt{\varepsilon})$ around the line $x = 0$. In order to prove this estimate outside the strip we have to compute explicitly the α-dependence of estimate (24a) of theorem 6.5. As in estimate (4.61) of theorem 4.10 we find that estimate (24a) remains true if the subdomain F_α depends on ε and if it is equal to Ω minus a strip of width $O(\sqrt{\varepsilon})$ around the line $x = 0$.

REFERENCES

[1] ABRAHAMSSON, L.R., *A priori estimates for solutions of singular perturbations with turning points*, report 56, Department of computer sciences, Uppsala University, Sweden, 1975.

[2] ABRAMOWITZ, M. & I.A. STEGUN, *Handbook of mathematical functions*, Dover publication, inc., New York, 1965.

[3] ACKERBERG, R.C. & R.E. O'MALLEY, Jr., *Boundary layer problems exhibiting resonance*, Studies in Appl. Math. 49 (1970), p. 277-295.

[4] ADAMS, R.A., *Sobolev spaces*, Academic Press, New York, 1975.

[5] BESJES, J.G., *Singular perturbation problems for linear elliptic differential operators of arbitrary order* I & II, J. of Math. Anal. & Appl. 49 (1975) p.24-46 and p.324-346.

[6] CODDINGTON, E.A. & N. LEVINSON, *Theory of ordinary differential equations*, Mc.Graw-Hill, New York, 1955.

[7] COOK, L. PAMELA & W. ECKHAUS, *Resonance in a boundary value problem of singular perturbation type*, Studies in Appl. Math., 52 (1973) p. 129-139.

[8] ECKHAUS, W. & E.M. DE JAGER, *Asymptotic solutions of singular perturbation problems for linear differential equations of elliptic type*, Arch. Rat. Mech. & Anal. 23 (1966) p. 26-86.

[9] FRIEDMAN, A., *Partial differential equations*, Holt Rinehart & Winston, Inc., New York, 1969.

[10] GARABEDIAN, P.R., *Partial differential equations*, J. Wiley & Sons Inc., New York, 1964.

[11] GRASMAN, J., *On the birth of boundary layers*, tract 36, Mathematisch Centrum, Amsterdam, 1971.

[12] GROEN, P.P.N. DE, *An elliptic boundary value problem with non-differentiable parameters*, Arch. Rat. Mech. & Anal. 42 (1971) p. 169-183.

[13] GROEN, P.P.N. DE, *Critical points of the degenerate operator in elliptic singular perturbation problems*, report ZW 28/75, Mathematisch Centrum, Amsterdam, 1975.

[14] GROEN, P.P.N. DE, *Elliptic singular perturbations of first order operators with critical points*, Proc. of the Royal Society of Edinburgh, 74A (1974/75) p.91-113.

[15] GROEN, P.P.N. DE, *Spectral properties of second order singularly perturbed boundary value problems with turning points*, J. of Math. Anal. & Appl., 56 (1976), to appear (report 39, Wiskundig Seminarium der Vrije Universiteit, Amsterdam, 1975).

[16] GROEN, P.P.N. DE, *A singular perturbation problem of turning point type*; New developments in differential equations, proceedings of the second Scheveningen conference on differential equations, ed. W. Eckhaus, North-Holland Mathematics Studies 21, North-Holland publ. co., Amsterdam, 1976, p.117-124.

[17] HARTEN, A. VAN, *Singularly perturbed non-linear 2nd order elliptic boundary value problems*, doctoral thesis, University of Utrecht, The Netherlands, 1975.

[18] HARTEN, A. VAN, *On an elliptic singular perturbation problem*, Proceedings of the 4th conference on differential equations, Dundee, 1976, *Lecture Notes in Math.*, Springer Verlag, Berlin, to appear.

[19] KATO, T., *Perturbation theory for linear operators*, Springer-Verlag, Berlin, 1966.

[20] LIONS, J.L. & E. MAGENES, *Problèmes aux limites non homogènes*, vol.I, Dunod, Paris, 1968.

[21] LIONS, J.L., *Perturbations singulières dans les problèmes aux limites et en contrôle optimal*, Lecture Notes in Math. 323, Springer-Verlag, Berlin, 1973.

[22] MATKOVSKY, B.J., *On boundary layer problems exhibiting resonance*, SIAM Review, 17 (1975) p. 82-100.

[23] O'MALLEY, Jr., R.E., *Introduction to singular perturbations*, Academic Press, New York, 1974.

[24] PROTTER, M.H. & H.F. WEINBERGER, *Maximum principles in differential equations*, Prentice-Hall, Englewood Cliffs, New Jersey, 1967.

[25] RUBENFELD, L.A. & B. WILLNER, *The general second order turning point problem and the question of resonance for a singularly perturbed second order ordinary differential equation*, to appear.

[26] SCHWARTZ, LAURENT, *Théorie des distributions*, Hermann, Paris, 1966.

[27] SLATER, L.J., *Confluent hypergeometric functions*, Cambridge University Press, Cambridge, 1960.

[28] STERNBERG, S., *Local contractions and a theorem of Poincaré*, Am. J. of Math., 79 (1957), p. 809-824.

[29] YOSIDA, K., *Functional analysis*, Springer-Verlag, Berlin, 1965.

[30] WASOW. W., *Asymptotic expansions for ordinary differential equations*, Interscience Publ., New York, 1965.

[31] WILKINSON, J.H., *The algebraic eigenvalue problem*, Oxford University Press, Oxford, 1965.

OTHER TITLES IN THE SERIES MATHEMATICAL CENTRE TRACTS

A leaflet containing an order-form and abstracts of all publications mentioned below is available at the Mathematisch Centrum, Tweede Boerhaavestraat 49, Amsterdam-1005, The Netherlands. Orders should be sent to the same address.

MCT 1 T. VAN DER WALT, *Fixed and almost fixed points*, 1963. ISBN 90 6196 002 9.

MCT 2 A.R. BLOEMENA, *Sampling from a graph*, 1964. ISBN 90 6196 003 7.

MCT 3 G. DE LEVE, *Generalized Markovian decision processes, part I: Model and method*, 1964. ISBN 90 6196 004 5.

MCT 4 G. DE LEVE, *Generalized Markovian decision processes, part II: Probabilistic background*, 1964. ISBN 90 6196 006 1.

MCT 5 G. DE LEVE, H.C. TIJMS & P.J. WEEDA, *Generalized Markovian decision processes, Applications*, 1970. ISBN 90 6196 051 7.

MCT 6 M.A. MAURICE, *Compact ordered spaces*, 1964. ISBN 90 6196 006 1.

MCT 7 W.R. VAN ZWET, *Convex transformations of random variables*, 1964. ISBN 90 6196 007 X.

MCT 8 J.A. ZONNEVELD, *Automatic numerical integration*, 1964. ISBN 90 6196 008 8.

MCT 9 P.C. BAAYEN, *Universal morphisms*, 1964. ISBN 90 6196 009 6.

MCT 10 E.M. DE JAGER, *Applications of distributions in mathematical physics*, 1964. ISBN 90 6196 010 X.

MCT 11 A.B. PAALMAN-DE MIRANDA, *Topological semigroups*, 1964. ISBN 90 6196 011 8.

MCT 12 J.A.TH.M. VAN BERCKEL, H. BRANDT CORSTIUS, R.J. MOKKEN & A. VAN WIJNGAARDEN, *Formal properties of newspaper Dutch*, 1965. ISBN 90 6196 013 4.

MCT 13 H.A. LAUWERIER, *Asymptotic expansions*, 1966, out of print; replaced by MCT 54 and 67.

MCT 14 H.A. LAUWERIER, *Calculus of variations in mathematical physics*, 1966. ISBN 90 6196 020 7.

MCT 15 R. DOORNBOS, *Slippage tests*, 1966. ISBN 90 6196 021 5.

MCT 16 J.W. DE BAKKER, *Formal definition of programming languages with an application to the definition of ALGOL 60*, 1967. ISBN 90 6196 022 3.

MCT 17 R.P. VAN DE RIET, *Formula manipulation in ALGOL 60, part 1*, 1968. ISBN 90 6196 025 8.

MCT 18 R.P. VAN DE RIET, *Formula manipulation in ALGOL 60, part 2*, 1968. ISBN 90 6196 038 X.

MCT 19 J. VAN DER SLOT, *Some properties related to compactness*, 1968. ISBN 90 6196 026 6.

MCT 20 P.J. VAN DER HOUWEN, *Finite difference methods for solving partial differential equations*, 1968. ISBN 90 6196 027 4.

MCT 21 E. WATTEL, *The compactness operator in set theory and topology*, 1968. ISBN 90 6196 028 2.

MCT 22 T.J. DEKKER, *ALGOL 60 procedures in numerical algebra, part 1*, 1968. ISBN 90 6196 029 0.

MCT 23 T.J. DEKKER & W. HOFFMANN, *ALGOL 60 procedures in numerical algebra, part 2*, 1968. ISBN 90 6196 030 4.

MCT 24 J.W. DE BAKKER, *Recursive procedures*, 1971. ISBN 90 6196 060 6.

MCT 25 E.R. PAERL, *Representations of the Lorentz group and projective geometry*, 1969. ISBN 90 6196 039 8.

MCT 26 EUROPEAN MEETING 1968, *Selected statistical papers, part I*, 1968. ISBN 90 6196 031 2.

MCT 27 EUROPEAN MEETING 1968, *Selected statistical papers, part II*, 1969. ISBN 90 6196 040 1.

MCT 28 J. OOSTERHOFF, *Combination of one-sided statistical tests*, 1969. ISBN 90 6196 041 X.

MCT 29 J. VERHOEFF, *Error detecting decimal codes*, 1969. ISBN 90 6196 042 8.

MCT 30 H. BRANDT CORSTIUS, *Excercises in computational linguistics*, 1970. ISBN 90 6196 052 5.

MCT 31 W. MOLENAAR, *Approximations to the Poisson, binomial and hypergeometric distribution functions*, 1970. ISBN 90 6196 053 3.

MCT 32 L. DE HAAN, *On regular variation and its application to the weak convergence of sample extremes*, 1970. ISBN 90 6196 054 1.

MCT 33 F.W. STEUTEL, *Preservation of infinite divisibility under mixing and related topics*, 1970. ISBN 90 6196 061 4.

MCT 34 I. JUHÁSZ, A. VERBEEK & N.S. KROONENBERG, *Cardinal functions in topology*, 1971. ISBN 90 6196 062 2.

MCT 35 M.H. VAN EMDEN, *An analysis of complexity*, 1971. ISBN 90 6196 063 0.

MCT 36 J. GRASMAN, *On the birth of boundary layers*, 1971. ISBN 90 6196 064 9.

MCT 37 J.W. DE BAKKER, G.A. BLAAUW, A.J.W. DUIJVESTIJN, E.W. DIJKSTRA, P.J. VAN DER HOUWEN, G.A.M. KAMSTEEG-KEMPER, F.E.J. KRUSEMAN ARETZ, W.L. VAN DER POEL, J.P. SCHAAP-KRUSEMAN, M.V. WILKES & G. ZOUTENDIJK, *MC-25 Informatica Symposium*, 1971. ISBN 90 6196 065 7.

MCT 38 W.A. VERLOREN VAN THEMAAT, *Automatic analysis of Dutch compound words*, 1971. ISBN 90 6196 073 8.

MCT 39 H. BAVINCK, *Jacobi series and approximation*, 1972. ISBN 90 6196 074 6.

MCT 40 H.C. TIJMS, *Analysis of (s,S) inventory models*, 1972. ISBN 90 6196 075 4.

MCT 41 A. VERBEEK, *Superextensions of topological spaces*, 1972. ISBN 90 6196 076 2.

MCT 42 W. VERVAAT, *Success epochs in Bernoulli trials (with applications in number theory)*, 1972. ISBN 90 6196 077 0.

MCT 43 F.H. RUYMGAART, *Asymptotic theory of rank tests for independence*, 1973. ISBN 90 6196 081 9.

MCT 44 H. BART, *Meromorphic operator valued functions*, 1973. ISBN 90 6196 082 7.

MCT 45 A.A. BALKEMA, *Monotone transformations and limit laws*, 1973. ISBN 90 6196 083 5.

MCT 46 R.P. VAN DE RIET, *ABC ALGOL, A portable language for formula manipulation systems, part 1: The language*, 1973. ISBN 90 6196 084 3.

MCT 47 R.P. VAN DE RIET, *ABC ALGOL, A portable language for formula manipulation systems, part 2: The compiler*, 1973. ISBN 90 6196 085 1.

MCT 48 F.E.J. KRUSEMAN ARETZ, P.J.W. TEN HAGEN & H.L. OUDSHOORN, *An ALGOL 60 compiler in ALGOL 60, Text of the MC-compiler for the EL-X8*, 1973. ISBN 90 6196 086 X.

MCT 49 H. KOK, *Connected orderable spaces*, 1974. ISBN 90 6196 088 6.

MCT 50 A. VAN WIJNGAARDEN, B.J. MAILLOUX, J.E.L. PECK, C.H.A. KOSTER, M. SINTZOFF, C.H. LINDSEY, L.G.L.T. MEERTENS & R.G. FISKER (Eds), *Revised report on the algorithmic language ALGOL 68*, 1976. ISBN 90 6196 089 4.

MCT 51 A. HORDIJK, *Dynamic programming and Markov potential theory*, 1974. ISBN 90 6196 095 9.

MCT 52 P.C. BAAYEN (ed.), *Topological structures*, 1974. ISBN 90 6196 096 7.

MCT 53 M.J. FABER, *Metrizability in generalized ordered spaces*, 1974. ISBN 90 6196 097 5.

MCT 54 H.A. LAUWERIER, *Asymptotic analysis, part 1*, 1974. ISBN 90 6196 098 3.

MCT 55 M. HALL JR. & J.H. VAN LINT (Eds), *Combinatorics, part 1: Theory of designs, finite geometry and coding theory*, 1974. ISBN 90 6196 099 1.

MCT 56 M. HALL JR. & J.H. VAN LINT (Eds), *Combinatorics, part 2: graph theory, foundations, partitions and combinatorial geometry*, 1974. ISBN 90 6196 100 9.

MCT 57 M. HALL JR. & J.H. VAN LINT (Eds), *Combinatorics, part 3: Combinatorial group theory*, 1974. ISBN 90 6196 101 7.

MCT 58 W. ALBERS, *Asymptotic expansions and the deficiency concept in statistics*, 1975. ISBN 90 6196 102 5.

MCT 59 J.L. MIJNHEER, *Sample path properties of stable processes*, 1975. ISBN 90 6196 107 6.

MCT 60 F. GÖBEL, *Queueing models involving buffers*, 1975. ISBN 90 6196 108 4.

* MCT 61 P. VAN EMDE BOAS, *Abstract resource-bound classes, part 1*. ISBN 90 6196 109 2.

* MCT 62 P. VAN EMDE BOAS, *Abstract resource-bound classes, part 2*. ISBN 90 6196 110 6.

MCT 63 J.W. DE BAKKER (ed.), *Foundations of computer science*, 1975. ISBN 90 6196 111 4.

MCT 64 W.J. DE SCHIPPER, *Symmetrics closed categories*, 1975. ISBN 90 6196 112 2.

MCT 65 J. DE VRIES, *Topological transformation groups 1 A categorical approach*, 1975. ISBN 90 6196 113 0.

MCT 66 H.G.J. PIJLS, *Locally convex algebras in spectral theory and eigenfunction expansions*. ISBN 90 6196 114 9.

* MCT 67 H.A. LAUWERIER, *Asymptotic analysis, part 2.* ISBN 90 6196 119 X.

MCT 68 P.P.N. DE GROEN, *Singularly perturbed differential operators of second order.* ISBN 90 6196 120 3.

* MCT 69 J.K. LENSTRA, *Sequencing by enumerative methods.* ISBN 90 6196 125 4.

MCT 70 W.P. DE ROEVER JR., *Recursive program schemes: semantics and proof theory*, 1976. ISBN 90 6196 127 0.

MCT 71 J.A.E.E. VAN NUNEN, *Contracting Markov decision processes*, 1976. ISBN 90 6196 129 7.

* MCT 72 J.K.M. JANSEN, *Simple periodic and nonperiodic Lamé functions and their applications in the theory of conical waveguides.* ISBN 90 6196 130 0.

* MCT 73 D.M.R. LEIVANT, *Absoluteness of intuitionistic logic.* ISBN 90 6196 122 x.

MCT 74 H.J.J. TE RIELE, *A theoretical and computational study of generalized aliquot sequences.* ISBN 90 6196 131 9.

* MCT 75 A.E. BROUWER, *Treelike spaces and related connected topological spaces.* ISBN 90 6196 132 7.

MCT 76 M. REM , *Associons and the closure statement.* ISBN 90 6196 135 1.

* MCT 77

* MCT 78 E. de Jonge, A.C.M. van Rooij, *Introduction to Riesz spaces*, 1977. ISBN 90 6196 133 5

MCT 79 M.C.A. VAN ZUIJLEN, *Empirical distributions and rankstatistics*, 1977. ISBN 90 6196 145 9.

* MCT 80 P.W. HEMKER, *A numerical study of stiff two-point boundary problems*, 1977. ISBN 90 6196 146 7.

MCT 81 K.R. APT & J.W. DE BAKKER (eds), *Foundations of computer science II*, part I, 1976. ISBN 90 6196 140 8.

MCT 82 K.R. APT & J.W. DE BAKKER (eds), *Foundations of computer science II*, part II, 1976. ISBN 90 6196 141 6.

* MCT 83 L.S. VAN BENTEM JUTTING, *Checking Landau's "Grundlagen" in the automath system*, 1977. ISBN 90 6196 147 5.

MCT 84 H.L.L. Busard, *The translation of the elements of Euclid from the Arabic into Latin by Hermann of Carinthia books vii-xii*, 1977. ISBN 90 6196 148 3

An asterik before the number means "to appear".